Praise for *Moral Ambition*

"A terrific read. There are so many things in here that made me think, 'Yes, exactly!' With *Moral Ambition*, Rutger Bregman has pulled off something remarkable: a lively and entertaining read that is full of important wisdom about some of life's most important questions. I hope everyone who wants to make the world a better place will read it."

—Peter Singer, Professor of Bioethics, Emeritus,
Princeton University and author of
Animal Liberation and *The Life You Can Save*

"A refreshing antidote to both cynical fatalism and naive idealism. If you're willing to trade a life of comfort for a life of meaning, Rutger Bregman is your guide and this book is your map."

—Daniel H. Pink, bestselling author of
The Power of Regret, *Drive* and *When*

"Another barnstorming, transformative book by one of the greatest thinkers of the twenty-first century. It is uplifting, inspiring, informative and entertaining in equal measure. I defy you to read it and not be motivated to act."

—George Monbiot, bestselling author of
The Invisible Doctrine

"What an inspiring book! A tremendous trumpet call to clear our heads of the current inward-looking obsessions with self-realisation and all those selfish life-coaching motivational goals, aims and targets that we are told will bring us happiness, and to think instead about satisfying that part of us that can make a difference to the world. And as Rutger Bregman brilliantly demonstrates, that, in the end, is where our true happiness and fulfilment is most likely to be found."   —Stephen Fry

"Fresh, lucid and persuasive, *Moral Ambition* gives us hope, humour and guidance at a time when all are in short supply. Bregman's version of our century is ever so much better than the one around us, and so we should all read, consider and act."
—Timothy Snyder, bestselling author of *On Tyranny*

"This practical and inspiring book is the best antidote to the pessimists and cynics who make you believe that nothing can be done about the problems we face today. Bregman helps you to expand your ethical ambitions and discover how you can contribute to a better world. *Moral Ambition* is the practical handbook for anyone ready to dedicate their life to making real change. Imagine what we could achieve together if everyone read Rutger's book!"
—Max Roser, founder of Our World in Data

"An essential guide for those who are determined to make a difference. Packed with powerful insights, inspiring stories, and data to back it up, Bregman challenges us to think and act bigger. Read it, then go out and change the world."
—Hannah Ritchie, bestselling author of *Not the End of the World*

"This is one of very few books in my life that has changed how I view the world (and my world, too!). It is a true bible of realistic idealism. It takes awareness of 'getting things done' to a new level, with a dynamic invitation to up each of our games. This is a must read."
—David Allen, bestselling author of *Getting Things Done*

"Do you want to read a book about the most important decisions of your life? Rutger Bregman has produced that book and you should read it."
—Tyler Cowen

"A fierce and brilliant call to arms for anyone who has been wondering whether there's more to life. (There is.) Bregman wants to change you, and he just might succeed. This is a wonderfully dangerous book."

—Tim Harford, bestselling author of *How to Make the World Add Up* and *The Undercover Economist*

"A new look at how to make the world a better place, guided by reason, balance and engaging case studies. Bregman avoids easy moralising and lazy conventional wisdom to offer a fresh and practical guide to idealism."

—Steven Pinker, Professor of Psychology, Harvard University, and author of *Enlightenment Now*

"Clear, brave, important and provocative. Forcing us to reassess and defend the most fundamental moral principles and purposes of our lives."

—Rory Stewart, bestselling author of *Politics On the Edge*

"This book is the wakeup call that our world sorely needs. With his signature clarity and conviction, Rutger Bregman boldly and brilliantly challenges us to hold ourselves to higher standards — and do more for others. *Moral Ambition* is the rare read that might actually help you become a better person."

—Adam Grant, bestselling author of *Think Again*

"Rutger Bregman challenges the reader to use their lives to improve the world. A bracing but ultimately uplifting wake-up call for a culture increasingly drowning in distraction and consumption!"

—Cal Newport, bestselling author of *Slow Productivity* and *Deep Work*

"Rutger Bregman's latest work isn't merely a book; it's a call to action for humanity to re-evaluate our paradigms of success and impact in the world. It serves as a stark wake-up call, urging us to truly utilise our talents to create the future we all wish to live in."
—Trevor Noah

" 'Find something worth doing' seems like sage advice for us all — and on this beleaguered planet, as this book makes clear, that means digging into the very biggest problems."
—Bill McKibben, author of
The End of Nature

"The key to solving our biggest problems isn't just awareness, political will, or money — it's ambitious individuals willing to dedicate their time and skills to improving the world. This book will inspire you to become one of them."
—Boyan Slat, founder and CEO of The Ocean Cleanup

"A life-changing book. It will lead you to re-evaluate your life — and radically raise your game. As soon as you finish it, you will want to buy it for everyone you love."
—Johann Hari, bestselling author of *Stolen Focus*

"A beautiful and courageous book about one of the most important questions each of us will face: what will we do with our one life? Rutger Bregman calls for a seismic norm shift in how those of us with the privilege to consider our career choices think about where we put our greatest resources — our time and energy."
—Wendy Kopp, founder of Teach for America

"We have come to accept so many things as normal — skyrocketing inequalities, gargantuan firms ruling our lives, virtue signalling on social media instead of democratic participation, all of us just worrying about our image while the world is on fire. We need to dream of and articulate to each other an alternative vision for a society in which we have control over our lives and can still speak truth to power via the democratic process and free media. I hope this readable, audacious book calling for greater moral ambition can be a first step."
—Daron Acemoglu, Institute Professor, MIT and Nobel Prize laureate

"There are many things to admire about this book. Just one of them is the way Rutger Bregman's inspiring array of dedicated people who changed the world around them spans continents and centuries. Meeting them all, some of whom I had not known before, gave me hope — at a moment when we need that."
—Adam Hochschild, author of *King Leopold's Ghost*

"Rutger Bregman, reliable and articulate voice of pragmatic solidarity, is back with a book offering guidance for well-intended do-gooders like me. His advice on how to build movements with achievable goals and see them through to tangible success is heartening and has given me much energy and wisdom for the years ahead."
—Abigail Disney

"Rutger Bregman has become the voice in my head. A disruptive revolutionary armed with an actual, tangible plan. At last."
—Jameela Jamil

"Every now and then something tumbles from a brave mind and clangs at your feet like a full metal gauntlet. *Moral Ambition* is a book of weight, wit and incitement. There is something Socratic about Bregman. His works set off a mechanism that expands the reader's ability to deal with and accept the vast and beautiful potential of humanity. I believe he calls himself a historian, he's not. He's a revolutionary in a sensible coat."   —Russell Crowe

"A thought-provoking exploration of humanity's potential for good ... Bregman's research-backed insights offer a refreshing perspective on prioritising, taking action ethically, making this book a must-read for the young activists curious about building a better, more compassionate future ... This book is an additional reminder for me that empathy and collaboration are at the heart of innovation."
—Gitanjali Rao, award-winning inventor, scientist
and *TIME*'s first Kid of the Year

"Do you want to use your talents and ideals to make a meaningful difference? Here is an inspiring and powerful call to action: why pursuing an altruistic career is not only vital for our shared future but can also bring you deeper personal fulfilment and happiness."   —Princess Mabel of Orange-Nassau

Moral Ambition

Stop Wasting Your **Talent**
and Start Making a **Difference**

Rutger Bregman

Translated from the Dutch by Erica Moore

LITTLE, BROWN AND COMPANY

New York   Boston   London

Little, Brown and Company
Hachette Book Group
1290 Avenue of the Americas, New York, NY 10104
littlebrown.com

First Edition: May 2025

Little, Brown and Company is a division of Hachette Book Group, Inc.
The Little, Brown name and logo are trademarks of Hachette Book Group, Inc.

The publisher is not responsible for websites (or their content) that are not owned by the
publisher.

The Hachette Speakers Bureau provides a wide range of authors for speaking events. To find
out more, go to hachettespeakersbureau.com or email hachettespeakers@hbgusa.com.

Little, Brown and Company books may be purchased in bulk for business, educational, or
promotional use. For information, please contact your local bookseller or the Hachette Book
Group Special Markets Department at special.markets@hbgusa.com.

ISBN 9780316580359
LCCN is available at the Library of Congress

Printing 1, 2025

LSC-C

Printed in the United States of America

CONTENTS

CONTENTS

PROLOGUE

I cannot believe that the purpose of life is to be "happy." I think
the purpose of life is to be useful, to be responsible, to be
honorable, to be compassionate. It is, above all, to matter: to
count, to stand for something, to have it make some difference
that you lived at all.
Leo Rosten, *writer (1908–1997)*

The neurologists could scarcely believe their eyes. Never before
had they seen a brain like this one. It was early morning on
May 22, 2001, and at a laboratory at the University of Wisconsin,
the team stared at the latest MRI scans.[1]

What in the world was going on? The subject showed a level
of gamma waves unknown to neuroscience. The left side of the
prefrontal cortex — the part of the brain associated with happiness — was bursting with activity, while the right-hand side —
associated with negative thoughts — registered next to nothing.[2]

When the scientists shared their results, the press proclaimed
they'd found the man with the most beautiful brain on earth. "His
level of mind control is astonishing," wrote a British reporter,
"and the upbeat impulses in his brain are off the scale."[3]

Who was this man? And how did his brain get this way?

The man in the MRI scanner was a Buddhist monk named Matthieu Ricard. He'd grown up in Paris and earned a PhD in molecular genetics at the prestigious Pasteur Institute. But at the age of twenty-six, with a promising scientific career ahead of him, Ricard left it all behind and went to Tibet. There, in the rarefied air of the Himalayas, he studied under the great Buddhist masters.

Ricard would end up clocking more than 60,000 hours of meditation. Year in, year out, he fed his brain with thoughts of love and compassion, to staggering effect. By the time he ended up in that scanner, according to headlines around the globe, Ricard was "the happiest man in the world."

What this monk achieved is something millions of people chase as the ultimate goal in their lives. We can't get enough of the mantras, methods, and life hacks that promise greater mindfulness, prosperity, and well-being. You can easily spend 60,000 hours on the thousands of books about the seven habits, twelve rules, or that one big secret to living a long and happy life. All in the hopes of someday having a brain as beautiful as the illustrious Frenchman's.

But you can also look at Mr. Ricard in a different light. Here's a guy who spent 60,000 hours — that's 7,500 workdays, or a solid thirty years of full-time work — inside his own head. Thirty years in which he did little for others, thirty years in which he didn't lift a finger to make the world a better place.

Maybe you dream of doing something else with your limited time on this planet. Maybe your own happiness isn't the prime objective, let alone your ultimate life goal. Maybe you don't want to find yourself on your deathbed with the gnawing feeling you had more in you — perhaps *much* more.

In that case, you'll need a book that's more than the latest guide to finding happiness. Not a book that makes life easier, but one that makes life a little harder. Not a book that offers solace, but one that causes friction. The kind of book you half-wish you'd never picked up at all because once you put it down, you might just have to change your life.

This is that kind of book.

No, you're not fine just the way you are

People may spend their whole lives climbing the ladder of success
only to find, once they reach the top, that the ladder is leaning
against the wrong wall.
Allen Raine, *writer (1836–1908)*

I

Of all things wasted in our throwaway times, the greatest is wasted talent. There are millions of people around the world who could help make the world a better place, but don't. Why is that? First there's the obvious reason: they don't get the chance. After all, half the world's people have to make do with less than seven dollars a day.[1] How many lost Einsteins walk among them?

But I'm talking here about the people who've been given every opportunity. About the ones who've got the power to shape their own careers, though you'd never know it from their utterly unsurprising résumés. About the talented folks with the world at their feet who nonetheless get stuck in mind-numbing, pointless, or just plain harmful jobs.

There's an antidote to that kind of waste, and it's called *moral ambition*. Moral ambition is the will to make the world a wildly better place. To devote your working life to the great challenges of our time, whether that's climate change or corruption, gross inequality or the next pandemic. It's a longing to make a difference — and to build a legacy that truly matters.

Moral ambition begins with a simple realization: you've only got one life. The time you have left on this earth is your most precious possession. You can't buy yourself more time, and every hour you've spent is gone forever. A full-time career consists of some 80,000 hours, or 10,000 workdays, or 2,000 workweeks. How you spend that time is one of the most important moral decisions of your life.

So what do you want on your résumé? Going for a respectable, if bland, list? Or do you set the bar higher? Morally ambitious individuals don't move with the herd, but believe in a deeper

3

form of freedom. It's the freedom to push aside conventional standards of success, to make your own way along life's path, knowing it's a journey you can only make once.

Those looking to do some good in today's world don't have to look far. Still reeling from a global pandemic, we're seeing hunger surge for the first time in years.[2] Meanwhile, autocracy is on the rise, while the number of people forced to flee their homes has topped 100 million for the first time.[3] And as temperatures hit one record high after another, climate scientists are stressing the need for "the biggest and most fundamental transformation" of society ever attempted in peacetime.[4]

In short: these times call for moral ambition.

Now you might be thinking: *That's all well and good, but I've got a full-time job, two kids, and a mortgage. I'm happy to recycle and eat some tofu now and then, but a "fundamental transformation"? No thanks.*

In that case, this book may not be for you. I mean, once you have a labradoodle, a set of cheese knives, or a robot mower, there's generally no going back. But if that's irritating to hear — and I imagine it might be — then by all means, prove me wrong. I've learned there are always exceptions, and in this book I want to show that you can be that exception.

When it comes to moral ambition, it's never too late to step up.

2

Let's start with a simple model of what you can do with your talents. Whether you've got your whole career ahead of you or are looking to make a change, it seems to me you've got roughly four options:

	Not-so-idealistic	Idealistic
Not-so-ambitious	I Bullshit job, independently wealthy	III Passionate part-timer, online activist
Ambitious	II Corporate lawyer, consultant, in finance or tech	IV Moral ambition

Category I jobs: not that ambitious, not that idealistic

Some jobs simply don't add much value. These are people writing reports nobody reads or managing colleagues who don't need managing. Recent research shows that about 8 percent of all employees think their own job is pretty pointless. Another 17 percent confess to having some doubts about whether their job contributes to society.[5]

The late anthropologist David Graeber (1961–2020) had a highly technical term for such positions: *bullshit jobs*.[6] What jobs are we talking about here? Well, we know which ones they're *not*. In 2020, at the start of the Covid-19 pandemic, lists of "essential workers" popped up everywhere: from cleaning staff to trash collectors, from teachers to firefighters, and from bus drivers to registered nurses. These are the people who keep the world running; they don't need a lecture on moral ambition.

But there's also a class of not-so-useful jobs. A class of influencers and marketeers, of lobbyists and managers, of consultants and corporate lawyers — all people who could go on strike and the world would be just fine. Remarkably enough, this group includes many men and women with impressive credentials and equally impressive salaries. Reminds me of that Facebook employee who said, "The best minds of my generation are thinking about how to make people click ads."[7]

Who thinks their own job is bullshit?

The percentage of people who think their job is pointless or who have doubts about its value for society, by occupation

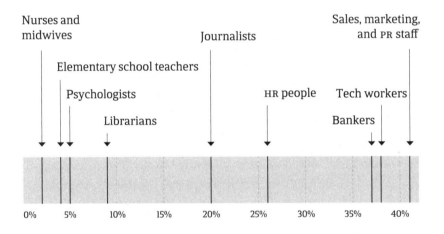

Source: Dur and Van Lent (2019)

But it can be even worse. Some jobs are outright harmful and fall into what are sometimes called the "sin industries." Here we find accountants helping the rich avoid taxes, marketers promoting addictive meds, brokers peddling dubious financial products, and anyone working for the gambling industry or Big Tobacco.

These jobs often get a lick of PR paint. (At tobacco giant Philip Morris, for instance, they claim to be working toward a "smoke-free future.") But make no mistake, we're talking here about people getting paid to do real damage to the rest of society.

Unless cornered, many of these employees won't cop to having a pointless or harmful job. It's not exactly the kind of thing you chat about at parties. (*Yeah, I'm in the addiction business. You?*) That may be why such positions pay so well. You'd want extra compensation for having to admit you do that kind of work. In fact, there's a striking correlation between the level of pay in a given industry and how moral or immoral we think it is.[8] See for instance this graph from a Swiss study:

The higher the pay, the more immoral the work?

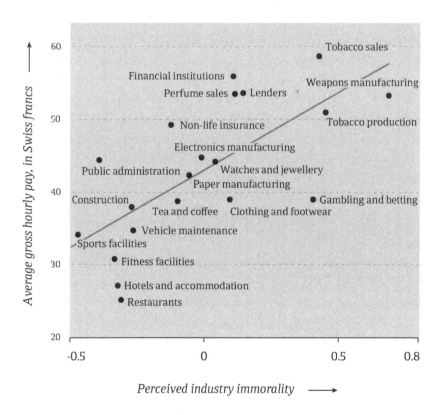

Source: Schneider, Brun, and Weber (2020)

7

For some people in this not-all-that-ambitious, not-all-that-idealistic category, there's also an escape hatch: becoming financially independent. Countless self-help books lay out how to get rich with minimal effort, so you can get out as soon as possible, then kick back and relax. You've now got loads of people in their twenties or thirties who dream of accumulating *passive income* — income from real estate, stock, or cryptocurrency — so they can "earn" enough to retire early.[9]

Nothing wrong with having some savings and investments, of course. But at its core, this kind of thinking always seems a little sad to me. It means you're chasing a form of freedom where you won't have to lift a finger. The dream is to make the transition from office serf to person of independent means, so you can delegate all the annoying work and no longer have to contribute to society.

Category II jobs: ambitious, but not all that idealistic

The second category of wasted talent consists of people who are ambitious but not so idealistic. Or put another way, these people want to reach the top, but use soulless indicators for success: a fancy title, fat salary, corner office, or other perks.

Take graduates from the world's most prestigious universities. Some 45 percent of Harvard alumni go into finance or consulting.[10] A poll from a few years back shows that in my country, the Netherlands, 40 percent of "high achievers" (college students with excellent grades) aspire to work for major consulting firms like McKinsey or the Boston Consulting Group.[11]

We're talking colossal waste of talent here. Economist Benjamin Lockwood, who studied at Amherst, the elite private school in Massachusetts, noticed that many of his fellow students went into fields with no clear added value to society.[12] And in 2017, Lockwood and two colleagues published a groundbreaking study showing that many of those former classmates now *cost* society money. (Think banking executives who need bailing out with public money.)[13]

A corporate lawyer, for instance, does some $30,000 of damage to society each year, a commercial banker more than $100,000.[14] That's a lot of money, but if you ask Lockwood, he stresses that the *opportunity costs* are well higher. That's economic jargon for: *just think how much better shape our world would be in if these bright people had done something useful with their lives.*[15]

Take consultants. Most consultants certainly contribute to society, but — and this is crucial — far less than they could. They help an organization develop a better workflow or clearer HR policies, or they advise one company after another on compliance with new legislation. The work's all right and isn't hurting anyone. But consider this: these talented people are at best helping others be a little more productive. They see to it that things run more smoothly; rarely do they get things rolling. They don't start new organizations, don't come up with new innovations, and generally don't concern themselves with the most pressing challenges facing us today.

Choose this career path, and you can count on a nice salary. If you're among the top in your field, you can afford to go skiing regularly or buy that beach house you always dreamed of. But is that really all you want out of life? Surely there's more to it. Many young consultants, according to the *Financial Times* a few years back, "feel they add little value to the world and lack a sense of personal growth, community, and purpose."[16]

You can hear similar frustrations even among doctors, professionals we usually think of as essential. Our best physicians are now able to do much more to help ever fewer patients. We have brilliant cardiologists who no longer have to perform invasive open-heart surgery but can replace a damaged heart valve through a small incision in the patient's groin.

9

Fantastic, right? But in practice, high-dollar operations like this one are often performed on wealthy, well-insured patients in their eighties in an effort to extend their lives by a few years. What's more, international studies show that up to one-third of medical interventions (not just procedures but tests, prescriptions, everything) turn out to be unnecessary or even harmful.[17]

More doctors ≠ longer lives

Life expectancy vs. number of physicians per 1,000 people

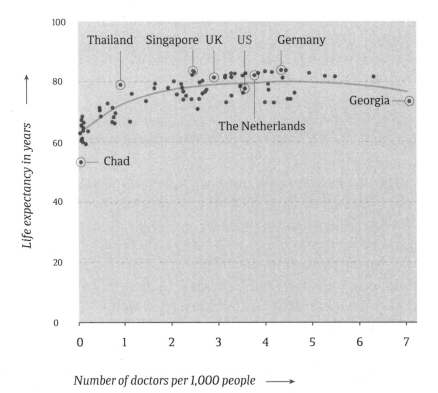

Number of doctors per 1,000 people ⟶

Source: World Bank (2019)

Things aren't much different for entrepreneurs. I was scrolling through lists of successful startups recently and spotted a couple of inspired initiatives — like a company working on cultivated meat, an enterprise that's building a solar-powered car, and an organization developing a nasal spray that protects against viruses. Very promising stuff.[18]

But more often than not, we're offered solutions for problems we didn't know we had. Take the category "best young entrepreneurs," where I came across the electric toothbrush toothbrush-head subscription.[19] Or what about a new investment app, or the next big online fashion outlet? Or yet another food delivery app, a personalized vitamin service, or that mattress startup that advertised on what seemed like every podcast in my feed a while back. ("A mattress is the most boring product you can imagine," according to the founder.)[20]

Now, I don't have anything against mattresses, and getting a new head for my toothbrush in the mail every other month sounds handy, honestly. But you've got to wonder what the founders of companies like these could have achieved if they'd taken on a challenge like, I don't know, the 5.4 *million* infants and children worldwide who die each year from diseases we can easily — *easily!* — prevent.[21]

What if they'd put their talent toward something that really matters?

Category III jobs: idealistic, but not all that ambitious
And then there's a third category, made up of people who're idealistic, but not that ambitious. It's a combination often seen in Gen Z — people born since 1996.

One survey after another shows that today's teenagers and twentysomethings make up the most progressive generation yet.[22] That's wonderful news. Most young people are far more idealistic than their parents and are focused on a number of the big challenges of our day, whether that's climate change or racism, sexual harassment or inequality.

But something seems to be missing. You see it in young people's take on their careers: with no interest in joining the capitalist rat race, many want work they're passionate about — and then preferably part-time.[23]

The rise of the phrase 'Follow your passion' in books published between 1970 and 2020

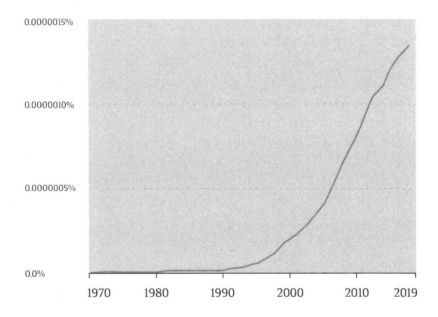

Source: Google Ngram

Sometimes it seems "ambition" has become a dirty word, incompatible with an idealistic lifestyle. Many people are more preoccupied with the kind of work they do than with the impact that work has. As long as it feels good. "Small is beautiful," you'll then hear. Or "think global, act local" — as if achieving little is somehow a virtue.

In some circles, you'd think the highest good is not to have any impact at all. A good life is then primarily defined by what you *don't* do. Don't fly. Don't eat meat. Don't have kids. And whatever you do, don't even think about using a plastic straw. Reduce! Reduce! Reduce! The aim is to have the smallest footprint possible, with your little vegetable garden and your tiny house. Best-case scenario? Your impact on the planet is so negligible, you could just as well not have existed.

Don't get me wrong — it's a fine idea to align even your smallest deeds with your biggest values. (And not eating meat from factory farms seems to me a moral minimum.) But surely a good life consists of more than what you *don't* do? One would hope that on your deathbed, you can chalk up your life's work to more than simply all the harm you didn't cause?

Seen this way, even the most moralistic movement of our times shows a serious lack of ambition. I'm talking about those called "woke." Often accused of going too far, woke activists in many cases don't go far enough. Take the preoccupation with the words we use to describe the world. Yes, words matter, and to some extent they even shape our reality. But in the end, what you *do* matters far more.

If we look at the concrete successes of these kinds of activists, the results seem meager. True, you can reach millions these days in no time with an online rant against sexism, racism, or capitalism. *Kill the patriarchy! Defund the police! Tax the rich!* But what happens next? Having lots of followers on Instagram isn't the same as building an effective organization. Going viral isn't the same as winning a majority in the legislature. Modern protest sometimes seems little more than a collection of clicks and likes, in the hopes someone higher up will take notice.[24]

"People don't understand," writes Patrisse Khan-Cullors, one of the founders of Black Lives Matter, "that organizing isn't going online and cussing people out or going to a protest and calling something out."[25] For actual change, far more is required. How do you build a coalition? How do you lobby effectively? Where's the money coming from? Who plays a key role in that commission at the local, state, or national level? How can you find out what buttons to push, and when? And who has the know-how to tweak legislation in clever ways to great effect?

The trouble with idealists who lack ambition is they tend to prize awareness more than action. Words and intentions take precedence over deeds and consequences, and what something's *really* like gets eclipsed by what it *feels* like. But here's the thing: awareness alone won't help a soul. Awareness doesn't put food on the table. Awareness won't keep a roof over your head. With awareness, you don't cool down the planet, you're not finding shelter for those 100 million refugees, and you won't make a bit of difference for the 100 billion animals at factory farms worldwide.[26]

Awareness is at best a starting point, while for many activists, it seems to have become the end goal.

Category IV: *idealistic* and *ambitious*

Is there another way? Say you take the ambition of a highflier and add a generous dose of idealism. What do you get?

Let me introduce my personal hero — someone I'll come back to often in this book — the author and activist Thomas Clarkson. In 1785, as a 24-year-old college student, Clarkson decided to enter an essay contest in Latin at Cambridge University. To take part, he had to answer a short question: *Anne liceat invitos in servitutem dare?*

That is, *Is it okay to force others into slavery?*

At the time, winning a Latin essay contest was *the* way to make a name for yourself at school. "I had no motive but that which other young men in the University had on such occasions,"

Clarkson would later recall, "namely the wish of being distinguished, or obtaining literary honor."[27]

There was just one small problem: Clarkson didn't know a thing about slavery.

Students had two months to put their thoughts to paper, and while most only started to feel the pressure once the deadline was imminent, Clarkson was different. He got straight to work.

The earnest student loved an intellectual challenge and thought he would enjoy the research process. But the facts hit hard. "In the daytime I was uneasy. In the night I had little rest. I sometimes never closed my eyelids for grief." Clarkson kept a candle near his bed in case anything occurred to him at night, because he believed that "no arguments of any moment should be lost in so great a cause."[28]

A few weeks of hard work later, his essay was finished. In powerful prose, Clarkson concluded that slavery was "contrary to reason, justice, nature, the principles of law and government . . . and the revealed voice of God."[29] And you guessed it: he won first place. Clarkson was invited to present his winning essay in the majestic Senate House at the University of Cambridge. There he stood, a towering young man with fiery hair and bright eyes. All signs indicated Thomas Clarkson had a glorious career ahead of him.

But on the way back to London, he couldn't get the subject of his essay out of his head. He got down from his horse and walked, distracted. He tried to convince himself he'd made some mistake, that the grisly facts couldn't be right. But the longer he thought about it, the deeper the truth sunk in. When the little village of Wade's Mill came into view, he stopped and sat down, glum, at the side of the road. "Here a thought came into my mind," he would later write, "that if the contents of the essay were true, then it was time some person should see these calamities to their end."[30]

If the end of the slave trade started anywhere, it started here, in the summer of 1785, at the side of the road outside Wade's Mill.[31]

Of course, there had been others who protested the most heinous forms of slavery. And certainly, history is filled with acts of resistance by enslaved people, who time and again worked to throw off their chains.[32] But the fact of the matter is that for centuries, victims of the system weren't able to overthrow that system. The very notion of *abolitionism*, the idea that the whole institution of slavery could be abolished once and for all, long seemed unthinkable.

And so Clarkson initially thought he was alone in his ambition. In the months following his revelation, he wandered around in a daze. "I walked frequently into the woods, that I might think on the subject in solitude, and find relief to my mind there. But there the question still recurred, 'Are these things true?' Still the answer followed as instantaneously 'They are.' Still the result accompanied it, 'Then surely some person should interfere.'"[33]

The young Englishman had few connections, but it occurred to him he could translate his winning Latin essay into English. He went to a printer in London, who was interested in publishing it for "persons of taste," but Clarkson was no longer interested in literary fame among a small elite. He wanted his essay to reach as many people as possible.

Disappointed, he walked back outside and ran into an old family friend. Crucial detail: this family friend belonged to the Religious Society of Friends, also known as Quakers. Clarkson didn't know that this peculiar church had been campaigning against slavery for some time. What he also didn't know was that they had their eye on him.

The Quaker took him to a small bookseller and printer in the heart of London. Clarkson discovered that day that he wasn't alone at all. England already had a burgeoning network of abolitionists.[34] One evening, at a dinner with his new friends, the young man made a decision. Clarkson knew someone had to dedicate their life to the fight against slavery, and so he stood up and announced to everyone there: "I'm ready to devote myself to the cause."[35]

That may sound a little melodramatic. And if you read Clarkson's memoirs today, you can't help but think, *Easy there, Clarkson, you seem mighty impressed with yourself.* But make no mistake, idealism often comes with a shot of vanity. With many a world-saver, it's tough to say where the idealism ends and the vanity begins. What's more, if Clarkson had been less self-assured, if he hadn't seen himself as a history-making hero, would he have devoted his life to abolitionism? Not likely.[36]

Later Clarkson would write that he'd obediently given up his worldly ambitions to follow the path God laid out for him. Quite the humblebrag. Clarkson was of course sincere in his empathy with the plight of enslaved people, but he hadn't suddenly lost all sense of ambition. Far from it. He'd simply traded in his literary dreams for something much, much bigger, for what could be more momentous than the fight to end slavery?[37]

Real-world deeds are more important than intentions, and when it came down to it, the ambitious college student kept his word. For the rest of his life, for sixty-one more years, Clarkson continued to fight for his ideals. He grew to be one of the greatest reformers of his time. What the apostle Paul was to Christianity, and Martin Luther to the Reformation, Thomas Clarkson was to abolitionism.

A "moral steam engine," a contemporary called him, a "giant with one idea."[38]

3

In this book, I'd like to introduce you to some of the Thomas Clarksons of our time: a parade of activists and entrepreneurs, doctors and lawyers, engineers and innovators, all bursting with moral ambition.

What they have in common is a refusal to see their own deeds as mere drops in the bucket. They believe they can make a difference and are prepared to take risks to get there. They don't just think, "Someone really should do something about that," but take action themselves.

What many of these people also share, is a certain degree of privilege. Not everyone can devote their life to the world's biggest problems. Thomas Clarkson could never have been a full-time abolitionist without the inheritance his father left him. Elizabeth Cady Stanton (1815–1902) would likely not have become a leading women's rights activist without the education paid for by her wealthy parents.

But I don't want to generalize. People suffering from poverty and illness, racism and sexism can move mountains, too. Helen Keller (1880–1968) was blind and deaf, and became a legendary advocate for people with disabilities. Malcolm X (1925–1965) grew up in deep poverty and became an iconic leader in the struggle for civil rights.

True, people with moral ambition often pay a price for their ideals. Malcolm X paid with his life. And even for those blessed with long lives, moral ambition can take its toll. Thomas Clarkson traveled 35,000 miles in a period of seven years — on horseback and often at night — to bring his pamphlets and petitions to the people. At thirty-three, he suffered a nervous breakdown, or what we'd now call burnout. Year in year out, he'd filled his brain with the horrors of slavery, in facts and figures and brutal images. "I am often suddenly seized with giddiness and cramps," Clarkson wrote in his journal. "I feel an unpleasant ringing in my ears, my hands frequently tremble. Cold sweats suddenly come upon me."[39]

What if they'd stuck this guy in an MRI scanner at that point, like the French Buddhist monk? Likely he'd have the most pitiful gamma waves ever. Because my lord, this man must have had some hideous gray matter. The left side of his prefrontal cortex didn't register the faintest spark of happiness, while the right was abuzz with negative energy. And picture the press. BREAKING NEWS: WE'VE FOUND THE UNHAPPIEST MAN ON EARTH! "His level of mind control is abysmal, and the negative impulses in his brain are off the charts."

So no, Clarkson wasn't exactly mindful, and he really should have done his breathing exercises. Or maybe just slowed down a little. It's in nobody's interest for the folks making the world a better place to collapse at age thirty-three and have to be carried off the field mid-fight. But at least he didn't get burned out from scrolling through never-ending spreadsheets or sitting through yet another PowerPoint. "I was therefore obliged, though very reluctantly," he wrote in his memoirs, "to be borne out of the field where I had placed the great honor and glory of my life."[40]

So ask yourself the question: What's the "great honor and glory" of your life? What do you hope one day to look back on? "A person of honor cares first of all not about being respected," writes the philosopher Kwame Anthony Appiah, "but about being *worthy* of respect."[41] Your honor is not the same as your reputation. It's not about looking good; it's about doing good.

One thing's for sure. If you want to lead a morally ambitious life, there's no time like the present. Fear of change is often the first sign of aging, and before you know it, you're in golden handcuffs: stuck in a ho-hum job with no time to spare and all your money earmarked for things like that replacement toothbrush-head subscription.

But make the leap, and the possibilities are endless. Because so many others waste their talents, people with moral ambition can make a world of difference.

Lower your threshold for taking action

At critical moments in time, you can raise the aspirations of other people significantly, especially when they are relatively young, simply by suggesting they do something better or more ambitious than what they might have in mind. It costs you relatively little to do this, but the benefit to them, and to the broader world, may be enormous. This is in fact one of the most valuable things you can do with your time and with your life.

Tyler Cowen, *economist (b. 1962)*

I

It's easy to think moral ambition isn't for you. Maybe you feel you're not cut out for it, that you're not hero material. But what sets some people apart? What makes them open to following their moral ambition?

There's a well-known photograph taken in 1936 of German shipyard workers doing the Nazi salute. If you look closely, you can see one man in the crowd who's not joining in. As over a hundred people stretch out their right arms toward the führer, this man stands there, coolly defiant, arms folded across his chest.

Who was this man? And where in the world did he find the courage? The photograph sat in the archives gathering dust for decades, until a German historian came across it by chance. On November 15, 1995, he placed an ad in Hamburg's evening paper: Does anyone recognize this man? That same week, a reader responded that it must be her father, August Landmesser.

His story was heartrending. In 1931, a young Landmesser joined the Nazi party, in the hopes of landing a job. But only a few years later, he met nineteen-year-old Irma Eckler. She was Jewish, and as an Aryan, he wasn't allowed to get involved with her. Yet the two fell in love. Against all the rules, they had two daughters together, Ingrid and Irene.[1] There's one photo of the family, taken in June 1938. We see a smiling father with his older daughter, and a mother holding her baby close.

A month after this picture was taken, the Gestapo pounded on the young family's door. The children were taken away to an orphanage, the parents convicted of *rassenschande*.* Irma was sent to a concentration camp and murdered in a gas chamber; August was ordered to the front to fight, where he was killed in 1944.

More than half a century later, their younger daughter opened the newspaper and spotted her father. The picture taken at the

* The Nazi term for sexual relations with a non-Aryan, a crime under the Nuremberg Laws in Nazi Germany, where unions between Jews and other Germans were prohibited.

shipyard went viral, and August Landmesser ended up on millions of buttons and postcards, t-shirts and posters. You can come across him today in dorm rooms, bars, and cubicles, and the photo still makes the rounds online every so often, usually with the same commentary: BE THAT GUY!

After all those years, the man who wouldn't salute still seems to confront us with the question, *What would you have done in my situation?* Would you have been as brave? Or would you have gone along with the crowd? We hope the former but fear the latter. "He's the only person in the entire scene," a historian later wrote, "who's on the right side of history."[2]

The story of August Landmesser reminds us of a simple fact: most humans are herd animals. We do what we're taught to do, we accept what we're handed, we believe what we're told is true. Though we may feel free, we're sticking to the script that goes with our kind of life.

The fear of being different runs deep in human nature. We may tell earnest tales of our personal convictions, but what we actually *do* is mostly a matter of mimicry. The longing to belong is like a magnet, interfering with our inner compass. If we focus only on our own lives, it's easy to confuse freedom with being free to do as you please. But doing what you feel like often means little more than going with the flow.

There's a quote from the anthropologist Margaret Mead that I think of often. "Never doubt that a small group of thoughtful, committed citizens can change the world. Indeed, it's the only thing that ever has." That may sound like a happy little motto for idealistic do-gooders, but it's really a cold hard observation.

What Mead is saying is that most people stand on the sidelines. The majority leave behind but a fleeting footprint and are soon forgotten because they made little difference. Only a small minority of dedicated citizens choose a more difficult life. They set the bar high and forge their own path.

Along the way, they change the world.

2

But how can you make a difference? What can you, as a lone warrior, bring to bear on the biggest challenges of our time, whether that's poverty or hunger, war or climate change? On a planet of 8 billion and counting, it's easy to feel insignificant. Even as part of a group, it can seem impossible to make your mark.

The opposite is true.

A small group of committed individuals can have enormous influence, in part because most people are busy living their lives. It's actually an old law of statistics. In 1906, economist and gardener Vilfredo Pareto made a startling discovery: some 80 percent of his peas grew in a mere 20 percent of his peapods. That is to say, two out of ten peapods contained far more peas than the other eight put together.

That 80/20 rule seemed to apply to more things, and today it's called the *Pareto principle*. Top athletes score more points than the rest of the team added up. Hit records are played more than all other songs put together. The most devastating wars cause more casualties than all other conflicts combined.

For those of us who grew up in a democracy, where "the people" are said to rule, the news that most citizens stand on the sidelines can come as a shock. Imagine you lined up all the people in the world in order of influence. Then you might picture a graph with a gently rolling curve:

You might think influence in the world
is distributed like this:

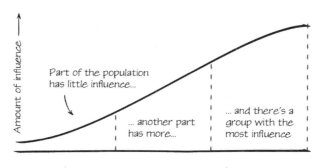

But according to Margaret Mead, the reality is neither gentle nor rolling. The reality is extreme. The most influential individuals aren't two or five or ten times as influential, but a hundred, a thousand, or a million times. In statistics, that kind of phenomenon is said to follow a *power law*, and the associated graph doesn't look like a hill at all — more like a plateau with one towering peak. On the left, you see the masses with negligible influence; on the right, the small minority that wields power.

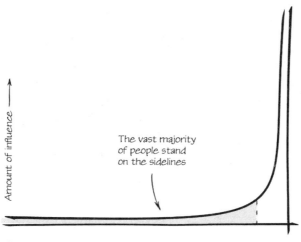

If you let that reality sink in, you may again feel small. Is the whole world ruled by a select group of rich and powerful elites?

It's not that simple. Extreme inequality persists, of course, in how wealth and income are distributed. And with millions in the bank, you can exercise a lot of influence. But most rich people don't do much that's interesting with their money. Their desires are pretty predictable: fancy cars, luxury homes, the biggest yacht they can buy — all to fill the void inside. No surprise there.

History, meanwhile, is full of people without deep pockets who still manage to have a lasting impact. What about abolitionists fighting to end slavery, or the suffragettes working for women's right to vote? Were they the richest or most powerful groups of their time? Hardly. But they changed the world.

The statistician Nassim Nicholas Taleb speaks of an "intransigent minority." The world is shaped by stubborn, obstinate, headstrong, hell-bent, willful, relentless advocates. "The most intolerant wins," Taleb dryly observes.[3]

3

I know few stories that illustrate the power of relentless advocates as clearly as the tale of Nieuwlande, a tiny town in the Netherlands close to the German border. During World War II, nearly one hundred Jews secured a hiding place there. The concentration of people in hiding was higher than nearly everywhere else in Europe.

What was Nieuwlande's secret? Why did so many in this little community have the courage to hide someone in danger? To understand what happened in Nieuwlande, you first have to hear the story of Arnold Douwes, a man from the town of Boskoop, on the other side of the country. Arnold had been a willful child, suspended from school on three occasions. Later

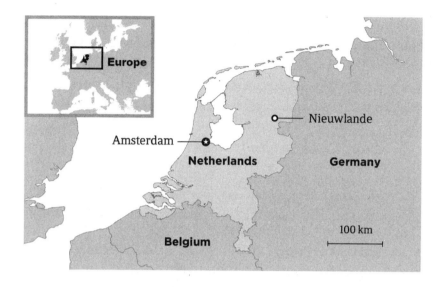

he couldn't land a job and failed to find a wife. As a young man, Arnold didn't in any way meet society's expectations.

Until May 10, 1940, when the Nazis invaded. That week, the 34-year-old freewheeler was stopped by a German officer on a motorcycle, looking for the way to Leiden. "Immer geradeaus," replied Arnold, *keep going straight*, as he pointed in the wrong direction. "Danke schön," the soldier said and rode off.[4]

It was the first act of resistance by a man who was a bit of a drifter in ordinary life but now found his calling in wartime.

If you'd told Arnold Douwes that "most people, deep down, are pretty decent," he would've laughed out loud, because he thought most people were cowards.[5] Few in the Netherlands dared resist Nazi occupation, while after the war, many claimed to have been part of the resistance.

Dutch historians speak of the *resistance myth*, the fiction that this brave little land rose up as one to challenge the Germans.[6] In reality, there were few serious attempts to resist their authority. Many Dutch people thought resistance was futile and adapted accordingly.[7] And so a civilized country largely stood by and watched as its Jewish population was carted off to camps. Public officials willingly took part, the police helped nab Jews in hiding, and the national railways took care of transit.

No, most Dutch people weren't Nazis or members of the Dutch National Socialist party. The majority did not approve of how Jews and other minorities were treated and hoped Germany would be defeated.[8] But when it came down to it, most Dutch people remained passive under occupation.

Arnold Douwes was different. He got his start in the resistance by delivering underground newspapers, then soon moved on to chores like cutting the cables powering German searchlights. Once the authorities were on to him, he trekked cross-country, his bicycle his sole possession. That's how he ended up in Nieuwlande in the summer of 1942. There, he led what would become one of the country's largest networks for Jews in hiding. In no time, Nieuwlande was full of what Arnold called *duikelaars* — Jews gone underground, primarily from Amsterdam.

To see how that worked, we can consult a unique source: Arnold's journal. It's the only known account written in real time by someone who helped hide Jews in Western Europe. Arnold filled thirty-five little notebooks with his writings, stuffed them into jelly jars, and buried them in the yards of homes in his secret network. After the war, he typed up his notes into a 247-page volume. The result is a wartime diary of astounding detail, at times providing an hourly play-by-play.

Arnold seldom wrote about his feelings, except for his frustration with cowardly countrymen. Maybe that's why his account is so powerful. It's the story of a man who didn't rationalize or make excuses, didn't stand around hemming and hawing, but who took action.

Life in the resistance required the endurance of an athlete. Reading his journal, I was amazed at the distances Arnold biked each day. For sixteen months, he rode his bicycle along the Dutch backroads — seven days a week, rain or shine, and often with a passenger hitching a ride — asking everyone he could find if they'd take people in.

I say "asking," but Arnold didn't really ask questions. That way he wouldn't get no for an answer. He and comrade Max Léons did the "good cop, bad cop" routine, with Max politely testing the waters and Arnold taking the direct approach. Arnold told off one farmer after another in the local dialect, which he'd picked up quickly. He was especially ruthless with ministers. He'd call them out as cowards, or what was worse in their eyes, *ye of little faith.*

Arnold wrote in his journal that people tended to defer to others who might help. *Couldn't they go to Mrs. So and So? Surely she had room. Or maybe the farmer up the road, with the big farmhouse?* When that didn't work, some tried to offer him money — anything to avoid taking someone into hiding.

Even today, people in the Netherlands debate the question of whether we "*gewusst haben*" — whether we knew what the Nazis planned to do to Jews.[9] But if you read about the people who resisted, you realize there are two forms of "knowing." You can know something and then do something about it. Or you can know something and look away, afraid to face the consequences of what you know to be true.

Those who helped Jews refused to look away. They believed they could make a difference. They didn't see themselves as simple onlookers or cogs in the machine, but as autonomous people who could choose to do the right thing. They asked themselves the question, *Can I live with myself if I do nothing?*[10]

People who remained on the sidelines during the war kept their heads down and told themselves they were powerless.[11] They had more of a tendency to doubt the gruesome tales of gas chambers in the east, maybe because those reports seemed too horrific to be true, or because disbelief was more comfortable. As two American researchers have reported:

> Although rescuers and nonrescuers knew similar facts, at some point rescuers began to perceive them in a personal way. At some point, information was no longer merely recorded or vaguely apprehended [. . .] At some point, for rescuers, awareness became attention, and attention became focused concentration on what was happening to particular people in a specific context.[12]

This tendency to face up to the truth can cause resentment. Those who helped Jews were regularly deemed selfish during the war because they put their neighbors' lives in danger.[13] Arnold and Max took a lot of heat for what they were doing. They were thought to be far too reckless, bringing way too many Jews into hiding in Nieuwlande.

But there was no stopping Arnold. He figured if everyone in town was hiding people, no one could snitch. As for how he ran up the numbers? There's a telling anecdote in Max's memoirs about the time he and Arnold stopped by the home of a certain Farmer Nienhuus to get him to take in two people.[14] Over a cup of coffee, they broached the touchy subject, whereupon the farmer immediately started to object.

But Max assured him, "They're man and wife — very sweet people." He added, "Just a moment. I'll go get them."

LOWER YOUR THRESHOLD FOR TAKING ACTION

And to the surprise of Nienhuus and his wife, a Jewish couple appeared in the living room. Before the farmer could protest, Arnold stood up to go.

"So, that's settled. Good night!"

The Jewish couple survived the war.

4

What makes some people capable of going against the flow and standing up to tyranny? What explains the moral choices of an August Landmesser or an Arnold Douwes? Was it their upbringing, or an innate quality? Was it the people around them, or something deep inside?

In the 1970s, the first in-depth studies were conducted into the psychology of resistance heroes. The pioneers of this new field were the professors Dr. Samuel Oliner and Dr. Pearl Oliner, a husband-and-wife team. Together, they founded the Altruistic Personality Institute at what was then Humboldt State University in California.[15] The Oliners interviewed more than 400 people who helped protect Jews during World War II and compared their psychological profiles with those of bystanders who did nothing.

The biggest surprise? How little the study found. Turns out heroes and mere mortals were hard to tell apart, which raised the question: Did the altruistic personality even exist? A resistance hero could be shy or self-assured, silly or serious, young or old, pious or scandalous, rich or poor, left-wing or right, and so on and so on.

The American psychologist Eva Fogelman, who interviewed over 300 rescuers for a similar study, regularly attended ceremonies in Israel in the 1980s honoring resistance heroes. She was struck by how, at a distance, they always looked like a random group of people, like "subway riders who are seated in the same car."[16]

And yet both Fogelman and the Oliners reached a couple of tentative conclusions. First, feelings are overrated. Very few rescuers reported being motivated by deep-felt sympathy. Empathy isn't the same as courage, after all. You can feel all kinds of things about the suffering of others, but that doesn't mean you'll *do* anything about it. Confronted with images of starving children on television, you can make a generous donation to an aid organization. Or you can change the channel. We usually go with the latter.

And besides, many of those who helped save Jewish lives said they put aside their emotions in order to function effectively. As part of the resistance, you had to be able to steal, falsify, bribe and manipulate, break into buildings, and sometimes even take a life. Above all, you had to be a good liar — to lie to the authorities, but also to the people you were trying to help.

Arnold lied to just about everyone about just about everything. He told Amsterdam Jews, who weren't sure whether they should go into hiding, that life in little Nieuwlande was a fine, comfortable existence. He told people in town who took in Jews that the risks weren't all that high.

Second, psychologists have concluded that many rescuers had similar upbringings. Their parents instilled in them a strong sense of self-worth and taught them to think for themselves.[17] When speaking with the Oliners, one man described himself as "completely independent and relatively invulnerable to the opinion of others." A woman said she "asked too many questions" as a child and another said she was "always vehemently and openly objecting" to the strictures of the church.[18]

A certain amount of self-confidence is needed to take action. You have to believe you can make a difference. Psychologists speak of the *internal locus of control* — the sense that you're in charge of your own life. Many resistance heroes were strong-willed children.[19]

The third and perhaps most striking conclusion of the psychological research into resistance heroes was that communists and the super-religious were both overrepresented, at least in the Netherlands.[20] It wasn't the middle-ground majority who rose up to resist the Nazi occupiers, but those on the flanks. Made little difference whether they were Christian or communist, left-wing or right.

As one survivor said about his devout Christian rescuers: "They won't patronize the shop of a grocer who in their eyes is too left-wing, but they will take in the Jews he was hiding, as part of the shared struggle."[21]

Still the question remains: What was so special about the tiny town of Nieuwlande? How could it be that so many Jews found a hiding place there? Did it just happen to be home to lots of people with an altruistic personality?

In the 1990s, a new generation of researchers came along, who were critical of the earlier studies. Samuel and Pearl Oliner were seen to rely on circular reasoning. Why did some people risk their lives for others? Answer: because they were good people. Why were they good people? Because they risked their lives for others.[22]

But what explains all those folks raised in loving families, with cherished ideals, who did nothing? Why does this gap open up between the ideals we subscribe to and the things we do? To answer this question, the new researchers wanted to look not at rescuers' motives, but at their circumstances. The focus shifted from the psychology of the resistance to its sociology.

Were resistance heroes generally friends, family, or acquaintances of those they hid, perhaps? They were not. More than half had no prewar relationship whatsoever with any of the

Jews they helped, and nearly 90 percent helped at least one total stranger.[23] What about having a basement, an attic, or some savings tucked away? Did that play a role? Again, no. The only thing that seems to have made any difference was how many rooms your house had, and that effect was minimal.[24]

Turns out there was one circumstance that determined almost everything. A new analysis of data gathered by the Oliners showed that when this condition was met, nearly everyone took action — 96 percent to be precise.[25]

And what was that condition? Simple: you had to be asked. Those who were asked to help someone in danger almost always said yes. In many cases, the question seems to have been a turning point, with people then helping other Jews afterward. And many who were asked to help went on to ask others.

The resistance worked like a virus. Those who got involved then passed on the resistance bug to others, and some individuals, like Arnold Douwes, were superspreaders, asking hundreds of people to take action. Many such superspreaders were ministers or teachers who were respected members of the community. Some two-thirds of resistance heroes were initiated into sheltering Jews by one of these superspreaders, while few people made a hiding place available of their own accord.[26]

That may be it: the key to moral ambition. Everyone has their own *threshold to act*, a tipping point to taking action.[27] There's a minuscule minority that needs zero encouragement to stand up. Psychologist Cass Sunstein calls these pioneers the *zeros*, and Arnold Douwes clearly falls into this category. But most of us only dare to act once others have led the way. The *ones* need only one person ("If you go, so will I"), the *twos* take action if

36

they have two allies, and the *millions* will only act if half the country has taken to the streets.

This theory also explains why revolutions can gain momentum so quickly. The zeros ignite the ones, the ones ignite the twos, and then there's no stopping it. Take the revolution sparked and stoked by Thomas Clarkson, as he galloped across England spreading antislavery propaganda. He saw up close how the country caught fire and took every chance he got to fuel the flames. At the start of 1787 almost no one was talking about it, but a year later, a British newspaper proclaimed that abolishing the slave trade, "like the celestial fire, appears to electrify every worthy spirit."[28]

In the French town of Le Chambon-sur-Lignon — like Nieuwlande, teeming with people in hiding — the role of the zero was filled by minister André Trocmé. "I think his message was so strong [. . .] that it became like an infection," his daughter said after his death. "It inspired the community. Maybe some people who normally wouldn't have done anything like hiding a persecuted person found that: yes, they could do it."[29]

It's important to stop and think about the implications of this infection theory because they are far-reaching. There are libraries full of books about the question of what distinguishes the doers from the non-doers, the builders from the non-builders, and the heroes from the rest. But what if moral ambition isn't a personal quality or attribute, but rather a frame of mind? And what if that mindset is contagious — something everyone can catch?

The British historian Anton Howes conducted an extensive study into the origins of the industrial revolution, which brought us wonders like the train, the lightbulb, and the steam engine. Howes sifted through the biographies of 1,452 British inventors, but initially couldn't make anything of his data. There were rich and poor inventors, rural folks and city dwellers, heretics and devout churchgoers, professors and amateur tinkerers.[30]

But then Howes noticed something. "After staring at my data for long enough," he writes, "I began to notice a pattern."[31] Time and again, people would only innovate after being inspired by other inventors — be it a coworker, teacher, or friend, a neighbor, family member, or acquaintance. It was as if they were "infected" by a belief in progress.

According to Howes, it wasn't about spreading a specific idea or design but more a way of looking at the world, an attitude that's transmitted from one person to the next. In other words, you have to be exposed to this outlook. So, find the hotspots where the virus thrives and breathe in deep. Get yourself infected and then pass it on.

To get going, you need only the smallest of beginnings.[32] Johtje Vos, who saved thirty-six Jews with her husband, Aart, said after the war: "You don't just get up one morning and say, 'Now I'm going to hide Jewish people.' It's something that grows."[33] Many rescuers went far beyond what they originally planned to do.

In that sense, the most important thing was starting. Once you started resisting, you generally didn't stop. A mere 3 percent of the people interviewed by the Oliners took part for less than a month. For the bulk of the rescuers, resistance lasted longer than two years, and the majority — 65 percent to be precise — helped more than five Jews survive.[34]

During interviews with resistance heroes, it's striking how many talk of getting swept up in the work after a hesitant start. In December 1956, shortly after the historic bus boycott in Montgomery, Alabama, the 27-year-old Martin Luther King Jr. said, "If anybody had asked me a year ago to head the movement, I tell you very honestly that I would have run a mile to get away from it. I had no intention of being involved in this way."[35]

Not long ago, Marianne Birthler, a dissident in 1980s East Germany, described her radicalization to historian Anne Applebaum:

> The choice to become a dissident can easily be the result of "a number of small decisions that you take" — to absent yourself from the May Day parade, for example, or not to sing the words of the party hymn. And then, one day, you find yourself irrevocably on the other side. Often, this process involves role models. You see people whom you admire, and you want to be like them. It can even be "selfish." "You want to do something for yourself," Birthler said, "to respect yourself."[36]

If you want to change the world, then it's not so much about whether you're "cut out for it," with your precise mix of personal traits. It's not about who you are; it's about who you can become. You don't do good things because you're a good person. You become a good person by doing good things.

Most of us, of course, aren't zeros like Arnold Douwes. But if you're open to being inspired by others, you can lower your own threshold for taking action. So, expose yourself to the virus. Get started. And once you've started, ask others to join in.

3

Join a cult (or start your own)

We are here, not because we are law-breakers; we are here
in our efforts to become law-makers.
Emmeline Pankhurst, *suffragette (1858–1928)*

I

So. Let's say you've been infected with the moral ambition mindset. The next question is: What are you going to do with that ambition of yours? What role can you play?

When it comes to go-getter idealists, we often think of the people who march and protest, orate and chant, motivate and inspire. But what if that kind of activism isn't your thing? What if you want to fight for a better world, but would rather, I don't know, digest dense reports, work in a laboratory, or start your own company?

There's a simple truth that I'm going to point out repeatedly: moral ambition can take many forms. Take these folks, for instance:

A photographer from *Life* magazine captured this group in the summer of 1969, posing on the steps of the Capitol building in Washington DC. It's a portrait of one of the most influential action groups of the twentieth century, also known as the Radical Nerds.

To stretch your idea of what moral ambition can do, I'd like to tell you the story behind this legendary photograph.

2

On a Friday evening in November 1968, a young lawyer addressed a full lecture hall at Harvard Law School. His name was Ralph Nader and his message was clear: you're about to throw your life away.

The average law student, said Nader, is being conditioned into spending the rest of their career doing mind-numbing work. Every year, another cohort of brilliant young minds is snapped up by law firms to help their clients dodge legislation and avoid taxes.

But it wasn't too late, Nader emphasized. He invited the students to join a new movement, made up of the brightest students at the top law schools: Princeton, Harvard, Yale. A movement that wouldn't fight for the haves, but for the have-nots. Not for big business, but for the people.

Ralph Nader, the son of Lebanese immigrants, knew the cause needed dogged individuals — people who were willing to throw themselves into the fight and weren't afraid of the riot police. It was the sixties, after all. College students were taking to the streets worldwide to protest racism, inequality, and the Vietnam War.

But Nader understood that other skills were also needed. Making the world a better place demands a range of disciplines. Maybe you enjoy lobbying behind the scenes. Maybe you're crazy about complex statistical analysis. Or maybe you know everything there is to know about Penal Code Title 6 §162.2 and how it applied to that one obscure arrest on November 5, 1965.[1]

Then the good news is that you, too, can be a big activist. You might even be precisely the kind of activist we need most, because in many a movement, there's a surplus of derring-do and a dearth of hard skills. In many cases, nerds and hairsplitters make the difference.

What's tragic is that lots of nerds and hairsplitters are stuck in relatively useless jobs. The best attorneys, consultants, programmers, accountants, and bankers seldom work on solutions to big problems — whether that's human trafficking or a lack of clean drinking water, antibiotic resistance or climate change. All too often, in fact, they're part of the problem.

But as Nader assured his young listeners on that Friday evening in 1968, there's an alternative.

Let's first go through his life story, because it's full of fantastic anecdotes. Like Arnold Douwes, Ralph Nader was a zero — but a zero in a suit instead of coveralls. At fourteen, he was already reading long transcripts of Congressional debates, and as an undergraduate at Princeton he'd devour at least a book a day, on top of the required reading for classes.[2]

Nader's next step was Harvard Law School, where he soon grew thoroughly bored and "increasingly disdainful of the typical law student's track."[3] He saw the corporate law route as the road to a fat wallet and a feeble mind. "They made minds sharp by making them narrow," he'd later say of Harvard Law.[4]

If you were idealistic in the early 1960s, you might head for Alabama or Mississippi to join the civil rights protests being led by Rosa Parks and Martin Luther King. But when Nader graduated from law school, he hitched a ride in the other direction: to Washington DC, the heart of political power. Nader had a pressing reason for doing so. As a student, he'd often hitchhiked around the country and seen countless accidents. In those days, some 50,000 Americans died in traffic accidents every year, and car manufacturers were doing next to nothing to make their vehicles safer.

Car safety became Ralph Nader's first mission. He wrote a ripper of an indictment targeting the auto industry and one manufacturer in particular: General Motors. The industry giant topped the Fortune 500 list at the time, with annual revenue greater than most countries. But that didn't deter Nader.[5] His indictment — which grew into a bestselling book — mercilessly exposed the problems with the Chevrolet Corvair, a car that seemed designed to kill its driver.[6]

GM soon saw Ralph Nader as Public Enemy No. 1. Management sicced private investigators on him, who proceeded to tap Nader's phone and hire prostitutes to sully his squeaky-clean reputation. Their efforts failed. Nader realized he was being tailed and tipped off a couple of journalists: the public was outraged, and Nader's book shot to the top of the bestseller list.

The CEO of General Motors was called before the Senate to testify on the matter in a televised hearing, where he apologized to the young Ralph Nader. Five months later, President Lyndon B. Johnson signed the Traffic Safety Act and the Highway Safety Act into law. LBJ SIGNS TWO ROAD SAFETY BILLS AS NADER LOOKS ON, read the headline in the *Washington Post*.[7] It's not overstating things to say that Ralph Nader's name should be on every seatbelt in every American car. In 2015, a couple of traffic experts calculated that these two federal laws had saved more than 3.5 million lives.[8]

But the young lawyer, at age thirty-two, was just getting started. Nader didn't want to be a lone David, slaying one Goliath a year; he wanted to train a whole team of Davids.

3

How do you build an elite corps of driven idealists?

Think back for a moment to Margaret Mead's words. "Never doubt," she said, "that a small group of thoughtful, committed citizens can change the world. Indeed, it's the only thing that ever has."

History is full of small action groups with enormous impact. Not only rebels who take to the streets, but entrepreneurs and engineers, scholars and public servants, attorneys and — you name it. Such groups often operate as tight, driven units. Venture capitalist Peter Thiel writes that we can speak of *cults*. That may sound over the top, but just think about the traits of cults and sects.

First of all, members are completely devoted.[9] Next, they have little time for a normal life, but work tirelessly in pursuit of their mission. The outside world usually views them as slightly insane, in no small part because they often *are* slightly insane.

Thiel went to Stanford Law School, worked briefly as an attorney, and then raised $1 million from friends and family to launch his career in venture capital. (Important career advice: choose your family carefully.) Next, he set out to find the most promising "cults" in Silicon Valley, or the most obsessive and fanatic startup founders.

You could say the search went alright: Thiel was the first outside investor in Facebook and grew into perhaps the most influential venture capitalist in Silicon Valley.[10] What's more, he became the godfather of the "PayPal Mafia" — a small group of entrepreneurs who were involved with payment platform PayPal and went on to set up immensely successful businesses like Tesla and SpaceX (Elon Musk), LinkedIn (Reid Hoffman), and YouTube (Steve Chen, Chad Hurley, and Jawed Karim).

A photographer from *Fortune* magazine made a group portrait of the men, dressed as mobsters.

Question: What's the opposite of a cult? Thiel's answer: a consulting firm. A company like Deloitte or Accenture isn't driven by one mission; employees hop from client to client. To put it bluntly, the big firms are full of highly talented individuals who don't know what to do with themselves. And so they shrug and become consultants.

If you want to change the world, you'd do better to join a cult. Or start your own. Regardless, you can't be afraid to come across as weird if you want to make a difference. Every milestone of civilization was first seen as the crazy idea of some subculture or another, from the Pythagorean theorem to the conviction that slavery is depraved.

The fact that we now learn $a^2 + b^2 = c^2$ at school is thanks to an ascetic sect of Greek vegetarians from the sixth century BCE. And historians agree that the early abolition movement was led by a group mentioned in Chapter 1, the Quakers — one of the most consequential sects in human history.

Let's take a moment to consider these fascinating folks.

The Quakers were always modest in number. Around 1660, the cult had some 60,000 members in Great Britain, no more than 1 percent or so of the population. But the world would look very different today without these weird Christians.

And yes, early Quakers were truly weird. To give you an idea, they'd streak naked through other churches and set Bibles on fire in public. They were dubbed "quakers" because they'd sometimes physically tremble and quake during prayers — and because they had some shocking convictions.

It didn't take long for the Quakers to become known for disrupting church services throughout England. Quakers then traveled the world to convert others to their alternative Christian faith. One had an audience with the Sultan in Constantinople. Another told off the Pope, saying "Thou art indeed the Antichrist!" (That Quaker was hanged the next day.)[11]

If the Quakers had one mission, it was equality. They would not bow or kneel, even when standing face to face with the King of England. They took their hats off for no man and refused to address nobles as "my Lord." They didn't want to pledge loyalty to anyone, and they certainly didn't swear oaths, because Quakers insisted they always spoke the truth.

Equality among Quakers also applied to women, who could hold leadership roles in the church — exceptional for the times. Women Quakers worked as preachers or prophets, missionaries or activists.[12] A whopping one in five books written by women in seventeenth-century England were from the pen of a Quaker.[13]

What did a Quaker meeting look like? Quakers thought it blasphemous to have their portrait made, but in 1690, the Dutch master Egbert van Heemskerck managed to paint a Quaker congregation in London. Art historians disagree as to whether this group portrait was intended as factual portrayal or satire of a bizarre cult.[14] Either way, the image shocked contemporaries, mostly because a woman had the floor.

In the eighteenth century, the Quakers also came out against slavery. Even as the ruling classes found it acceptable to buy and sell Africans, the abolitionist movement got going as a sort of Quaker startup.

The ultimate pioneer — a true zero — was the hermit Benjamin Lay (1682–1759). Described by his biographer as a "class-conscious, gender-conscious, race-conscious, environmentally conscious, vegetarian ultraradical," Lay was a little, humpbacked man, who smashed teacups if they contained tea or sugar harvested by enslaved people.[15] He insulted slaveholders, calling them everything under the sun, and was even thrown out of four different Quaker meeting houses.

And then there was the Quaker and schoolteacher Anthony Benezet (1713–1784), who was like a writer-in-residence for the abolition movement. Benezet penned hundreds of letters, books, and pamphlets to alert as many people as possible to the horrors of slavery. He was also a follower of what he called "practical Christianity." Benezet gave away the lion's share of his income and would consume nothing harvested by the enslaved. (Convictions declared in the meeting house, he lamented, were "too much contradicted in practice.")[16]

The writings of Lay and Benezet, in turn, greatly influenced British activists like Thomas Clarkson (from Chapter 1), who would take part in the Cambridge essay contest at age twenty-four. Clarkson found a book in a London bookshop written by Benezet, which he then essentially copied over to win first prize. (This wasn't unusual. Other abolitionists also plagiarized entire passages from Benezet's books, a practice the schoolteacher was fine with. As far as he was concerned, it wasn't about him; it was about the message.)[17]

Who would've suspected that this odd collection of individuals — the hermit, the schoolteacher, and the recent graduate — would unleash one of the greatest revolutions in human history? But that's precisely what happened.[18] In Great Britain, where big money was being made off the slave trade and less than 3 percent of the population could even vote, millions stood up to overthrow one of the oldest economic systems.

"In all of human experience," a modern historian notes, "there was no precedent for such a campaign."[19]

And so the UK officially banned the slave trade in 1807 — at a time of peak profits, no less. The British then forced other countries out. The Royal Navy launched a campaign called the "blockade of Africa," where they captured some 2,000 slaving vessels and freed those aboard. "In the end," two experts estimate, "direct British efforts accounted for eliminating approximately 80 percent of the slave trade." From 1807 to 1867, the British put an astronomical amount of money into enforcing the ban: nearly 2 percent of the national income, or four times the UK's current foreign aid budget. The researchers speak of the "most costly international moral action in modern history."[20]

Now back to Peter Thiel and his PayPal cult. It's debatable, of course, whether those guys have made the world a better place. Silicon Valley has countless startup incubators who measure success not in terms of beauty, wisdom, or justice, but in dollars, dollars, and dollars.[21] And Thiel today may well be one of the most dangerous men in America, given his massive influence, deep pockets, and deeply authoritarian views.[22]

But that doesn't mean he's wrong about the power of cults. And morally ambitious entrepreneurs can most definitely change the course of history: ten of the twelve men who in 1787 founded the British Society for the Abolition of the Slave Trade were entrepreneurs.[23] And nine of them were Quakers. Go through the archives of that group today, and you'll mostly find to-do lists, action plans. While the abolitionist movement in France was led by writers and intellectuals (and didn't get much done), the British movement was powered by merchants and businessmen.

4

Pragmatic revolutionaries can make all the difference — something you also see reflected in Ralph Nader's next career moves and the cult he founded in the 1960s.

After his victory over General Motors, Nader continued to work as a one-man crusader, a "self-appointed lobbyist for the public interest."[24] During those years, he learned his first big lessons about how to get things done:

1 Most reporters are lazy and don't investigate things for themselves. You get press coverage by handing them ready-made scoops, preferably along with telephone numbers for your sources.
2 Don't bother contacting members of Congress directly because politicians are chronically short on time. You'd do better lobbying their staffers. They're younger, more idealistic, and better prepared.
3 The best whistleblowers are found from middle management on down. Folks lower on the company ladder know more about how things really work than the big bosses in the boardroom. They'll generally also have a stronger moral compass.
4 The drier something seems, the more exciting it is. If your eyes glaze over while reading policy, then you know: here's where the money is.
5 The less praise you need, the stronger your position. "If you want to be effective in Washington, put your own ego aside," Nader said. "Feed other people's egos."[25]

Nader preferred to go where it was quiet and focus on issues that hadn't yet made the news. He was principled in his ideals, but pragmatic in his methods. "I try to figure out how best to use what I have," he explained. "A speech? A magazine article? A congressman? A letter to a corporation? There's no formula."[26]

As long as it worked.

And Nader's approach was crazy effective. Within a few years, he had a hand in four sweeping new laws — everything from upping food inspection standards to making gas pipelines safer. Next he wanted to scale up his legal activism, as there was still so much that needed doing. Freeways were being plowed through urban neighborhoods, natural areas destroyed and wild rivers poisoned.[27]

And so Nader came up with his idea of recruiting a whole brigade of Davids, which he'd pay with the royalties from his bestselling book on General Motors. Nader sought ambitious people in their twenties or thirties who could "combine moral indignation with laborious research."[28] The first ones applied in the summer of 1968. "Your work is most appealing to two disgusted Harvard graduate students," two of them wrote, "who must endure endless years of drivel in order to mechanically defend the guilty and profitably screw the consumer."[29]

Nader hired these two immediately, along with five others. He'd already set his sights on his next target: the Federal Trade Commission, or FTC. This then-obscure government agency was tasked with cracking down on dangerous products and dubious advertising claims, but according to Nader, was far too lax. And he believed that when you want to accomplish something, you shouldn't attack your archenemy, but your lazy friend.[30]

His bombshell report on the FTC came out in January 1969. "So far as anybody can remember, nothing quite like this has happened in Washington before," one journalist noted.[31] Nader and his crew deemed the FTC a watchdog with no teeth, staffed by sleepy bureaucrats. The organization was characterized by "cronyism, institutionalized mediocrity, endemic inaction, delay, and secrecy," not to mention an "iceberg of incompetence and mismanagement."[32] The *Washington Post* called the findings "totally devastating."[33]

It made the young crusaders hungry for more. In the months to follow, hundreds of students reported to Nader, and at one point, a third (!) of Harvard Law School had applied for a job with him.[34] And not only law students, but also aspiring doctors, biologists, chemists, and engineers jumped at the chance to work with Nader.

Nader hired the top applicants and grouped them into teams of seven to fourteen researchers. Each team dug into a complex issue, like food safety, environmental pollution, or energy policy. Meanwhile, Nader sued General Motors for invasion of privacy by those private detectives. He settled for what at the time was the unheard-of amount of $425,000 — money he put back into his growing army.

Then the legal bombardment began in earnest. The teams published one report after another, with titles like *Vanishing Air* (on air pollution and full of "incriminating facts, figures, and failures"), *Water Wasteland* (on water pollution, a "crime against humanity"), and *The Chemical Feast* (on the Food and Drug Administration, and what *Time* magazine said "may well be the most devastating critique of a U.S. Government agency ever issued").[35]

The reports Nader and his people put out were bone dry but sold half a million copies as books. And the proceeds? That was used to fund more research.

Which brings us back to the beginning of this chapter. In the summer of 1969, the young lawyers — now dubbed Nader's

Raiders by the press — posed for a photographer from *Life* magazine on the steps of the U.S. Capitol. In the accompanying article, Nader said he wanted to bring a new dimension to the legal profession. "Lawyers are never where the needs are greatest. I hope a new generation of lawyers will begin to change that."[36]

No, they wouldn't get rich off their investigations and activism, but Nader thought riches were for the weak-minded anyway. He lived in modest quarters in a boardinghouse, sharing a phone line with three housemates. He didn't own a car or a television and was known for his secondhand suits. (A New Hampshire paper once described Nader as a "conscientious objector to fashion.")[37]

When asked what his perfect workweek would be like, Nader answered: "One hundred hours a week is ideal."[38] He only slept a few hours a night and didn't have much of a personal life. He demanded the same level of devotion from his followers. It pushed some Raiders "to the brink of revolt," according to the *New York Times* in 1971. Nader, for his part, complained that many of his recruits were too soft.[39]

"They wanted people to sit with them in the morning and say, 'How are you doing?' Hand-holding."[40] One of the jokes around the office was that Nader "must be an ardent capitalist: How else could he exploit his workers so mercilessly?"[41]

And yet. Despite the meager pay, despite the long hours, Nader held tremendous appeal for young, ambitious America. Working for him became the ultimate job to land. Sure, he had high expectations, but as a Raider you had the freedom to chase your own leads. ("The function of leadership is to produce more leaders, not more followers," according to Nader.)[42] More importantly, working as a "radical nerd" was far more interesting than working at some stuffy old law firm. As a Raider, you made things happen.

I mean, millions of people write reports. The world is overflowing with researchers, consultants, and academics who produce stacks of books, articles, and policy papers, then chuck them into the "public debate," as if there's someone just sitting there, waiting to convert any fresh insight into a new law, new product, or new agency. There's not. In reality, most papers end up shelved or shredded.

But Nader's Raiders knew how to turn their words into deeds and their deeds into results. The publication of *Vanishing Air* was followed by the Clean Air Act of 1970. After *Water Wastelands* came the Clean Water Act of 1972. And many more pieces of legislation bear Raider fingerprints. One historian estimates that Nader's Raiders directly influenced or inspired twenty-five federal laws on air and water pollution, energy production, wildlife protection, hazardous chemicals, and safety in the workplace.[43] The Clean Air Act alone has saved hundreds of millions of life-years, and counting.[44]

All that time, Nader's method remained the same: expose an injustice, come up with solutions, and then bring together a coalition of activists, lobbyists, politicians, and experts to make those solutions happen. The Raiders weren't staging protests or rioting in the streets; they were supernerds, taking on mountains of memos, letters, transcripts, and reports. They didn't hit their adversaries with stones or Molotov cocktails but with motions or a well-timed court summons.

Nader was quickly becoming a household name. In 1971 alone, the *New York Times* ran 141 articles on him, and he was swamped with thousands of letters from across the country. "I think Ralph got more mail than the Beatles," one of his Raiders would later quip.[45]

Nader ended up founding or inspiring dozens of organizations, many of which still exist today.[46] "Public interest lawyer" became an actual career path. One of Nader's nonprofits even put out a jobs guide in 1980, listing hundreds of places where people could "bring their conscience with them" to the office.[47] In the foreword, he wrote that students no longer had to opt for "trivial jobs chasing manipulated wants."[48] Instead, they could do something useful for society.

To this day, numerous attorneys, consultants, marketeers, programmers, managers, accountants, and bankers are stuck in well-paid but relatively useless or even harmful jobs. Meanwhile, the world is facing enormous challenges that can't be solved with slogans and banners alone. We need protesters in the streets *and* bookworms in the bureaucratic trenches who can take what Nader started and run with it.

In September 2015, Ralph Nader was back on campus at Harvard Law. Much had changed since his day. The law students then were almost all white men; now, the student population was more diverse.

But other things were the same, much to Nader's frustration. At least 80 percent of the law school graduates worked on behalf of less than 20 percent of the population. Most lawyers stood on the side of the landlords, not the renters; the debt collectors, not those in debt; the perpetrators, not the whistleblowers. At best, the chance of landing a well-paid, yet soulless, position had been somewhat democratized.

"You have 2,500, maybe 3,000, weeks left," Nader said to his young audience.[49] What did these students want to do with the rest of their lives? How did they hope to look back on their career? Don't diminish yourself, the lawyer argued, by selling your talents to the highest bidder to work on "lucrative trivia." It's the same message as forty-seven years earlier, on that Friday evening in 1968, when he recruited his first Raiders:

You're about to throw your life away. But it's not too late.

5

You may have been wondering as you read this chapter: Is he going to talk about the havoc Nader wreaked in 2000? And you're right, there's more to his story. If Ralph Nader had retired in the early 1990s, he would have gone down in history as one of the greatest Americans of all time. But today, his reputation has taken a huge hit.

Nader started to lose influence in the late seventies, in part because adversaries adopted his tactics. He fell out with many of his friends and distanced himself from the Democrats — Nader thought them little different than the Republicans. At the close of the century, he made a decision that would have dramatic results: he ran for president.

Many ex-Raiders looked on in horror as their old hero ran a popular campaign as the Green Party candidate, which threatened to shift millions of votes away from the Democrats. In October 2000, a month before the election, they begged him to pull out of the race. "Dear Ralph," they wrote, "You have sacrificed for the benefit of the common good your entire adult life, as we, your friends and colleagues, know well. There have been countless occasions where you stayed in the background when that helped achieve the maximum benefit for others. It is time for you once again to step aside in the best interests of our nation."[50]

But Nader wouldn't let up. With an army of young activists, he continued to campaign in crucial swing states right up to election day, winning nearly 100,000 votes in the state of

Florida. And indeed, a few months later, Republican George W. Bush was sworn in as the 43rd president of the United States. Bush had defeated Al Gore in Florida by the thinnest of margins: 537 votes.

Mention the name Ralph Nader today, and many Americans think of the dramatic outcome of the November 2000 election. That, and everything that came out of the Bush administration: tax cuts for the richest Americans, human rights violations at Guantanamo Bay, and the wars in Iraq and Afghanistan.

The tragic thing about Nader was that he morphed into the kind of cult leader who's deaf to all criticism. He clung to his old methods, even when they started to backfire. He continued to attack his friends, even when he had almost no friends left.[51] And while he had an admirable capacity for taking setbacks in stride, he seemed to forget that defeat wasn't in itself a virtue.

Which brings us to the most important lesson of the next chapter.

4

See winning as your moral duty

God spare me the purists.
Joe Biden *on Ralph Nader in November 2000,*
a few days after the presidential election Al Gore lost

I

When it comes to the question of how cults can change the world, it never takes long in academic circles before Joseph Overton's name comes up. Overton (1960–2003) was an American political scientist who wondered how — over time — radical dreams could become reality.

Picture a window, said Overton, framing all the ideas taken seriously at a given point in time. These are the opinions you can voice at dinner parties without people giving you the side-eye. If you hold dear a conviction that lies outside this frame, you'll promptly be dismissed as a nut or a fool. Politicians in particular have to stay inside the frame if they want to get reelected.

But then how do you change the world? If you have to stay inside the frame, how do you change the view? Overton wrote that the key is to shift the whole window. Many activists conclude this means pushing the limits — being unreasonable, unbearable, and unrealistic, to stretch the boundaries of what society finds acceptable.[1] Over time, standpoints that once seemed radical can become mainstream. At least that's the idea.

But let's face it: most mavericks couldn't make a dent in a stick of butter. Most nuts on a mission don't change the world; they spend their lives shouting from the sidelines. Yes, radical dreams *can* become reality, but that doesn't mean that push push pushing is always the best strategy.

Effective idealists, on the other hand, may be pie-in-the-sky when it comes to their goals, but they're pragmatic in making them happen. If they need to hobnob with wealthy types to raise money for a good cause, then hobnob they will. If they must forge tough compromises in order to forge ahead, that's what they'll do. If their carefully cultivated curly mustache

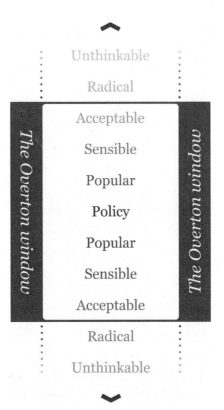

threatens to compromise their credibility, they're the first to grab the clippers.

In Chapter 3, we saw that in every movement, there's a variety of roles to play. We often have a personal preference for a given type of activist: we may think protesters are brave and lobbyists useless; perhaps we have a weakness for poetic professors, but a distaste for slick influencers. Or vice versa.

But change is not that one-dimensional. All these people can play an essential part. The intellectual *and* the influencer. The networker *and* the agitator. The bureaucrat *and* the entrepreneur. Someone who writes in academic jargon, someone who brings ideas to a wider public. Someone who's polarizing, someone who brings people together. Someone who lobbies behind the scenes, someone who lets themself get dragged away by the riot police.

The only kind of person we *can't* use in this fight is the fool who thinks good intentions are enough. Someone whose clear-eyed convictions put them squarely on the right side of history, but who achieves little in the here and now. Let's call this figure the Noble Loser.

How to avoid this fate? To answer that question, it's time for a masterclass by one of the greatest resistance heroes of the twentieth century.

On December 1, 1955, a 42-year-old woman boarded a bus in Montgomery, Alabama. After three stops, the driver announced that the Black passengers needed to make room for the white folks who had just got on. But one Black woman remained seated.

"Are you going to stand up?" barked the driver.

"No," she said.

"Well, I'm going to have you arrested," he said.

"You may do that," she replied.[2]

Her name, of course, was Rosa Parks, and her protest prompted a citywide bus boycott, soon supported by the as yet largely unknown Reverend Martin Luther King Jr. Her flat-out refusal in the face of arrest grew into one of the most consequential and well-known moments in U.S. history.

But Rosa Parks was much more than the woman-who-wouldn't-give-up-her-seat. Often portrayed as a kindly seamstress, Parks had long been a committed activist. By the time she got on that bus, she'd been involved with the civil rights movement for years. That very summer, she'd discreetly traveled to Tennessee to attend the Highlander Folk School for activists, where she had taken part in workshops on all kinds of protest tactics.[3]

And a long line of Black women went before Rosa Parks. The eighteen-year-old Mary Louise Smith had been arrested a month earlier for refusing to surrender her seat on a Montgomery bus. Six months before that, fifteen-year-old Claudette Colvin was taken into custody because she didn't want to stand up for a white woman. And there were more: Aurelia Browder, Viola White, Geneva Johnson, Katie Wingfield, Susie McDonald, Epsie Worthy . . . [4]

It was no coincidence that for months, the idea of a bus boycott had been making the rounds among the Black women of Montgomery. The Women's Political Council in particular — a small, well-run action group — had run out of patience. Chair Jo Ann Robinson was the mastermind behind the whole thing. "We planned the protest long before Mrs. Parks was arrested," she later explained.[5]

The women were just looking for the right moment. When Colvin was arrested, they made the tough decision to hold off a little longer. Colvin had been violently pulled off the bus, but wasn't the ideal icon for large-scale protests. At fifteen, she was seen as too young, she came from a poor neighborhood, and she also turned out to be pregnant. The white press would have eaten her alive.

But after Parks was arrested, the decision was quick. Now was the time. In the dark of night, Robinson and her team mimeographed some 35,000 leaflets calling on Black residents to boycott Montgomery's bus system.[6] The next morning, a group of twenty women from the Women's Political Council went out to spread the word. Male church leaders — including Martin Luther King, who had at first been reluctant — decided to join the boycott.

Only then did Rosa Parks take on the role of the demure heroine. She knew she couldn't come across as too radical, or white

Americans would turn against the movement. "Strategically," a historian later wrote, "the success of Parks as the symbol of the boycott turned, in part, on obscuring her longstanding political activity."[7] To this day, many people still think of Rosa Parks as a kindly seamstress — that's how effective the mythmaking was.

Meanwhile, an action group made up of radical nerds was elsewhere working behind the scenes. Ever heard of Pauli Murray? She published the seminal work *States' Laws on Race and Color* in 1950, also called the "bible for civil rights attorneys."

Or what about Fred Gray? He led the legal team who filed a lawsuit against the mayor of Montgomery, and won. On November 13, 1956 the U.S. Supreme Court ruled that segregation on city busses violated the constitution, and with that decision, the 381-day boycott in Montgomery came to an end.

One thing that stands out about the activists of the American civil rights movement is how strategically they went to work. They made use of all kinds of carefully chosen methods, from bus boycotts to sit-ins, and from lawsuits to marches on Washington. In the years following the victory in Montgomery, they managed to get five major pieces of legislation through Congress.[8] That's the polar opposite of the Noble Loser, whose good intentions fail to yield any meaningful results. Women like Rosa Parks and Jo Ann Robinson were convinced of a simple truth: in the fight against injustice, winning is a moral duty.

2

Maybe we should take another look at that famous photo of August Landmesser, the man who refused to do the Nazi salute (see Chapter 2). Because honestly, Landmesser's action didn't make much difference. His open resistance was brave but futile. His daughter Irene even wrote that he put his family at "exceptional risk" by continuing to appear in public with his Jewish fiancée.[9]

Landmesser was more of a Noble Loser. He was clearly in the right, but where did it get him? He was on the right side of history, but he didn't make history. His courage was and is admirable, no question. But if you really want to change things, then someone like Rosa Parks is a better role model.

To avoid the fate of the Noble Loser, we have to get rid of some persistent illusions. As I see it, there are at least five myths about how social change works.

I: The illusion of awareness

To put it bluntly: awareness is overrated. The fact that people are aware of various injustices doesn't mean they'll act on that knowledge — on the contrary. We hold all kinds of opinions on all kinds of matters, but we generally do little with our viewpoints.

Psychologists speak of the *belief-behavior gap*. Take people who think it's awful how animals are treated but still eat meat; progressives who think planes are too polluting but fly all the same; churchgoers who scarcely give to charity, despite the scripture's call to tithe.[10]

We also see this gap between word and deed in our involvement with politics. Most of what we call political engagement looks an awful lot like a love of football or Formula 1. Scroll through your newsfeed, read up on the latest political scandal, rant about a politician who never fails to get under your skin. All too often, politics is treated as entertainment. A political scientist at Tufts University speaks of "political hobbyism."[11]

Most news junkies who consider themselves "politically engaged" don't do anything remotely resembling true political activity. Sure, they vote every few years, maybe sign a petition every now and then, but that's about it. Politics is reduced to a spectator sport you watch from your couch. Politics as pastime. It has little to do with lobbying, protesting, organizing, or mobilizing — the building blocks of democratic power.

This might also help explain why opinion polls don't always mean all that much. More than half the country was still against gay marriage in 2010, while today the overwhelming majority considers it a constitutional right.[12] Or what about the fight over abortion? For decades now, most Americans have agreed abortion should be legal in most cases.[13] But a small group of committed activists set out in the 1990s to get that right revoked. They built a network of nearly 5,000 lawyers and brought case after case, chipping away at the legal basis for reproductive rights. The culmination of this strategy? The 2022 Supreme Court decision in *Dobbs v. Jackson Women's Health Organization*, which ruled abortion was not a protected right, reversing the law of the land.[14]

That is to say: it's not what you think is right that counts, but what you're prepared to do about it.

II: The illusion of good intentions

The second misperception of the Noble Loser is that good intentions are enough. Nothing could be further from the truth. Take the world of charities. We open up our wallets if an ad moves us, forgetting that loads of promising initiatives have little effect. They're rarely seriously evaluated, and when they are, the results often fall short.

Here are just a few examples:

- Each year, nearly 10 billion dollars' worth of *fair-trade* products are sold. But researchers agree a mere fraction of that money reaches poor farmers, the people it's designed to help.[15]

- In a 2019 *metastudy* (analyzing a large group of other studies on the topic), Australian researchers concluded that an estimated "40 to 70% of donated medical devices are not used, as they are not functional, appropriate, or staff lack training."[16]
- A global analysis of 1,500 climate policies put in place between 1998 and 2022 found that only 63 of them — a mere 4 percent — led to a significant drop in emissions.[17]
- A team of U.S. researchers came to the conclusion that most social programs and services (from fighting poverty to treating addiction to crime prevention) have never been rigorously evaluated, and at least 75 percent of the ones that were "produce small or no effects, and in some cases negative effects."[18]

Of course you can't always quantify the effects of an initiative, but you still have to take a critical look at whether good intentions also generate good results. It's tempting to believe that all good deeds count, however small — that every little effort, every protest, every bumper sticker somehow matters in the end.

But that's not how it works. Opportunities can be squandered, and time wasted. History is full of idealists with good intentions who achieved little, while the problems they could have fixed instead fester.

Bear in mind, it takes courage to admit that your idealistic plans have failed. One of my favorite examples is the U.S. charity No Lean Season, which once seemed effective at helping farmers in Bangladesh find jobs in town during the off-season. "A bus ticket out of poverty," was the idea. But turns out it didn't work. The organization's own research showed that the money was not helping relieve poverty.

So, what did No Lean Season do? In 2019, they disbanded their own organization. "It's sad when something you thought might actually solve a problem turns out not to," one of the program's initiators said. "But it's much sadder to waste resources."[19] I wish we held an annual awards show for those who dare to share such failures.

III: The illusion of the right reasons

Focus too much on intentions, and you can lose sight of something else: the right thing often happens for the wrong reasons. And clever activists can make use of that fact. Take the young abolitionist Thomas Clarkson (from Chapter 1), who never would have been able to start a movement against the slave trade if he'd focused solely on the suffering of the enslaved. For most Britons in the eighteenth century, that seemed a remote concern, far removed from their daily lives.

Clarkson knew he needed other arguments against the slave trade, so he turned his attention to the fate of British sailors on slave ships. That's right, one of the greatest abolitionists of all time shifted his focus to the suffering among the perpetrators. Psychologists call this tactic *moral reframing*.[20] The idea is to find new arguments for the same standpoint — arguments that resonate with people outside your cult and fall within the Overton window.

An example: a left-wing politician who wants to raise taxes on the rich isn't likely to convince a right-wing voter by talking about how everything is so unfairly distributed. But what happens if they show that — aside from some industrious types — the very rich by and large don't work for their money? That they generally inherit it or collect substantial income from investments like stocks and real estate? Or perhaps an appeal to patriotic sentiment works better, laying out an argument for how the country can use those extra tax dollars to lead the way in wiping out poverty.

Clarkson's find, in any case, turned out to be a winning move. Enslavers asserted that a stint on a slaving vessel was good training for any sailor, but Clarkson discovered that some 20 percent of the white crew died during any given voyage.

What's more, sailors died in greater proportions than the enslaved.[21] British seamen were especially vulnerable to tropical illnesses and subject to a brutal economic logic. "Because they were laborers rather than a capital investment," a historian later wrote, "slave ship sailors were more disposable than the captives."[22] If a great deal of his crew was dead on arrival, many a captain was not bothered. After all, you didn't have to pay a dead sailor.

This grisly fact is often forgotten today, but it turned out to be crucial in the fight against slavery: the life of a sailor on a slave ship was truly horrific. To be clear: the suffering of the guards was not remotely comparable to the suffering of their captives. But the sympathy Clarkson managed to summon for the fate of these sailors turned out to be one of his smartest moves. When British politicians learned of the death toll among British sailors, many were deeply shocked and came out against the slave trade.

There was another brilliant abolitionist, a friend of Clarkson's, who also understood that good things often happen for the wrong reasons. In the spring of 1789, he published his autobiography, which would grow to be the biggest bestseller of the British antislavery movement. His name was Olaudah Equiano.

The Interesting Narrative of the Life of Olaudah Equiano is the story of a Black boy snatched and subjugated, shackled and shipped across the Atlantic Ocean. It's the story of a man who threw off his chains, survived a sea battle and shipwreck, and went on to have extraordinary adventures on three continents plus the North Pole. It's the story of a citizen of the world who settled in England and — to the shock of many — married a white woman. (The word "interesting" in the title is the understatement of the century.)

If you want to know how to write a bestseller, you can always look to Olaudah Equiano. He wasn't the kind of writer who submits his manuscript and then nervously awaits the reviews (and blames the publisher if the book flops). Equiano was his own publisher, editor, and marketing department. For five years, he traveled to towns and cities in England, Wales, Scotland, and Ireland to promote his book. That is to say: he went on the first political book tour ever.[23]

For many Britons, it must have been their first time seeing a Black man. His very existence was a blow to the pro-slavery lobby. Here was this intelligent, charismatic, and deeply religious African man — an impossibility, in the racist worldview of slaveholders. Even worse, Equiano presented himself as a true gentleman. For the cover of the book, he had a stately portrait of himself printed, complete with jacket, vest, and silk cuffs. (The second edition — more painful still — portrayed him as a maritime hero, saving a couple of white figures from drowning.)

This was the cover of the biggest bestseller of the British antislavery movement. The author was known for years as Gustavus Vassa, the name his former owner had given him. But now he chose to publish under his original African name, too: Olaudah Equiano.

Equiano was a master communicator and persuader. His book
was a mix of the three most popular genres of the time: a spec-
tacular travelogue, a moving conversion story, and an inspiring tale of heroism.[24] At times, *The Interesting Narrative* also
sounds like a self-help book. Equiano emphasized the will of
the individual because he believed that people had the power
to change themselves and their lives. His own life served as an
example: Equiano had bought himself out of slavery, converted
to Christianity, and become an abolitionist, and now he was
challenging his readers to follow in his footsteps.

Equiano also understood that to achieve his goal, he had to
stroke the egos of his public. He mastered the art of redraw-
ing the moral framework. He wrote extensively, for instance, on
the horrors of the slaving vessel, but also emphasized his love
for England, "where my heart had always been."[25] He told of his
surprise when he saw that the British "did not sell one another
as we did." (He wrote that his father in Africa owned slaves.) "I
was astonished at the wisdom of the white people in all things
I saw."[26]

It was exactly what the British wanted to hear, and just what
the abolitionist movement needed. But it also raised the question: Was Equiano's story too good to be true?

For slaveholders, it was clearcut. They crowed that this
so-called autobiography was made up by a white ghostwriter
and that Equiano wasn't born in Africa at all. Such accusations
were long considered pure slander, but in 1999 an English professor named Vincent Carretta found a ship's roster and a record
of baptism. Both seemed to suggest Equiano wasn't born in
Africa, but in South Carolina.

Note that Carretta also showed that the vast majority of
Equiano's autobiography was corroborated by other sources.
But the professor had doubts about the first few chapters. Could
they be made up? "Equiano knew," according to Carretta, "that

the anti-slave-trade movement needed precisely the kind of account of Africa and the Middle Passage that he, and perhaps only he, could supply."[27]

Carretta's find, of course, was a bombshell discovery. For years, Equiano's memoirs had been *the* source about life on a slave ship. His life story inspired children's books, graphic novels, movies, and a television series. Not surprising, then, that some historians were outraged at Carretta's detective work. During an academic conference, he was accused of doing "anti-Equiano science," with money, fame, and racism as possible motives.[28]

The plain truth is we'll likely never know for sure where Equiano was born. Carretta's evidence is strong, but not conclusive.[29] And maybe it doesn't matter much anyway. Equiano was one of the greatest abolitionists of all time, hands down. Even if he drew on the experiences of others to craft his incredible account of a slave journey, Equiano gave the movement exactly what it needed at exactly the right time.

Maybe he was even more of a genius than we thought.

IV: The illusion of purity

If you want to change the world, sooner or later you'll face a dilemma. How do you deal with people who seem less committed to their beliefs or their practice? What Noble Losers tend to forget is that every successful coalition is a pact among people who *disagree* on any number of things.

Again, take the eighteenth-century campaign against slavery. "This is a cold and dead place," a British abolitionist wrote about the Netherlands when he found zero interest there in starting a Dutch antislavery society.[30] The Calvinists there didn't want to join forces with the liberals because the latter didn't open their meetings with prayer.[31] The chair of the Calvinist club thought that "upholding Christian principles is more important than attracting new members."[32]

In England, meanwhile, the campaign gathered steam once the Quakers joined forces with other Christians, including pious politician William Wilberforce. To attract as many other people as possible, the Evangelical Wilberforce even tried to come across as less devout than he was, afraid that "the dread of an over-righteous man would deter people."[33]

A century later, during British women's struggle for the right to vote, all kinds of suffragettes came together, "from fishwives to aristocrats, mill girls to Indian princesses."[34] This fragile coalition held just long enough to see victory in 1918: women over the age of thirty who owned property got the vote.[35] True, only privileged women got the vote initially. But making that compromise seems to have been a good call, because after that first difficult step, the next step — the right of all women to vote, won in 1928 — came much more easily.

In the run-up to the Montgomery bus boycott in 1955, members of the Women's Political Council also knew they had to build a coalition. The small organization needed the support of Black churches and their still-hesitant ministers. Some preachers didn't even want their names associated with the boycott, for fear of retaliation from the white community.[36] It was one of the reasons chair Jo Ann Robinson decided not to set up a campaign around the young Claudette Colvin. She knew that conservative ministers — sad but true — would never rally around a pregnant teen.

Why does it seem so hard these days for activists to forge a coalition? I suspect it has something to do with a key doctrine of modern progressives: *intersectionality*. That's the understanding that people are often discriminated against on the basis of multiple, overlapping factors, like gender, ethnicity, class, education, age, sexual orientation, disability, and so on.

Intersectionality means we can't study different forms of discrimination and oppression separately, but only as interrelated phenomena. That's without a doubt an important insight. Countless social issues are woven together in complex ways, and you'd think this realization would provide the basis for a broad movement to fight inequality and discrimination.

But there's also a risk associated with centering this tenet. What if intersectional thinking turns into a litmus test for every form of collaboration? What happens if the duty to declare your solidarity with anyone and everyone is just too much, stifling cooperation instead of facilitating it? And what if you then lose sight of your original goal?

In June 2022, three days before the U.S. Supreme Court scrapped the right to abortion, the country's main pro-choice organization, NARAL, tweeted this:

> If your feminism doesn't include trans women and girls, it's 👏 not 👏 feminism 👏

> If your feminism doesn't understand how anti-trans policies disproportionately impact BIPOC folks, particularly Black trans women and girls, it's 👏 not 👏 feminism 👏

So you want to fight for the right to abortion? First tell us what you think about trans women and girls. Want to fight for climate? Great. But what's your opinion on reparations for centuries of colonialism?

The problem with this uncompromising attitude is that you shut out loads of potential allies. Then you end up with a movement that's 100 percent pure, but 0 percent effective. And no, the pursuit of purity isn't just a theoretical problem. Left-wing journalism outlet the *Intercept* published a high-profile investigation in 2022 on how nearly all progressive interest groups in the U.S. had "more or less, effectively ceased to function" due to internal disputes. Activists continued to write each other off for all manner of minor missteps and mistakes.

"So much energy has been devoted to the internal strife," said one manager who recently resigned, "that it's had a real impact on the ability for groups to deliver."

"Most people thought that their worst critics were their competitors," another activist noted, "and they're finding out that their worst critics are on their own payroll."[37]

V: The illusion of synergy

That brings us to the final myth that keeps Noble Losers from hitting their goals. Years ago, the economist Albert Hirschman (1915–2012) concluded that idealists often get swept up in the *synergy illusion*. They think that all their ideals reinforce one another. "Progressives are eternally convinced," Hirschman wrote, "that 'all good things go together.'"[38]

Take the climate crisis. Many an activist believes we'll only beat it when we solve a bunch of other problems, too.[39] We shouldn't only fight against fossil fuels, but also for affordable healthcare, free schooling, universal childcare, a basic income, a jobs guarantee, a four-day workweek, reparations for centuries of colonialism — and shoot, while we're at it, how about we do away with capitalism entirely. And oh yeah, we really should do all that in a radically reformed democracy, with citizen councils selected by lot to be fair, and could we get it done within ten years, please? Otherwise it's too late. The whole system has to be rebuilt right now from the ground up. It's all or nothing — utopia or the apocalypse.

But what about when reality is messier — when you have to make all sorts of difficult compromises to get anything done? Precisely when time is short — say, when the planet's getting warmer — you have to make some sacrifices. The risk of an all-or-nothing approach is that you shoot for the moon, then don't even get off the ground.

Yes, it's important to look at the big picture, and to foster dreams, ideals, utopias. But we must also make choices — and fight tooth and nail for each concrete result. The serious idealist, as Dr. King said years ago, "never yields to the passive sort of patience which is an excuse to do nothing . . . He recognizes that social change will not come overnight, yet he works as though it is an imminent possibility."[40]

The strategic considerations of Thomas Clarkson and the British abolitionists are a good example. During one of their first meetings in June 1787, the question arose as to what goal they should pursue. Abolishing slavery altogether? Or imposing a ban on shipping and trading the enslaved?

The founders all agreed on the ultimate goal: a world without slavery. But was abolition doable in the here and now? To enforce a total ban, the British Parliament would have to severely limit the autonomy of its colonies overseas — a political nonstarter. Add to that the plantation owners whose property rights would be compromised, and the whole enterprise was unthinkable. Because if one thing was sacred for the British establishment, it was property rights.

Morally speaking, only completely abolishing slavery went far enough for the abolitionists, but in practice that was about ten bridges too far. And if something can't be done, does it make sense to waste everyone's energy? How does that help anybody? A single one of the twelve founders, the scrupulous theologian Granville Sharp, refused to make any concessions. Sharp declared his fellow abolitionists "guilty before God," a pronouncement he delivered "with a loud voice, a powerful emphasis, and both hands lifted up toward heaven."[41]

The rest of the group — largely entrepreneurs — nodded sagely, then promptly got to work as the Society for the Abolition of the Slave Trade. That's what their most effective arguments supported (remember the fate of the British sailor), and it was a step the Parliament in Westminster could take — with no consent needed from the colonies. Although Sharp's "most sacred feelings" were "wounded to the quick," he decided to take the loss and continue to serve the cause with his friends, leaving further judgment of his fellow abolitionists to the Almighty.[42]

And don't forget: the proposition to end the slave trade was itself an incredibly radical one. We're talking about a super-lucrative segment of the British economy, backed by a powerful lobby. Thomas Clarkson still hoped that abolishing the slave trade would be "laying the ax at the very root" of slavery as a whole (though he didn't — strategically enough — share that hope in public).[43]

Many activists think you have to hold on tight to your highest ideals. But sometimes you have to aim lower if you want to hit your target.[44]

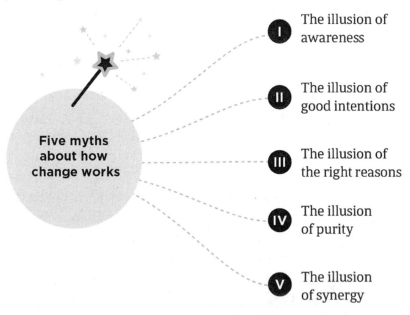

3

We live in revolutionary times. A recent study shows the number of protest movements increased threefold between 2006 and 2020.[45] In no other period in the history of humankind did so many take part in a demonstration.[46] From Occupy Wall Street to Extinction Rebellion, from the Arab Spring to the Chilean Protests: around the world, people have taken to the streets. This juncture calls to mind 1968, 1917, or maybe 1848 — other eras bursting with idealism and unrest.

But something seems to be missing. Something essential. Whether we're talking about the fight against climate change or inequality, about Occupy or Black Lives Matter — when you track actual progress made in terms of new laws or rights secured, the results look pretty meager.

Occupy protests popped up everywhere after the 2008 crash, but bailouts continued unabated and the income gap between the top 1 percent and the rest grew. More people protested in a single day during the Women's March of 2017 than ever before in the U.S., but the organization later fractured into multiple groups. The Black Lives Matter demonstrations of 2020 were even bigger — in a matter of weeks, over 15 million people took to the streets — but it didn't result in much concrete legislation.[47]

Of course every one of these protests was historic and awe-inspiring and served to wake up millions. But awareness isn't the same as change. In her 2017 book *Twitter and Tear Gas*, the sociologist Zeynep Tufekci argues that something fundamental has shifted since the time of Rosa Parks. "In the past," she writes, "a truly big march was the culmination of long-term organizing, an exclamation mark at the end of a sentence."[48] Today's protests more often stem from an impulse — a surge of outrage that can sweep across the globe in no time.

Compare that with the Montgomery bus boycott of 1955. Chair Jo Ann Robinson and her colleagues on the Women's Political Council had to sneak into the university at night to mimeograph 35,000 flyers. They had to hand them out among the city's sixty-eight Black organizations to get word out, whereupon they took on the formidable task — without email or cell phones — of putting together a citywide carpool roster for thousands of workers. And then kept it up for 381 days.

Tufekci emphasizes that the magic isn't found in the mimeograph machine or the carpool roster. The magic is found in the countless hours activists spend together — not via a screen, but face to face.[49] Activists back in the day had to build up this enormous capacity for organizing, and that close cooperation made them formidable opponents. When MLK gave his iconic "I have a dream" speech on August 28, 1963, his adversaries not only saw 250,000 people gathered for the March on Washington who came to listen. They also saw the incredible organizing strength behind that mass protest and realized how powerful the civil rights movement had become.

That very public success meant first lots of hard work in the shadows. The people working behind the scenes are never as famous, but they are — it bears repeating — at least as important as those in the spotlight. Take Bayard Rustin, the big strategist behind the March on Washington (and a Quaker, incidentally). Rustin was described by a contemporary as "one of the five smartest men in America."[50] Despite that, he was never pulled on stage by his fellow activists, because he was gay. They feared his sexual orientation would somehow prove a liability to the movement, though insiders knew Rustin was integral to its success.

Or take Rachelle Horowitz, the 24-year-old law student responsible for transportation to the march. She built a huge system of lists and index cards to keep track of all the travel. "You could call her at three o'clock in the morning, and say, 'Rachelle, how many busses are coming from New York? How many trains coming out of the South? How many busses coming from Philadelphia? How many planes coming from California?' And she could tell you."[51]

Or what about Patricia Worthy, the law student who'd worked so hard on the march, she slept through MLK's historic speech? Or Walter Fauntroy, the man who only hours before King was set to speak made sure the pricey sound system — sabotaged during the night — was up and running again in time. Without Fauntroy, only the first few rows of people would've heard anything about that dream.

Don't get me wrong. Mass protest can still spark massive change. Protests can topple leaders and create new ones; they can build solidarity and propel people into a lifetime of activism.[52] As the Women's March began to break apart, new groups emerged, determined to get as many women elected as possible. And they succeeded. Since 2016, the number of women in Congress has grown by more than 40 percent.[53] "Ultimately, a march in and of itself doesn't accomplish anything," one of the original activists said. "We have to focus on the continued work."[54]

And as for those five illusions: of course awareness and good intentions are a great starting point, of course the right thing can happen for the *right* reasons, of course you won't be happy working with everyone, and of course your ideals will find some synergy.

But still. Much of modern protest seems too fleeting. Heavy on intuition, light on strategy. Heavy on intentions, light on results. "Being on the right side of history," writes Tufekci, "doesn't insulate one from weak analyses."[55]

5

And then one last thing.

There's a sidenote to the story of August Landmesser that's usually left out, likely because it's not a pretty tale.

On November 15, 1995, someone *else* opened the evening paper in Hamburg, saw the photograph of the man who wasn't doing the Nazi salute, and thought he recognized his own father. It was Wolfgang Wegert, a German televangelist. He immediately called to his wife that his father was in the paper. But when that same newspaper published Landmesser's gripping tale a few days later, Wegert decided out of respect not to respond.[56]

We now have strong indications that it's Gustav Wegert, and not August Landmesser, in that famous photograph from 1936. We know for certain that Wegert (1) worked at that shipyard, (2) consistently refused to do the Nazi salute, and (3) resembled the man-who-didn't-salute even more than Landmesser.

The man-who-didn't-salute   *Gustav Wegert in 1948 (right)*

According to his son, the deeply religious Wegert thought it blasphemous to revere a fellow man as a saint, even when it was Adolf Hitler. Whenever someone said "Heil Hitler" to Wegert, he'd respond with a breezy "Guten Tag" (or "Good day").

And that was it. That's all there was to the famous photo. Nothing indicated Wegert was sympathetic to the fate of the Jews. He continued working for the German war industry until 1945, and differed little in that sense from most other Christians in Nazi Germany who did nothing to resist the regime.

More than seventy years ago, in one of his most famous sermons, MLK emphasized that nonconformity isn't in itself a virtue. It's not about what you think or say; it's about what you do to move that Overton window and win the fight against injustice. Nonconformity may inspire, but it can also get mired in exhibitionism. Reverend King preached of the need for "a tough mind and a tender heart" both. "The idealists are not usually realistic," he said, "and the realists are not usually idealistic."[57]

What we need is some realistic idealism.

Learn to weep over spreadsheets

Instead of comparing our lot with that of those who
are more fortunate than we are, we should compare it with
the lot of the great majority of our fellow men. It then
appears that we are among the privileged.
Helen Keller, *disability rights advocate (1880–1968)*

I

And now for a concrete case from our own times.

I'm going to tell you the story of a British executive who suddenly got fired up for a cause. His big change is extra-interesting because you likely wouldn't have seen it coming. He sure didn't. This guy had an established career, a comfortable life, and was well over thirty (which as we all know is the official cutoff for doing anything remotely radical). Already quite successful in a traditional sense, he one day asked himself: This is it? This is my life?

It all started late in the evening on June 9, 2003. Rob Mather was sitting on his couch in London watching the evening news. He'd wanted to turn off the television, but as he later explained, "I'm rubbish with a TV remote control, and that led to a major left turn in my life."[1]

The television jumped to a channel showing a documentary about a girl named Terri.[2] One evening in November 1998, when Terri wasn't yet two, her mother put the little girl to bed and tucked her in. Maybe it was exhaustion, maybe it was stress, but Terri's mother had done something she normally never did. She'd lit a cigarette in the house — a cigarette she then forgot at her child's bedside.

When firefighters rushed in not much later, they first thought there was a black plastic doll in the baby bed. Until they heard a soft whimper.[3]

For days, Terri was near death. She twice stopped breathing and was twice resuscitated. She lost fingers, toes, her ears, her nose, and a foot. Only the skin under her wet diaper remained intact.[4] But miraculously, she survived. After many weeks, she stirred and spoke her first word since the accident: "Mama."

It was all too much for Terri's mother, who was eaten up by guilt.[5] She broke with the family, and Terri's father was left to cope alone. He quit his job so he could care for his daughter. Every morning, he washed her and applied her ointment. He took her to endless hospital appointments, and he slept in her room on the floor next to her bed.[6] When Terri was scared, he held her close; when things looked bleak, he encouraged her.

All the while, there was one thing that kept him going: his daughter's incredible spirit. Terri was upbeat and mischievous, curious and determined. She seemed the only person in the world who could manage to forget her injuries, if only for a little while.

2

"I'm not an emotional person," the executive Rob Mather would later say about the night he watched that documentary on Terri. "But my wife and I had two children, and I'm not ashamed to say that I was streaming."[7]

Most people who see something sad on TV go on with their lives the next day. Not so Rob Mather. He couldn't get Terri out of his mind and decided he had to do something.

We live in a time where the happy few are increasingly made aware of their many privileges — and rightly so. But awareness alone isn't enough. What can you do with the realization that you're blessed? I don't think I know anyone with a better answer to that question than Rob Mather.

The first thing you notice when you contact Rob is how swiftly he answers his email. This is a man with lots of energy.

When Rob tells me about his childhood, it's almost cringey how successful he was — at everything.

At age eleven, he was awarded a scholarship to Hampton, a prestigious boys' school in southwest London. He soon rose to the top of his class. And as if that wasn't enough, Rob also turned out to be ridiculously good at sports. Track, soccer, the high jump — he did it all. After Hampton, he went on to study at Cambridge University because they had the best soccer team.

It's true that Rob occasionally didn't finish first. There was the time he applied for a scholarship, came in second, and said to a friend, "Bloody hell, just wait till I get my hands on the bastard who won." Turns out the winner was that same friend.

But Rob was used to winning. He'd run the 100 meters and notice as he crossed the finish line that the rest of the field was a good ten meters behind. That ten-meter lead was a metaphor for his life.

What followed was an equally successful career. First, four years in Italy as a consultant for a big U.S. company — and skiing every weekend — then two years of Harvard Business School, which Rob says was a wonderful experience. Next, he got the chance to be co-owner of a company that organized conventions, but decided after three years that growth wasn't fast enough and took an executive position at an international media conglomerate.

That's where Rob learned how to make some serious money. The corporation had forty-six divisions and 1,400 employees around the world. Some divisions had profit margins of 5 percent, others 20 percent. Rob's job was to figure out what the 5 percent divisions had to do to become 20 percent divisions, and he was good at it. Each quarter, the company's revenue went up — as did Rob's, who'd negotiated a solid share of the profits in his contract.

So, here's what we've got so far: a schoolkid who excelled at everything, a college student who thrived at Cambridge and Harvard, a man who had it made as a consultant and an executive. That's certainly impressive, but here's the thing: Rob Mather wasn't doing anything particularly unique. He was successful in the same ways many others are successful. He was a cliché of privilege, with his carefree youth, his glorious career, his comfortable life.

And yet I was fascinated to hear Rob recount the first half of his career. Because I knew what was coming next.

3

When Rob Mather woke up on June 10, 2003, he didn't yet know that his life was about to change dramatically. He'd been looking for a new job for a while now, but he couldn't stop thinking about Terri, the little girl who'd been so severely burned. And so he started a thread on the peerless UK parenting site Mumsnet. I could still find it twenty years later, under the title "Little girl suffered 90% burns. Charity swim? Email help?"[8]

Rob Mather had an idea. He wanted to raise money for little Terri and had already convinced two friends to join him for a sponsored 22-mile swim, the distance across the English Channel. When his friends were game right away, Rob thought, "Why not ask more people?"[9]

A few months later, 10,000 people from seventy-three countries took part in more than 150 swim-a-thons. They raised money in Fiji and Canada, Spain and Vietnam, Tonga and China. Oh, and also on an island in the Atlantic Ocean, where eight Royal Air Force cadets took part in the Swim for Terri.[10]

"What are we doing next year?" one participant asked.

"I wonder if we could get a *million* people to swim," Rob blurted out.[11]

But for what goal? Terri now had enough in savings to last the rest of her life, and this time Rob wanted to set the bar higher. Far higher. With the second edition of the swim-a-thon, he wanted to do as much good as possible for as many people as possible.

And so he started to brainstorm his next good cause. Heart disease? Nah, that's largely a first-world problem. Cancer research, then? Lots of money already goes to that. Landmines? Too political. Clean drinking water? You need at least a trillion for that. Diarrhea? Much too complicated. Tuberculosis? Also difficult. What about malaria? Let's see: malaria is a leading cause of death in pregnant women. One of the most common causes of death in children under five. Some 500 million cases a year, and 3,000 dead children every day.[12]

Wait. Three thousand dead children every day? That's the equivalent of seven full jumbo jets going down. Is there a solution? Yes, malaria pills. But then you're raising money for the pharmaceutical industry. Is there another solution? A mosquito net. Treat it with insecticide and you're good to go. What does something like that cost? A few bucks. That sounds simple. Great, I love simple. Does it work? Bloody hell, thought Rob, why isn't more money being put toward this?

Rob made a few calls to malaria experts and soon understood he'd stumbled upon a no-brainer. The world wasn't doing nearly enough to fight malaria. In 2004, only 5 million mosquito nets treated with long-lasting insecticide were distributed worldwide.[13] That may sound like a lot, but not when some 3.2 billion people lived places where they're at risk of getting malaria.[14] At the same time, scientific studies indicated that just a few hundred mosquito nets could — statistically speaking — save a child's life.

And that's how World Swim Against Malaria was born. Now Rob just needed to convince a million people to take part, so he applied the twenty-minute rule. "I often challenge myself in thinking: If I want to do this thing that I'm trying to do, how would I do it in twenty minutes?"[15] In this case, the answer seemed simple. He started with twenty phone calls to twenty well-connected strangers, asking each of them to find 5,000 swimmers.[16] If that worked, he'd have 100,000 people — a great start toward that one million.

"It's simple," said Rob. "If we swim, we save lives. If we don't swim, we don't save lives. So let's swim."[17]

Once Rob and his team hit the milestone of 100,000 swimmers, they paid a visit to a billion-dollar fund in Geneva, Switzerland. "Do you realize you are the largest malaria advocacy group in the world?" they said there.[18]

Rob was surprised. "Are you telling me that twenty phone calls out of the back room of my home in London has created the world's single largest advocacy group for the world's single largest killer of children?"[19]

The answer was yes. In 2005, more than 250,000 people from 160 countries took part in the World Swim Against Malaria. London newspaper *The Times* spoke of the "greatest charity splash in history."[20]

And that was just the beginning.

Rob initially intended to go back to his work in management. He'd had a lucrative offer to take over as director of a major chicken corporation. But the idea of selling dead birds suddenly seemed a tad depressing. And he'd only recently set up the Against Malaria Foundation, or AMF, to distribute all the money raised from swim sponsors. Could he maybe do something more there?

In the business world, Rob had seen that sweeping change often works like toppling dominoes. You just need to find out where the dominoes are set up and then give the first ones a push. Rob was brilliant at locating those first dominoes, and so his anti-malaria movement kept growing and growing. Time and again he'd apply his twenty-minute rule, which meant making the most phone calls he could in the least amount of time.[21]

In fact, those phone calls are key to Rob Mather's success. Like Arnold Douwes, the resistance hero from Chapter 2, Rob doesn't shy away from asking other people to help, even if he's never met them. The result? The AMF doesn't have to spend its funds on bookkeeping, the website, or legal advice, because that's all provided pro bono.[22] Everything can go to those in need.

At the same time, Rob is also critical of the nonprofit world — the lack of transparency, the lack of accountability, and the lack of in-depth evaluations. That's why he wants everyone who donates to be able to see exactly what's done with their money. Every donation is logged on the foundation's website, and you can follow each delivery. The mosquito nets are distributed by local partners, and an independent third party checks to make sure the nets reach their destination.

All this time, Rob hasn't spent a cent on marketing, focusing instead on building as efficient an operation as possible. He's also never sought the limelight for himself. This is the first time he's talked extensively — at my request — about his incredible career.

4

To make clear just how great an impact the Against Malaria Foundation has, I'd like to introduce another privileged young man. In 1999, Holden Karnofsky joined the freshman class at Harvard. He got good grades and took part in numerous edifying extracurricular activities, such as "pissing on the John Harvard statue and running naked through Harvard Yard."[23]

After graduating, Holden — like many of his talented classmates — went to work as an investor for a major hedge fund. He drew a six-figure salary, but for some reason wasn't content living the languid life of the rich. He decided to give away a sizable chunk of his income, and in the fall of 2006 started a charity club with some of his coworkers.

These men were used to researching company returns on investment, and Holden's idea was to do the same for nonprofits. The only problem? There was very little info out there on nonprofit results. When Holden and his colleagues asked for information, they'd get glossy brochures but no hard data.[24]

And so Holden, at twenty-six, decided to quit his well-paid hedge fund job. He cofounded the think tank GiveWell and started doing evidence-based assessments of all kinds of charities. It soon became clear that most charities didn't have any serious data to analyze. There was one former executive in London, however, who was happy to hand over folders full of figures, assessments, emails, memos. Guess who. Rob Mather.

Thanks to extensive analysis on the part of GiveWell, we know that the Against Malaria Foundation is one of the world's best-performing nonprofits. It's the Real Madrid of charities. As the spreadsheets made by Holden and his colleagues show, few foundations have saved as many lives or done so as cost-effectively. As I write this, the AMF has now raised more than 700 million dollars and distributed over 300 million mosquito nets to 600 million people — a colossal contribution to beating malaria.

What started as a swim-a-thon for little Terri has grown into a campaign that by conservative estimates has saved 100,000 lives.[25]

What would have happened if on that night in 2003, Rob Mather had hit a different button on his remote? Rob suspects he would still be running a mid-sized company. He likely would have continued to climb the conventional career ladder.

That element of serendipity in Rob's big career switch makes me hopeful. You don't have to play the Good Samaritan all your life to make a difference. You can be your average exec in your average company one day, and then take the lead in fighting one of the world's deadliest diseases the next. You can catch the moral ambition bug and start to transform your life and career. Seems not all is lost after all if there's a set of luxury cheese knives in your kitchen.

Every day in 2005, the equivalent of seven jumbo jets full of children died of malaria. Today, it's less than three jumbo jets.[26] It's still tough to grasp figures of that scale. The human brain simply isn't cut out to truly feel abstract statistics like that. But when I ask Rob what his most emotional moment has been in his time with the AMF, he tells me about the time they distributed 50,000 nets in Uganda's West Nile region. One day, Rob phoned a local Red Cross employee, who said, "We have one of the village elders here at the office. He'd like to speak to you."

Rob knew the numbers for the village. In the previous months, 357 cases of malaria had been reported, and that was in a community of only 700 people. Two young boys had died. Rob spoke briefly with the man, Mohammed, who thanked him for the mosquito nets. From his home office in London, Rob answered that he and his colleagues were happy they could help, even though they were thousands of miles away.

Six months later, new figures came in. Cases of malaria were now down to seven — a decrease of 98 percent. And the next month, there weren't any cases at all. It wasn't long before Rob got an email from Mohammed. The man had walked six miles to the Red Cross, where he'd dictated a brief message:

Mr. Rob,
Malaria no longer exists in our village.
Mohammed

When Rob Mather tells me about this message, the same thing happens as when he watched the documentary on the little girl with the burns twenty years earlier. Tears come to his eyes. It makes me think of something the philosopher Bertrand Russell once said. "The mark of a civilized man is the capacity to read a column of numbers and weep."[27]

How many people Rob Mather helped

When Rob organized the swim for Terri:

👤

When Rob took on malaria:

This would have to go on for another 38 pages to show
the number of lives saved: 100,000 and counting.

6

Enroll at a Hogwarts for do-gooders

In order to be irreplaceable, one must always be different.
Coco Chanel, *fashion designer (1883–1971)*

I

Imagine a school that produces a yearly class of effective ideal-ists, each one the caliber of a Rob Mather or a Rosa Parks. An academy that helps you start your own cult to make the world a wildly better place. A hotbed of innovation where you learn to avoid the illusions of the Noble Loser and turn your moral ambition into sound results.

Do schools like that exist?

The answer is yes. On a busy street in Kilburn, west London, across from a yoga studio and a mechanic's, you'll find one of the most magical schools in the world. Passersby walk right past the old office building, unaware it's the home of what some call the "Hogwarts for do-gooders." Each year, a new cohort of wizards is trained here to go out into the world and do as much good as they can.

To find out more about this school, I took the train across the Channel to London St. Pancras, the subway to Queen's Park, and then wheeled my suitcase down Kilburn Lane until I got to No. 253. And sure enough, a nameplate by the door read "Charity Entrepreneurship." This was the place.

And let me just say upfront: that night back at the hotel as I got into bed, I was still super-excited about everything I'd seen.

Let's start with the school catalog, because that's easy to summarize. Charity Entrepreneurship is a program for entre-preneurs — entrepreneurs with moral ambition. It's a startup incubator like so many you'll find in the world of tech and ven-ture capital, but here it's not about launching high-performing companies. This is where high-impact *charities* are hatched.

Each year, the school's staff probes the question of how you can help as many people and animals as possible. What are the best solutions to the world's biggest problems? Which investments provide the greatest good in return? What organizations don't exist yet, but should?

The answer can be all kinds of things. Take the charity calling for higher duties on tobacco in Mongolia and Lebanon, so that fewer people die of lung cancer.[1] Or the organization lobbying to better fund antibiotics research, so that fewer people succumb to bacterial infections. Or the team advocating for strict regulations on meat, fish, and dairy imports coming into New Zealand and the EU, so that foreign producers will have to comply with the same standards for animal welfare as domestic ones, prompting better animal treatment across the board.

What do all these problems have in common? They're sizable, they're often super-solvable, and they're sorely overlooked — *the three S's*, if you will. These large (and largely neglected) challenges are things we can tackle, as long as we land on the right approach. Think Thomas Clarkson's struggle against slavery, Ralph Nader's crusade against General Motors, or Rob Mather's fight against malaria. Such *triple-S challenges* offer untold new prospects for doing good. And that's a niche market endlessly more promising than the market for electric toothbrush paraphernalia.[2]

In baseball, scouts speak of VORP, which stands for "Value Over Replacement Player." Say you're an excellent batter, but there are ten other fantastic batters on the bench: your added value to the team is limited because there are ten others just like you, doing the same thing. At Charity Entrepreneurship, you're trained to score your highest possible VORP. To go where no one else is going.

Every year, there's a small army of idealists who can't wait to start the new Tesla of charities. As soon as the school announces the year's new causes on its website, thousands of prospective

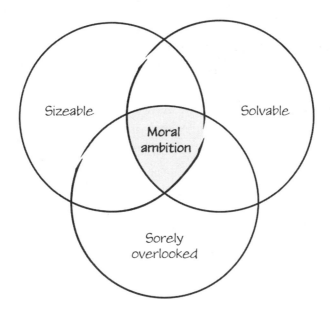

students from all over the world apply to attend. Following an extensive application process, a select group is invited to come to London. They're given a two-month crash course, matched with a cofounder and a cause, and provided with modest seed capital.[3]

The result? Since its founding in June 2018, the school has helped launch over forty organizations, making a difference to the lives of millions of people and animals.

Take someone like Lucia Coulter. After her crash course at Charity Entrepreneurship, she cofounded the Lead Exposure Elimination Project, a foundation that combats lead poisoning. That's a *sizable* problem, as one in three children worldwide have dangerous levels of lead in their bloodstream.[4] It's also *sorely overlooked*, as 52 percent of all countries don't have any laws in place to regulate lead in paint.[5] And the problem itself — lead in consumer products — is *super-solvable*. We can do something about it.

Lucia and her team buy and test paint from hardware stores in Madagascar, Zimbabwe, Angola, Sierra Leone, Bolivia, and Pakistan, and have successfully lobbied the government of Malawi to impose stricter regulations on lead in paint. That's expected to save thousands of lives.[6]

Another example is Anna Christina Thorsheim, one of the founders of Family Empowerment Media, an organization that helps prevent unwanted pregnancies through sex education. Again, we're talking big, big issue here, with more than 200 million women worldwide who don't have access to modern contraceptives.[7] It's also a sorely overlooked issue, particularly in sub-Saharan Africa, where far too little is offered in the way of sex ed.[8] Meanwhile this problem has proved solvable, too, when enough people join forces.

Together with local women, doctors, and religious leaders, Family Empowerment Media makes radio programs that convey reliable information on contraception. The foundation kicked off their efforts with a campaign in the state of Kano in Nigeria, and managed to reach over 5 million listeners in the first year. Contraceptive use in the region rose by a whopping 75 percent, saving some 200 women from dying in childbirth.[9] The foundation is now scaling up to cover another three Nigerian states.

And did I mention that Anna is twenty-four?

The director of this extraordinary school is a certain Joey Savoie. Granted, he doesn't look a thing like Dumbledore, the wise old wizard and Hogwarts headmaster of Harry Potter fame. Joey has a dark, modest little beard and can't be much past thirty. And yet he does have something in common with the elder wizard: he comes across as slightly nutty. In all honesty, he's one of the oddest people I've ever met.

When I ring the school's doorbell at No. 253, it's Joey who shows me around. Inside, it's not exactly a castle, more like a shared house for college students. There's a clunky old piano in the corner and a big map of the world on the wall, dotted with little labels with names. "That's where our students come from," Joey explains. And they come from all over: Egypt, India, South Africa, Spain, Argentina, Ireland, Nigeria, the Philippines, Mexico, the U.S., Mozambique, the Netherlands, and twenty-some other countries.

On the website, I'd already read up on the application process. There's no set number of spots; show enough potential and you're in. But make no mistake: it's easier to get into an Ivy League school. "People apply with PhDs from Harvard or Oxford all the time," Joey says. "Our bar's a lot higher."

To earn a spot, you must first of all be radically open-minded. Forget your passions. Abandon your pet causes. Odds are you'll soon be setting up an organization to do something you'd never ever considered. "I think the cause I'm now working on would have ranked lowest on my list going in," one graduate tells me. (He's involved with family planning in Ghana.)[10]

Second, you have to bring buckets of ambition — *moral ambition* to be precise, because plain old ambition isn't actually all that rare. "And it's really easy to be ambitious about the wrong thing," says Joey.

Third, you've got to be prepared to work incredibly hard. "You can set your own hours," Joey says with a smile. "As long as it's all of them." The school's alumni put in long days for modest pay. They're away from friends and family for extended periods, while the work itself is frequently far from glamorous. As Joey says, "All too often, you're stuck trying to fix the internet connection somewhere in northern Nigeria while the AC's gone out."

Other items on your résumé are less important. Academic degrees, for instance, are of little interest to Joey. Field experience is helpful but not necessary: the sooner you get started on a morally ambitious career the better.[11] And lose that startup stereotype of an extroverted founder who likes to listen to himself talk. Many talented folks here are full-on introverts.

It strikes me how diverse the school's students are. The youngest is twenty-one, the oldest fifty-five. There are lots of women and many people of color. One of the students tells me that when he was eleven, he wouldn't answer the door, afraid of yet another summons for yet another debt. With his skills, he could have pursued a career in banking, but he didn't want to end up being part of the system that squeezed his mom.

The school does its best to cast a wide net for new students; Joey is convinced there's a vast reservoir of untapped moral ambition out there. Loads of people think they're not good enough, when in reality they can change the world.

What can help is a mentor, to help lower the threshold for action. An Arnold Douwes, a Jo Ann Robinson, a Rob Mather — a wise old wizard who knocks on your door and tells you there's a spot for you at Hogwarts. Someone who points and says, "Hey, you. Yes, you! You're needed, right now. You have a mission to accomplish in this world."

It's how many a heroic tale begins.

2

To understand how the school for good causes on Kilburn Lane got its start, we have to go back to the beginning — to Joey Savoie's story.

Before my visit, I'd looked up videos of Joey, and at first I thought I must have inadvertently switched the playback speed to 1.5. But no, this was his normal speaking tempo. Next, I came across a website where Joey posted videos he made, sharing his favorite life hacks. He's got a video about the best way to care for your teeth (flossing is a waste of time, sugar-free mints underrated), and he's the proud originator of a method to dry yourself off using only an eighth of your towel.[12]

In short, this man loves his optimization. He likes to eat peanut butter and bananas because both are inexpensive, healthy, tasty, and efficient. Or take his love life. Joey swears by the dating site OkCupid because it's the "most analytical" one around. In his early twenties, he read through more than a thousand profiles, put all the information in a spreadsheet, and sent the most promising prospect a long message. That was a young woman with — surprise surprise — ambition, compassion, and an open mind. "Ended up dating that person for eight years," he says and grins.

This unusual guy's story starts in Vancouver, Canada, in the 1990s. Joey's mother, Lynn, was a child psychologist; his father, Mark, first and foremost a father. When people used to ask Mark what he did, he'd always say, "I'm a dad."

"The first thing my mom was attracted to in my dad," says Joey, "was that he was super-kind to everyone — didn't matter if you were the boss or the dishwasher or the homeless person who came by."

At elementary school, it was soon clear Joey was an exceptional kid. He found his first mission at age nine: the fight to end bullying. "Bullying was the first thing that I saw was bad for the world." And so little Joey looked into the scientific literature on bullying.[13] He discovered that instead of focusing on the bully or their target, you'd do better to turn to the bystanders. They're the ones who can make the most difference.[14]

Next, Joey put the theory into practice. Every time he detected even a whiff of bullying, he took action, and he encouraged his friends to do the same. There was only one time he didn't intervene, when someone he didn't like much was being bullied. That still haunts him.

In high school, Joey found his second mission. He thought classes were dreadfully dull and wondered one day: *what if it's not me, but the system?* The curriculum, for instance, makes no sense. You're taught all kinds of stuff you'll never use, while teachers don't say a word about things we clearly all need to know (like how to do your taxes).

And why did school have to be so monotonous? Why so little effort to serve different students who had different needs? Joey saw lots of talent going to waste. What's more, he was convinced the entire system needed to be overhauled, and so he again dove into the literature. Meanwhile, teenaged Joey joined all kinds of online forums for education experts. "I loved the internet because no one could tell my age."

After some time, he gathered that there were two main schools of thought in the world of education. On the one hand, you've got the folks who know everything there is to know about the hard science — the evidence-based methods shown to boost student test scores. On the other, you've got the people asking the question at the heart of it all, namely: how can education best prepare you for living a meaningful life?

Joey loved the quantitative approach of the first group, but thought their objectives ridiculous. (Those test scores are mostly "vanity metrics," according to Joey.) He also loved the second school of thought's vision, but got frustrated by the lack of evidence backing it up. And so he decided to take matters into his own hands.

In his final years of high school, Joey formulated a master plan for his career. When he looked around at his classmates, he couldn't believe how passive they were. He saw all these talented young people who got good grades in the hopes of making their parents proud. Meanwhile, they didn't dare give the future any thought. "Well, I get my best marks in biology," they'd say. "So, I guess I'll study biology." Why did no one seem interested in the rest of their life?

Joey, on the other hand, had always lived in the future. "I was always thinking five or ten years out." That's why he looked into what job he'd need if he wanted to unleash an education revolution in Canada. But turns out that job didn't exist. Even the chair of the highest educational board in the land had only nominal influence on school policies.

So then Joey thought: *What if I start my own school?* He invited his friends over for a roleplay — a Dungeons & Dragons–style scenario where you'd normally play an elf or a dwarf — but this time Joey had other roles in mind. Participants got the role of teacher or student at a school of the future. For Joey, it made perfect sense. "If you can play at being a dwarf or an elf, why not play your twenty-year-older future self?" He called the group the Scientific World Changers.

It was around this time that Joey had another realization. He'd been watching one documentary after another, on everything from extreme poverty to factory farming, and could hardly believe what he saw. He'd always thought that gross injustice was a thing of the past. He'd sometimes even felt like he'd missed out by not living in Europe during World War II, a time when you could follow your conscience and join the resistance.

But then it hit him: there's still a tremendous amount of suffering and oppression in the world today. We still have fundamental choices to make, and you can still be part of the resistance in one form or another. Why weren't we grappling with that at school every day?

After finishing high school, Joey Savoie chose to study psychology at a community college near Vancouver starting in September 2011. He had his whole future mapped out. He thought diplomas were overrated but knew he might need a couple of them for his education revolution. At the same time, he knew that people would generally only look at his most recent degree.

Joey's plan: get his first degree at a low-priced school, earn his master's at a more prestigious institution, and then go for a PhD at Harvard. That way, he'd retain as much time and money as possible for more useful matters, like developing the curriculum for the school he wanted to set up. His friends called him crazy, but Joey thought the plan made sense.

But then, in his sophomore year of college, Joey discovered something. He was googling "good ways to make a difference" and "how to change the world" — as you do — when he hit on the think tank GiveWell. That organization, founded by a certain Holden Karnofsky (see Chapter 5), did in-depth research into the most effective ways to help people.

Suddenly everything fell into place. For the first time, Joey understood there were other people like him. People with similar criteria for success, who wanted to make the world a far better place. That insight changed everything. On GiveWell's website, he read about extremely effective charities like the Against Malaria Foundation. Joey quit school and booked a one-way ticket to London with his girlfriend at the time (the one from OkCupid). One of the first people he called once he got there? You guessed it: Rob Mather.

3

As I sit in the school's kitchen and listen to Joey Savoie, two things keep coming to mind:

1 This guy is fantastic.
2 I can't do a thing with his story.

Joey is no use as a role model for moral ambition, I'm afraid, because it's like he's from another planet. And yet it's wonderful to hear how independent a life he lives, how little regard he has for traditional definitions of success.

Take his spartan lifestyle. When Joey and his girlfriend lived in London, they survived on £12,000 a year (roughly $18,000). Together. Half that amount was for rent, the other half for everything else. (This was also the period Joey discovered you could dry off with one-eighth of your towel.) The couple lived well below the UK poverty line, but for them it made sense. That £12,000 was in line with what your average person on the planet earned.[15]

Shortly after Joey arrived in London, Rob Mather, the founder of the Against Malaria Foundation, told him he didn't really need an extra pair of hands. But more money for the cause was always welcome, so Joey and his girlfriend started fundraising. And why did Joey like that so much? Because it's measurable. You know precisely how much or how little you've accomplished.

In the months that followed, Joey and his girlfriend tried out three strategies: applying for grants (didn't work at all), schmoozing with rich people (they weren't that good at it), and crowdfunding (which really took off). At some point, they had raised £200,000 and GiveWell got in touch. "Nice job," the GiveWell people said, "but shouldn't young, energetic people like yourselves start your own organization?"[16]

Joey was immediately enthusiastic. He asked Rob Mather to be his mentor, something Rob was happy to do. Now in his fifties, Rob thought it would be great if a couple of kids in their early twenties could knock him out of first place in the charity rankings.

The young people's plan was straightforward. As Joey put it: "Let's do six months of research, make a prioritization spreadsheet, and come up with the best possible thing." Along with a couple of friends, Joey immersed himself in the literature, and then all four of them booked a one-way trip to India. They thought the vast and varied land would be a perfect place to scale up their operation. And the startup now had a name: Charity Entrepreneurship.

In January 2016, they took off — four kids with little experience and even less money, but with big plans for setting up one of the best charities in the world. In the city of Lucknow (population 3.3 million at the time), they went from slum to slum interviewing hundreds of parents, doctors, and field staff about their lives and their work. "I wouldn't say it was fun," Joey said. "It was really challenging, but very good from a life satisfaction perspective."

They started with a list of twenty-eight ideas, and then crossed off more and more of them.[17] After a few months, they had five options left, and the best plan turned out to be the simplest: sending parents text messages to remind them to have their kid vaccinated. That intervention cost next to nothing, but it boosted vaccine coverage, which could save thousands of lives. (Worldwide, 14 million children don't get any of their basic shots.[18] And every minute, a child under five dies from a disease we can easily prevent with a vaccine, like measles or whooping cough.)[19]

Joey and his friends wanted to be sure this was the best idea, so the team devised a prize for anyone who could convince them otherwise. When nothing came in, and both Rob Mather and GiveWell were enthusiastic about the plan, they took the leap. Twenty-four-year-old Joey and his friends founded their first charity: Charity Science Health.

The four got straight to work. In no time, twelve hospitals in India were taking part, ten employees were hired, and they'd reached 200,000 parents. Once the organization was up and running, Joey was eager to move on to the next project. He wanted to become a serial entrepreneur, tackling one neglected global problem after another.

And then came his big lightbulb moment.

The team had taken the spreadsheet with all the ideas for new nonprofits and posted it online. A young Harvard student saw it and asked for a job, offering to set up one of the potential new organizations. That's when it occurred to Joey: what if I do for him what Rob Mather did for me? "Okay, here's what I'm going to do," Joey told him. "We'll give you a $30,000 grant and one hour a week of mentorship."

The student soon found a cofounder — a recent Oxford graduate — and together they did field studies in India. Next, the duo set up Fortify Health, a foundation that works with local millers to enrich wheat flour with iron, folic acid, and vitamin B12, protecting millions from anemia and congenital defects like spina bifida. Within a year, Fortify Health had helped more people than Joey's own Charity Science Health.[20]

At that point, Joey had to reevaluate. "I was looking at this project, which took me like no time and no money," he told me. "And then I was looking at Charity Science Health, which I killed myself doing." The two founders of Fortify Health said that Joey had lowered their threshold for action and that without his encouragement, they wouldn't have dared do what they did. He was their wise old wizard, who'd said, "Hey, you. Yes, you! You're needed, right now. You have a mission to accomplish in this world."[21]

Only now did Joey know what he wanted to do with his life.

It was time to start his own Hogwarts.

4

Lying in bed back at my hotel that night, I tried to figure out what I liked so much about the school on Kilburn Lane. Was it the inspired teachers, who could be earning three times as much elsewhere? Was it the mismatched office chairs, which gave off clear vibes that the actual work mattered more here than the packaging? Or was it the comradery among the students, which made the place feel like one big happy family?

In the end, I think it had to do with a unique combination of four characteristics you almost never find in a single person. But taken together, folks at the school have them all. Call them the four main ingredients of moral ambition:

1 the idealism of an activist
2 the ambition of a startup founder
3 the analytical mind of a scientist
4 the humility of a monk

You can't change the world by yourself, Joey continually emphasized during my visit. It always comes down to teamwork. The problem with a lot of idealists is they have towering expectations of themselves. They want to be a successful entrepreneur, skilled researcher, fundraiser, networker, and storyteller in one. "It's really nice to think you're super-important, that you're the one who's going to save everything," said Joey. "But you have to get down to earth and realize you need a team to get stuff done. You need a community."[22]

That was also true for Joey: he knew he needed a cofounder for his school. Through a friend of a friend of a friend, he came in contact with Karolina Sarek, who at twenty-one had just been named the youngest university lecturer in Poland. Joey and Karolina complement one another neatly. If he's the somewhat nutty Professor Dumbledore, she's more the meticulous Professor McGonagall.

Working together puts you in a stronger position when things go south. And startups are inherently risky: of the five organizations set up each year out of Charity Entrepreneurship, at least one is dissolved within a year. It takes courage to start something new, but perhaps more courage to pull the plug if a project fails to deliver.

New insight can also make you change course. A groundbreaking study came out in 2019 by economists Abhijit Banerjee and Esther Duflo, who would go on to win the Nobel Prize that year.[23] Turns out that if you want to boost vaccination rates in India, what works best is sending reminder texts *and* recruiting local ambassadors who can encourage young parents to get their children vaccinated.

Joey and his friends decided to take their first nonprofit, Charity Science Health, and merge with Suvita, an organization also hatched at the school for good causes. Suvita now combines both strategies in comical ways: staff members get their hands on a local phone directory, call someone at random, and ask who's the biggest gossip in the village.[24] Then they call that person and convey a simple message: "Hey, you. Yes, you! You're needed, right now. You have a mission to accomplish in this world."

And what do you know. More than 95 percent of the people they approach agree to help. Like Arnold Douwes and Rob Mather had discovered before them: nearly everyone takes action, as long as they're asked.

If you ask Joey Savoie about his ambitions for the future, you get treated to a grand vision. At Hogwarts, you've got four houses: Ravenclaw, Hufflepuff, Slytherin, and Gryffindor.

What if the school on Kilburn Lane also had four divisions that together take on the world's biggest problems? Four tracks for ambitious idealists?

The first house would be the equivalent of Gryffindor, known for courage and daring. Here, the founders of startup charities would be trained.

Next, you've got Ravenclaw, the division for the most analytical students with the highest IQs. They scour the literature for new ideas and do thorough assessments of startup results.

Third, we have Hufflepuff, the division that values patience, loyalty, and hard work. Here you'll find the idealistic all-rounders who excel at lobbying and communication — the people people who bring folks together to form coalitions and the "intrapreneurs" who have the persistence to change organizations from the inside out.

And finally, Slytherin. That's the division known for ambition, cunning, and pride. Here, advisers are taught to help big donors allocate their money effectively. Without Slytherin fundraising, the whole model would collapse, but you have to watch out you don't produce a Voldemort from time to time.

To keep their moral ambition from getting away from them, the Kilburn Lane students are trained to keep each other accountable and on track. It's essential to build in that kind of reflection: Am I doing what I say? Producing what I promise? You have to be on the lookout for moral corruption. People don't lose their ideals all at once, Joey says, but in little steps: "Gain one pound a year, and twenty years later you'll be twenty pounds heavier. I think something similar can happen to our altruism."

That's why the school director believes in short feedback loops, or concrete goals you can stick to. And he's even leery of getting too much funding for the school because that could make students and teachers lax. Nothing wrong with Joey's fundraising skills — he just prefers to bake in a certain measure of financial insecurity. He always wants to be able to show the school's donors that their money is being well spent.

As I write this, Charity Entrepreneurship already has over a hundred graduates. Some 65 percent of them have set up a non-profit, and the rest have found other work in the fight against poverty, disease, or animal suffering.[25] For Joey, that's just the beginning. "Even way back in my education reform days," he says, "I always had this idea of starting small and then scaling up."

Just imagine a world with many more idealistic schools that do magic. Academies for morally ambitious journalists and marketeers, one for lobbyists and politicians, another for lawyers and bankers, doctors and teachers, techies and engineers. Better yet, a school for school directors, so you can train twenty Joeys at once.

Joey Savoie dreams of a vast, international network of driven alumni that help each other out.[26] Slytherin raises the money, Ravenclaw comes up with the best ideas, Hufflepuff builds a movement, and Gryffindor jumps in at the deep end. It's a world with a new definition of success, a world where many more people use their skills to do as much good as possible.

As a wise old wizard says at the end of *Harry Potter and the Chamber of Secrets*: "It is our choices, Harry, that show what we truly are, far more than our abilities."

7

Find out what the world needs and make it happen

I find out what the world needs. Then I go ahead
and try to invent it.
Thomas Edison, *inventor (1847–1931)*

I

In 1836 the richest man in the world, Nathan Mayer Rothschild, died of a simple infection that we can cure today with a course of antibiotics for a few bucks. For thousands of years, just about anyone, just about anywhere, could suddenly keel over from diseases we now shrug off or which we've eradicated entirely.

Children were especially vulnerable. In most places in the twenty-first century, the death of a child is a rare tragedy, while it used to be a matter of heads or tails. Until the year 1800, nearly half — half! — of all children died before reaching adulthood.[1] Even princes and princesses dropped dead in droves, despite being attended by the best physicians.

Charlemagne (747–814), for instance, had seven brothers and sisters, but only two lived to see their eighteenth birthday. King Edward II of England (1284–1327) had eleven sisters, but only five survived childhood, and his three brothers all died before their twelfth birthday.[2] The Queen of Great Britain, Anne Stuart (1665–1714), was pregnant no less than eighteen times, and only one of her children survived early childhood: little Prince William.

Shortly after his eleventh birthday in 1700, William got sick.[3] The court doctors promptly advised bloodletting, and that treatment seemed to ease his fever, but during the night of July 29 to 30, he developed difficulties swallowing and breathing. With his desperate parents at his bedside, the young prince lost consciousness. A few hours later, he was dead.

These days, child mortality worldwide is ten times lower than in Prince William's day. In the U.S., it's more than fifty times lower, and in the EU, a hundred times lower.[4] The share of the world's population that lives in extreme poverty has gone down nearly 90 percent, and the poor in wealthy countries now enjoy a higher standard of living than kings and emperors a few centuries back.[5]

But the good news doesn't seem to have reached everyone. A survey in twenty-eight countries indicated that most people think child mortality has stayed the same or increased over the past twenty years, when in reality it's been cut in half.[6] Cut. In. Half. It's enough to make you want to shout it from the rooftops: *Millions and millions of children used to die, but not anymore! Do you hear me? Millions and millions . . .*

For years now, the world has been making swift and steady progress in the fight against death and disease, but when it comes to our views on the future, pessimism prevails. Countless movies and television series portray the varied ways that hurricanes, ice ages, asteroids, virus outbreaks, aliens, robots, and zombies threaten to wipe us out. Remarkably, it's largely inhabitants of wealthy countries that share this bleak outlook. In Finland and Norway, for instance, only 8 percent of people think things are getting better; in France and Australia, a mere 3 percent.[7]

True, it's not all that difficult to come up with scenarios that don't end well for humankind. At the same time, there's a chronic lack of imagination when picturing how much better the future can be. When half of all children didn't make it, people couldn't imagine a world where 96 percent live. Yet here we are. And likely our progeny will be appalled at what illnesses we now succumb to, saying things like: *back in 2017, the richest woman in the world, Liliane Bettencourt, died from Alzheimer's complications. In those days, they had no way to treat the disease.*

2

One thing's certain: scientific innovations have saved more lives than all the Malalas, Mandelas, and Mother Theresas combined. That's why it's especially tragic that so many whiz kids spend their time building pointless apps and algorithms. If we want to take on the big challenges of our time, we're going to need an army of morally ambitious science geeks.

There was a time, not so long ago, when pioneers in science and technology inspired greater admiration. A time when major advances were widely celebrated.[8] Take the discovery of the polio vaccine. Polio is a horrible illness that can lead to paralysis and suffocation. Up until the early 1950s, parents were terrified their children would catch the disease — only the nuclear bomb was feared more.[9]

But then Jonas Salk appeared on the scene. The virologist had studied medicine at New York University in the 1930s and soon decided he didn't want to go the clinical route. Instead of seeing one patient at a time, Salk wanted to treat humanity.[10] He ended up devoting seven years of his life to developing the polio vaccine.

Read anything about April 12, 1955, the day Salk's breakthrough was made public, and you're likely to get a lump in your throat. All across the country, Americans gathered around their radios. Shops set up loudspeakers, factories went quiet, and judges declared their courtrooms in recess. In hundreds of movie theaters, more than 50,000 doctors watched the news together.

Then came the official announcement: a team led by Dr. Jonas Edward Salk had developed a safe and effective vaccine against polio. The disease's days were numbered. In the auditorium where the press conference took place, people fell into each other's arms, crying. Motorists drove around honking, and thousands of people took to the streets to celebrate. One historian later wrote:

> A contagion of love swept the world. People observed moments of silence, rang bells, honked horns, blew factory whistles, fired salutes, kept their traffic lights red in brief periods of tribute, took the rest of the day off, closed their schools or convoked fervid assemblies therein, drank toasts, hugged children, attended church, smiled at strangers, forgave enemies . . . [11]

A massive vaccination operation got underway at once, and the quiet virologist became world famous overnight. Three Hollywood studios fought for the rights to his life story, and New York City offered to put on a parade in his honor, but Salk graciously declined.[12] When asked who held the patent to his vaccine, he famously replied, "Well, the people, I'd say. There is no patent. Could you patent the sun?"[13]

Today, polio is nearly eradicated.

Less well known, but at least as impressive, is the tale of Viktor Zhdanov, a Ukrainian virologist. He didn't develop a vaccine but had an enormous impact in 1958 when he called on the World Health Organization (WHO) to start an inoculation campaign against smallpox.

Smallpox was the deadliest virus of all time.[14] In the twentieth century alone, over 300 million people died of the disease. Compare that to World War II, which claimed some 80 million lives.[15] (Historians suspect that Anna Stuart's longest living son, little Prince William, also died of smallpox.)[16]

Zhdanov's plan was brimming with ambition. The small-pox vaccine had long been available, but humankind had never eradicated a disease before, and many experts simply didn't think it possible. But in 1966, with a margin of only two votes, the WHO gave Zhdanov the go-ahead.[17] Over a period of ten years, $300 million would be put into a worldwide vaccination campaign.[18]

The results were staggering. In October 1977, the world's last smallpox patient was diagnosed in Somalia. His name was Ali Maow Maalin, one of the volunteers with a local vaccination team. Maalin recovered, and when no other patient was found after months of searching, the WHO field office in Nairobi sent this historic telegram to headquarters in Geneva:

> Search complete. No cases discovered. Ali Maow Maalin is the world's last known smallpox case.

To this day, smallpox is the only human disease we've completely eradicated. UNICEF estimates that Viktor Zhdanov's campaign has saved 200 million lives. Perhaps the disease would have been eradicated without the Ukrainian virologist, but it would likely have taken far longer, and many more people would have died in the meantime. In other words, Zhdanov may well have the highest VORP in the history of healthcare ("Value Over Replacement Player," see Chapter 6).

Regrettably, he didn't enjoy as much acclaim as Jonas Salk. A solemn ceremony held in Geneva in May 1980 marked the eradication of smallpox worldwide, but the Russian regime didn't allow Zhdanov to attend. A Soviet apparatchik was sent in his stead.[19]

"Not a single good deed goes unpunished," was Zhdanov's ironic comment on the insult. He then added, with a flair for understatement: ". . . but good deeds are still cost-effective."[20]

These days, far more is possible with new vaccines. Take one of the main causes of death today: malaria. Yes, we have mosquito nets treated with insecticide, and people like Rob Mather (see Chapter 5) have shown how they can save many lives. But what if we had a vaccine? Could we beat malaria once and for all?

Well, here's some good news: we've got a vaccine. On October 2, 2021, the WHO greenlighted the first effective vaccine against malaria — a huge breakthrough. Looks like this disease that's plagued humankind for thousands of years, killing an estimated 5 percent of all the people who ever lived, is now something we could eradicate in the coming decades. [21]

Naturally, that's a fantastic prospect. But you've got to wonder: what took us so long?

Back in 1980, researchers at New York University identified a protein that's essential for the malaria parasite to develop.[22] They realized that the human immune system could be trained to recognize that protein. In other words: from then on, it was clear a malaria vaccine was within reach — as long as we invested in additional research.

The U.S. Army was briefly interested, because a shot seemed convenient for protecting troops stationed overseas. But the research required was never prioritized. It took until 1998 before the first results came in from a test with adult men in Gambia. By then, the army's attention had turned elsewhere, and other countries and companies likewise showed little interest.[23]

All that time, only a couple of million dollars a year was spent worldwide on developing a malaria vaccine.[24] Fifty times as much was invested in research into HIV/AIDS because, well, thousands of activists in wealthy countries had fought for funding.[25] For malaria, there was no such movement, likely because it primarily strikes poor people in poor countries.

In the end it was a tech billionaire, of all people, who took it upon himself to step in and finally revive research into a vaccine. Support from Bill Gates meant the next stage of development could start: looking into whether the vaccine was safe for children.

That stage lasted another twenty years.[26]

While all of this was happening — from 1980 to 2020 — more than 40 million people succumbed to malaria. That's about how many people died in Europe during World War II.[27] One of the victims was that Somalian volunteer, Ali Maow Maalin, who'd made a full recovery from smallpox in 1977. Since 2004, he'd helped eradicate polio in his country because, as he told a British journalist, "Somalia was the last country with smallpox. I wanted to help ensure that we would not be the last place with polio, too."[28]

But in 2013, polio cropped up again in Somalia. Maalin immediately joined the latest vaccination campaign but was bitten by a mosquito on the job. He developed a fever and died a few days later of malaria.

3

If the fight against smallpox, polio, and malaria shows us anything, it's that we can't make the world a wildly better place without science. Moral ambition needs technology, and new discoveries and inventions can make a world of difference in the struggle to tackle our biggest problems. So why don't we talk more about the promise of such developments?

We stage demonstrations against inequality and poverty — and rightly so — but seldom for more research into vaccines. You see protests against factories that pollute or pipelines that leak — and rightly so — but never people marching with signs

that read FUND NUCLEAR FUSION! INFINITE CLEAN ENERGY NOW!
In left-wing circles, it's hipper to be a tech cynic than a techie.
And people of all stripes primarily tend to know good and well
what they're *against*.

But we also need to know what we're *for*. MLK never said, "I
have a nightmare." He had a dream. Yes, we need activists fighting injustice in the here and now, certainly, but we also need
people dreaming and creating and building the future. We need
people who hear "super-solvable," then go and think up solutions that don't yet exist.

Naturally, the word *tech* may call up an image for you of a
tax-dodging billionaire who shoots himself into space to fill the
gaping hole in his soul. You're not wrong, but that's a limited
view of what tech can do. New technology proved crucial for
those who fought for freedom in centuries past. What's more, it
can set off moral revolutions.

Take the women's movement. The invention of the bicycle gave
women more freedom of movement than ever, and the famous
suffragist Susan B. Anthony considered a woman riding a bike
"the picture of untrammeled womanhood."[29] The bicycle did
away with "old-fashioned, slow-going notions of the gentler
sex," according to a Nebraska newspaper in 1895, and paved the
way for "some new woman, mounted on her steed of steel."[30]

Around the same time, Josephine Cochrane of Illinois
wondered why there wasn't yet a machine to do the dishes.[31]
Cochrane came from a family of inventors, but male engineers
of the time had little interest in the home.[32] "If nobody else is
going to invent a dishwashing machine," Cochrane said, "I'll do
it myself."[33]

Inventions like Cochrane's sparked a revolution in American
households. Home appliances like washing machines, vacuum

cleaners, and refrigerators are called the "engines of liberation" for a reason.[34] In 1900, the average homemaker spent fifty-eight hours a week on cooking, cleaning, and the wash. By 1975, that was down to eighteen hours.[35]

"Whenever I'm asked to name my feminist heroine," writes the British feminist Helen Lewis, "I'm tempted to answer: the washing machine."[36]

The engines of liberation

Time spent on household work by rural women in the US

■■■ Cooking, tidying, cleaning   ▒▒ Doing laundry
☐ Knitting, sewing, mending   ■ Gathering wood, fetching water, etc.

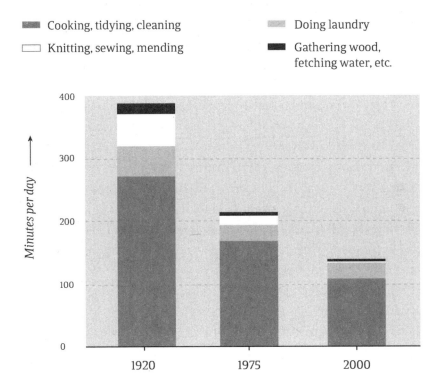

Source: Gershuny and Harms (2016)

I haven't even mentioned my favorite example yet: Katharine McCormick. In 1904, she was the second woman to graduate from the Massachusetts Institute of Technology, and the first with a degree in biology. McCormick would fight for women's rights her whole life, in particular for the right to contraception.

In McCormick's day, it was against the law to promote birth control or to send contraceptives through the U.S. mail. That would be officially "obscene." And in the state of Connecticut, until 1965, you could be arrested or jailed for using a condom, even if you were married.[37] (In my own country of the Netherlands, things weren't all that different: there you had the Morality Act, which prohibited the distribution of contraceptives as late as 1970.)[38]

But McCormick didn't let that stop her. She smuggled over a thousand diaphragms from Europe through U.S. customs by sewing them into her clothing.[39] She believed that women could only be free once they had control over their own bodies.

In 1947, McCormick inherited her wealthy husband's estate (his father had invented the mechanical reaper, a groundbreaking technology for harvesting grain).[40] She was now in her seventies, but as idealistic as ever. And she knew exactly what she wanted to do with the money. McCormick wrote a letter to an old friend, the feminist Margaret Sanger, asking whether she knew someone who could develop a safe, reliable, and inexpensive contraceptive for women.

Not much later, Sanger met a biologist who was already working on precisely that. Gregory Goodwin Pincus was a brilliant scientist, said to have an IQ of 210.[41] He'd been let go from Harvard due to controversial research into sex and reproduction, and even many activists thought him too radical.[42]

But then McCormick came to see him. She immediately wrote him a check, and in the end put more than $2 million toward his research. A few years later, Pincus's discovery of "Enovid" was approved by the U.S. Food and Drug Administration.[43] It was revolutionary — millions of women gained control over their own bodies, reshaping economies, transforming families, and upending centuries-old norms. Enovid's impact was so massive, and on such a historic, global scale, that it came to be known by a simple name.

The pill.

4

It's hard to imagine the feminist revolution of the 1960s without the vim and vigor and vision of pioneers like Josephine Cochrane and Katharine McCormick. Their stories show that technological progress is not a given; it has everything to do with the choices we make.

New technology can also spark the moral revolutions of the future, about how we treat animals, for instance. Every year now, we slaughter some 80 billion chickens, cows, turkeys, goats, and sheep.[44] Such immense numbers of livestock can't exist without antibiotics and modern mega-sheds, but fortunately, technology can also offer a solution.

Picture the highest quality meat imaginable, untainted by salmonella or traces of heavy metals, and produced using 90 percent less water and land. Picture a world with countless healthier, tastier, more sustainable, and inexpensive sources of protein. That's the future. "We shall escape the absurdity of growing a whole chicken in order to eat the breast or wing," wrote a certain Winston Churchill back in 1931, "by growing these parts separately."[45]

In 2020, Churchill's prediction came true. That year, in Singapore, the first chicken nuggets were served that required no chicken to be slaughtered.[46] The meat was grown in a laboratory from the stem cells of a chicken.

In a world where this kind of cultivated meat abounds, it will become much easier to have principles and refuse to eat meat from factory farms. In fact, it wouldn't surprise me if polluting, industrial-scale meat production is outlawed this century, like asbestos is now in many countries. "We once ate animals," we'll then tell our astonished children and grandchildren.[47]

To be sure: the fact that technology can play such an important role doesn't mean that the work of animal rights activists is no longer needed. On the contrary, it's thanks in part to activists that we've seen substantial investment in biotechnology in recent years. Josh Balk, founder of the company that served those first chicken nuggets in Singapore, started out as an undercover activist in slaughterhouses.[48]

But just like with the malaria vaccine, we could have had those nuggets years earlier. How soon we see further advances in cultivated meat depends largely on us: on how much time, attention, money, and talent we put into it.

It reminds me of something Jimmy Wales, who founded Wikipedia, once said. When he launched his online encyclopedia in 2001, the necessary technology had already been around for years. Web servers, browsers, and online databases were nothing new, so Wikipedia could have seen the light of day much earlier. "Think of all the technology we have today," Wales said, "and what could be created with it that nobody has even really thought of yet."[49]

Let me give one last example of a revolution unleashed by a cult of morally ambitious science geeks. It may well be the most inspiring example of them all: the rise of sustainable energy.

Energy is the foundation of modern society. No energy means no cars or computers, no fridges or phones. And turns out that per capita, we now consume 700 times the energy used two centuries ago. Put in terms of heavy physical labor, it's as if the average American has 240 adults working hard for them around the clock.[50]

Of course, we're now well aware of the huge downside to our unchecked fossil fuel use. But let's say we succeed in making our energy supply green and clean. And say we then have at our disposal 700 times as much energy per person.

Then the wildest fantasies can become everyday realities.

"The team that brings clean and abundant energy to the world," writes the psychologist Steven Pinker, "will benefit humanity more than all of history's saints, heroes, prophets, martyrs, and laureates combined."[51]

Clean drinking water for everyone on the planet? Check. With enough electricity, we can desalinate as much seawater as we need. Vacuum up two centuries' worth of carbon emissions? Sure thing. With essentially free green energy, we can remove as much carbon from the atmosphere as we want. And while we're at it, we can provide the entire world with fresh produce, as long as we plant everything under LED grow lights in skyscrapers where we can fine-tune the growing conditions. Then we'll need virtually no pesticides and can give almost all farmland back to nature.

And I'm probably not being bold enough here. With endless amounts of energy, we can move all roads underground, or build cities at the bottom of the ocean. We can start exploring the Milky Way and make planets like Mars inhabitable, too. Space docks — where you take an elevator to a launchpad a hundred kilometers up — shouldn't be a problem, so you can then hop over to another planet.[52]

Okay, maybe these aren't the best examples. I mean I'd personally rather go to the coast for a few days than spend the weekend on Saturn. But the point is we might just be on the verge of something very big indeed. If history teaches us anything in this regard, it's that every energy revolution comes with a burst of new technology. "The rapid progress true science now makes," wrote Benjamin Franklin back in 1780, "occasions my regretting sometimes that I was born so soon."[53]

You know how we see people in the Dark Ages? That may well be how our great-grandchildren will look back on us.

In the meantime, we have to stop with the fossil fuels — a scarce, dirty, and deadly source of energy that keeps many a dictator in power. At some point, we'll look back and think burning coal, gas, and oil was as primitive as burning peat.

Fortunately, there are far better options. With his famous formula, $E = mc^2$, Einstein already anticipated that you could turn a little bit of mass into an immense amount of clean energy. That energy gets released when atomic nuclei are split, or even better, when they fuse together. We got a glimpse into that future in December 2022, when U.S. scientists announced that for the first time, they'd managed to generate energy in this way.[54] The process at work, nuclear fusion, also takes place deep inside stars.

One small sidenote: those researchers produced just enough energy to make a pot of tea. So nuclear fusion on a grand scale still seems a long way away, but just how long it will take us isn't written in the stars. It depends on the choices people make, or in other words, how hard we push for it.

There's yet another candidate for the energy source of the future. I'm talking about the nuclear reactor we see rise every day: the sun. "I'd put my money on the sun and solar energy," Thomas Edison reportedly said back in 1931 to carmaker Henry Ford. "What a source of power! I hope we don't have to wait till oil and coal run out before we tackle that. I wish I had more years left!"[55]

Since the 1970s, the price of solar energy has dropped more than 99 percent.[56]

Cheap, cheaper, cheapest

The price of solar energy in US dollars per watt, adjusted for inflation

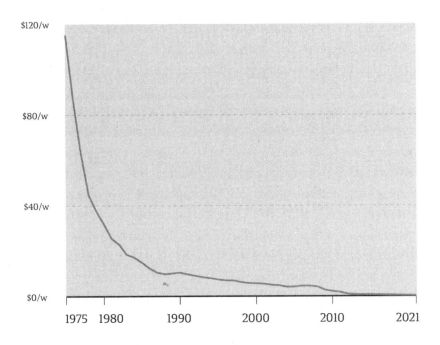

Source: Our World in Data

When you see the steeply sloping line of this graph, you could get the impression that the drop in solar energy prices was inevitable. Nothing could be further from the truth. Behind this graph lies a fascinating tale about a handful of determined individuals. I'm talking about three pioneers with towering VORPS: an Australian professor, a German politician, and a Chinese entrepreneur.

Let me start at the beginning of this incredible tale. As early as 1839, a French physicist described the basic principle of a solar panel, the photovoltaic effect. But it would take another hundred years before the *New York Times* reported in 1954 on a revolutionary development: NEW BATTERY TAPS SUN'S VAST POWER.[57] Researchers at Bell Labs succeeded in building the first usable panel that collected light particles and transformed them into electricity. The newspaper understood the revolutionary implications. "It may mark the beginning of a new era, leading eventually to the realization of one of mankind's most cherished dreams — the harnessing of the almost limitless energy of the sun for the uses of civilization."

Despite this enthusiasm, little was invested in the technology. As Ralph Nader put it in the seventies, "The use of solar energy hasn't been opened up because the oil industry doesn't own the sun."[58] Following the oil crisis of 1973, some money was freed up for a modest research program, but funding was cut again in the eighties. President Ronald Reagan acted as if research into renewables was typical Democrat spendthrift behavior and mocked it as "solar socialism." The solar panels installed at the White House during President Jimmy Carter's administration were removed under Reagan.[59]

In the years that followed, a small pilot light continued to flicker at the University of New South Wales in Australia. There, a team led by a professor named Martin Green kept at it, working to craft the solar panel of the future.

Meanwhile, on the other side of the world, another key figure came on the scene: the German city council member Hans-Josef Fell. Look up a picture of him, and you'll see a politician in a nondescript suit — nothing to suggest superhero status. And yet. Mr. Fell gave solar energy, our most important weapon to date in the fight against climate change, an enormous boost.

Back in the early nineties, he was already an affable environmentalist, or "solar freak" as he called himself. On a hillside in the town of Hammelburg, he built a sort of Hobbit dwelling entirely covered with grass and solar panels. Fell was known in the area as that nut who'd spent a fortune on pricey panels that generated next to no power.

But that nut could be pretty persuasive. He believed that solar energy could become far cheaper, once production was stepped up.[60] And so Fell proposed the world's first "solar premium." Local residents got a sizable subsidy for their solar panels, financed with a fee added to everyone's utility bill. Suddenly it became lucrative to join the cult of solar freaks.

In 1998, Fell's party *Die Grünen* ("The Greens") now made up part of the ruling coalition at the national level. He knew his chance had come. Fell wrote an ambitious plan for a national subsidy scheme, and the new coalition adopted it. In the years that followed, the Germans pumped a crazy amount of money — over 200 billion euros — into subsidies for solar panels. The world market increased thirty-fold, and in some years Germany bore more than half of all the costs.[61] Nowhere in the world did the electric bill go up as much.

People often used to scoff at silly Germany, where they paid a fortune to ever so slightly reduce emissions. But those who scoffed back then aren't laughing now. Because what Fell predicted came true: as the factories scaled up, production became more efficient and the price of solar panels plummeted everywhere. In other words, Germany paid the world's dues, thanks to the solar freak from Hammelburg, and now solar energy is super-cheap. Thank you, Mr. Fell!

And where were those millions of panels manufactured? Not in Germany, but China. One of Martin Green's exchange students (Green was that Australian professor) turned out to be not only an excellent researcher, but also a brilliant entrepreneur. His name was Shi Zhengrong, and he grew into the solar king of the world. Like Thomas Edison figured out a business model for the lightbulb, Shi developed a business model for the solar panel.

On the advice of his former professor, Shi went to a trade show in Germany, where Fell's subsidy scheme had just been unveiled. Shi was the only solar entrepreneur from China there, but managed to win everyone over with his perfect English and his PhD from the planet's preeminent school for photovoltaic engineering.

"We had to accomplish in a decade what many told me would take a century," Shi reflected in 2012. "Some believe that we grew too fast . . . but the world couldn't afford to wait a hundred years to solve our planet's energy and environmental crisis."[62] Shi would go bankrupt a year later. Turns out his billion-dollar company did grow too fast. But by then, dozens of competitors were already following his lead, and experts agree that Shi played a historic role.[63] Without him, advances in solar energy would have taken much longer.

There's no end in sight for the drop in solar energy prices. According to the International Energy Agency, it's now the cheapest source of energy in human history, even without subsidies, and it can be much cheaper still if we continue to scale up production. Every hour, enough sunlight reaches the planet to power the whole world for a year.

Looks like Thomas Edison was right when he said he'd put his money on the sun, and that solar could turn out to be our greatest source of energy. Once we get to that point, remember Martin Green, Shi Zhengrong, and Hans-Josef Fell — because nothing about it was inevitable.

5

Who among you dares to dream of a wildly better future?

We live in pessimistic times. The right longs for a return to a glorious past that never existed, while the left seldom looks beyond injustice today.[64] And of course there's a lot to reckon with in a swiftly warming world. You could fill a library with works on all the downsides of technology — on the profits gobbled up by reckless billionaires, on the frightening potential for digital surveillance, and on the unfathomable risks associated with nuclear weapons, artificial intelligence, and lab-grown viruses.

The last thing we need is blind optimism about technology. History is rife with innovations that failed to bring shared prosperity. Once sixteenth-century shipping technology improved by leaps and bounds, it was used to transport millions of enslaved people across the Atlantic. As nineteenth-century England filled up with factories, many laborers had to work longer and harder.

It took nearly a century before the incomes of regular workers started to go up.[65] And that had everything to do with the rise of political parties and unions, which pushed the industrial elite to share the wealth generated by all that new technology. Nothing says that tech progress will automatically benefit everyone. That depends on the choices we make as a society, and those choices have moral aspects we can't sidestep.

What this world needs is more innovative pioneers. People who start with the world's biggest problems and work on the most promising solutions — tapping into the full power of their imaginations as they go. We need inventors like Josephine Cochrane, politicians like Hans-Josef Fell, entrepreneurs like Shi Zhengrong, philanthropists like Katharine McCormick, and lobbyists like Viktor Zhdanov.

Technology isn't a force of nature; it's the work of people.

8

Save a life. Now only $4,999!

No one would remember the Good Samaritan if he'd only had
good intentions. He had money as well.
Margaret Thatcher, *UK Prime Minister (1925–2013)*

I

Whether as an activist, advocate, or innovator, inspired idealists can change the world. But the big question remains: what do you take on? What do you prioritize?

When choosing a direction, we often rely on our own intuition and experience, or that of the people around us. As a result, most of us are concerned about more or less the same things. Your average journalist is obsessed with what other news outlets are reporting. Your average entrepreneur is preoccupied with what the competition is up to. Your average academic is fixated on what peers think. (A common measure of scholarly success is tallying how often your peer-reviewed articles are cited by your peers.)[1]

In this world of conformity, it's an act of resistance to shift your focus. A scientist who poses a question others never think to ask can make the greatest discoveries. A journalist who covers what's *not* in the news can make all the difference. An entrepreneur who operates in a new market without competitors can fill that niche.

Changing the world often starts in the quiet places, where others don't think to go. To show you what I mean, let's take another look at Rob Mather, who founded the Against Malaria Foundation. This was his learning curve:

1 Rob's career switch started with empathy for someone on television who had been through something awful.
2 Rob was well aware of his talents and privilege and decided to put them toward this good cause.

3 But Rob's impact only went through the roof once he focused his efforts on malaria. He didn't choose the disease because he'd had it himself or because someone he knew had died of it. Rob simply wanted to help as many people as possible. So he did his homework and discovered that fighting malaria was his best choice.

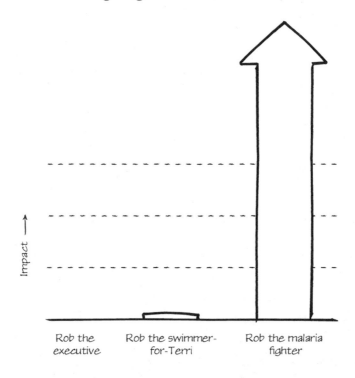

Impact →

Rob the
executive

Rob the swimmer-
for-Terri

Rob the malaria
fighter

I can't emphasize enough how important this third point is. During all phases of his career, Rob was equally talented, but only once he took a step back and carefully considered his options did he make the biggest difference. By far. So don't start out by asking, "What's my passion?" Ask instead, "How can I contribute most?" And then choose the role that suits you best.

Don't forget: your talents are but a means to an end, your ambition raw energy. What matters is what you do with them.

That's also true for something else. So far, I've talked mainly about wasting talent and ambition. But there's another aspect of privilege that we waste on a grand scale: money. In this chapter, I go back in time a little and tell you about a young cult that was overcome with that realization. It's a movement that took chasing impact to the extreme. A movement that's always on the lookout for the best financial investments with the highest returns for as many people and animals as possible.

Their story is about how much you can achieve with relentless prioritizing. But it's also a tale of how moral ambition can go completely off the rails.

2

We begin in 1969, when one Peter Singer went to study philosophy at the University of Oxford.

At the time, philosophy was quite an esoteric affair. As millions of people took to the streets to protest inequality, pollution, and the war in Vietnam, your average philosopher sat in a comfy armchair, pipe in hand, pondering the precise meaning of ordinary language. Philosophers filled bookcases with their thoughts on sentences like "It's raining," "The cat sat on the mat," and that classic, "The present king of France is bald."[2]

Most philosophers felt they had to remain morally neutral, which came with the pleasing side effect that they could remain comfortably seated.[3] But the students at Oxford? They'd had enough of stodgy professors. There were demonstrations against something or other every week. A few years earlier,

Malcolm X had paid a visit to the university. He'd made clear to students that they lived in "a time of extremism, a time of revolution."[4]

Peter Singer, too, thought that philosophy should go back to addressing real issues. He decided to devote his thesis to civil disobedience, using the protests in Northern Ireland and against the war in Vietnam as examples. And shortly after graduating, in November 1971, he penned his masterpiece. It was an article no more than fifteen pages long, published the following year in an obscure journal. The title was "Famine, Affluence, and Morality," and in it, Singer introduced a thought experiment that would become known the world over.

Picture seeing a toddler, he wrote, struggling to stay afloat in a shallow pond. You look around and realize no one else has noticed. The child can barely keep their head above water and you sense there's no time to lose. There's only one problem: you're wearing brand-new shoes and there's no time to take them off. They're gorgeous, your new favorites, and not exactly cheap. What do you do?

Nearly everyone says: are you kidding me? You jump! You'd have to be a monster to hesitate and let that child drown, all for your love of a pair of shoes. But what if, the philosopher then writes, *millions* of toddlers die every year from malaria, measles, or diarrhea — conditions we can easily treat or prevent? What if you can give a relief organization a relatively small donation — say, the price of your favorite pair of shoes — and save a child's life, even if no one's threatening to drown in your local pond? Isn't it then your duty to donate? And for that matter, isn't it your duty to keep on giving until you can't give any more?

Peter Singer was only twenty-five at the time. Now, half a century later, he's one of the most influential philosophers in the world, and the essay is still a compelling read. His later work is also interesting, but perhaps Einstein was on to something when he said geniuses do their best work before the age of thirty, when people still dare to do what later they're too wise to try.

As Singer worked on his article, a disaster was unfolding in East Pakistan, now Bangladesh. "People are dying," Singer began his piece, "from lack of food, shelter, and medical care. The suffering and death that are occurring there now are not inevitable, not unavoidable."

A famine, a civil war, and a cyclone had upended the lives of 9 million people, yet those in wealthy countries did little to help. How could you possibly justify that? Singer's answer was clear: you couldn't. "The whole way we look at moral issues," he wrote, "needs to be altered, and with it, the way of life that has come to be taken for granted in our society."[5]

When would you say you're a good person? Most people would say if you don't lie or steal, if you do your job and pay your taxes, if you're a good neighbor, a loyal friend, and a good brother, sister, parent, or spouse, if you put something in the collection plate, are more generous at Christmastime, and go on then, if you also do some volunteer work. Then you're doing all right in the good person department.

But what if we should be aiming higher — far higher? Singer felt that most people go too easy on themselves. Because when millions are suffering from hunger and disease, you can never really do enough. You'd have to keep giving until you're nearly as poor as a refugee from Bangladesh.

Does that sound like too much? Okay, well, Singer left the option open of not having to go quite that far. But even if we backtrack a little and decide we should continue to give as long as we're not causing ourselves any serious pain, then the practical implications of his reasoning are still huge. Our lives, after all, are one long succession of luxury goods. Well-off people in well-off lands buy heaps of clothing, food, toys, furnishings, jewelry, cosmetics, and electronic goods that bring little joy and mostly end up on the trash heap.

We're largely blind to our own extravagance. It's a lot easier to point out the unchecked consumerism of others. That person on benefits who's got the latest iPhone, six cats, and a Netflix subscription. Or perhaps a billionaire like Steven Spielberg and his 86-meter-long yacht worth $200 million, with pool, jacuzzi, screening room, dancefloor, gym, spa, helipad, and monthly maintenance costs of one cool million. (Or wait, I read that Spielberg now has a new yacht — word is he thought the old one wasn't big enough.)[6]

But if you live in a wealthy country and look in the mirror, you'll likely concede that your own life is also a series of things wasted. Most wealthy individuals don't consider themselves rich, but just to give you an idea: a single person with a median income in my country of the Netherlands turns out to be among the richest 3 percent of the world population.[7] And yes, that figure has been adjusted for the fact that prices in poorer countries are considerably lower. Half the world's people live on less than $7 a day, and more than 600 million live on at most $2.15 a day.

Now perhaps you're wondering: surely you can't live on so little? And you're right. People living in extreme poverty often die of malnutrition. They consume an average of 1,400 calories a day — that's half of what's recommended if you're physically active. They regularly skip meals, are frequently anemic and underweight, and they die twenty to thirty years earlier than people in wealthier countries.

So if you sometimes throw food out, order coffee to go, or buy clothes you seldom wear, then relatively speaking, you're stinking rich. And if you don't feel like you're among the richest people on the planet, think of the words of the old Russian writer Fyodor Dostoevsky: "Man grows used to everything, the scoundrel."[8]

Global Income Distribution

Net income per day in US dollars
(adjusted for cost-of-living differences)

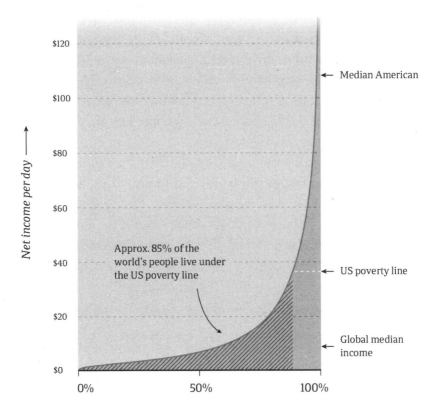

Source: Our World in Data

The global distribution of income has the form of a hockey stick and follows the form of a power law with one towering peak (a concept and shape you might remember from Chapter 2). More than half the world's income is deposited every month in the bank accounts of only 10 percent of the world's people.[9] And then to think that many people in wealthy countries dream of an even higher income. It doesn't seem to get through to us that we're already among the top earners.

Meanwhile, we've developed all kinds of excuses for not sharing the wealth. We convince ourselves that donating doesn't work, when you need only google "donate effectively" to come across GiveWell, which can point you to the Against Malaria Foundation and other outstanding charities. We mutter something about "overpopulation" when even a little background reading shows that fighting poverty is the best remedy against an overpopulated world (because when child mortality drops, so do birth rates).[10]

"But other people aren't doing much either," we sputter, when of course no one would say that if a kid fell into the neighborhood pond. Wait — now we don't have to lift a finger if others are just standing there watching? What about if ten children are drowning and nine bystanders do nothing but gaze at their own lovely shoes. Would you then only have to save one child — just your fair share — while letting the others go under?

There's really only one convincing objection to the philosophy of Peter Singer. It asks too much of us. People aren't capable of being constantly preoccupied with all the misery in the world. Yes, we manage to be concerned about a toddler drowning in the pond out back, or about a girl who suffered terrible burns and was the subject of a gripping documentary. But the 47 million children who according to the WHO at this very moment suffer from acute malnutrition?[11] We simply can't be personally moved by that scale of suffering. We humans are, well, human. We're not saints.

Psychologists suspect that our blinders are a form of self-preservation. Our empathy doesn't grow as we see more victims; it doesn't even plateau. Instead, empathy drops.[12] As Joseph Stalin reportedly said, "One death is a tragedy, a million a statistic."[13]

When it comes down to it, even the moral philosophers — the big experts who daily ponder the nature of good — fail to step up. A study of 200 professors of moral philosophy showed that your average ethics prof is roughly as righteous as your average historian or chemist.[14] The philosophers *believe* they should donate more money but don't actually do it.

"It's not that we try but fail, or that we have good excuses," notes one of the researchers, himself a philosopher.[15] No, most people are simply satisfied with their own mediocrity. They tend to go easy on themselves and aim for more or less the same moral status as their peers. Not worse, but certainly not better.

It's precisely that complacency that Peter Singer was fed up with.

3

A philosophy without practical implications is a dead philosophy, concluded the young Singer. "What is the point," he wrote, "of relating philosophy to public (and personal) affairs if we do not take our conclusions seriously?"[16]

Singer and his wife wanted to walk the walk. While still students, the Singers started giving away 10 percent of their income, a portion they've since increased to 40 percent. And still Singer thinks he could do more. "There's always a struggle," he says, "unless you're a complete saint and you've given away everything except what you need to live . . . Until you get to that point, I think you should be struggling."[17]

For years, the Singers were essentially alone in this struggle. Singer's sure to have influenced a few people, but his behavior wasn't terribly contagious. That changed in 2009, when the young philosopher Toby Ord also decided to take action. Like Singer forty years earlier, he'd had it with academic philosophy. "We mainly end up talking about things that are contentious rather than things that are important."[18] And Ord had done the math. As an academic, he could expect to earn about 1.5 million pounds (roughly 2 million dollars) over the course of his career. He figured he'd need about one-third of that to live a comfortable life, so he'd have 1 million pounds to donate.

But Toby Ord understood that he would make a still greater difference if he could persuade others to do the same. Someone recommended he meet an ambitious philosophy student by the name of William MacAskill.[19] MacAskill was also a big fan of Singer's and equally frustrated with all those philosophers who did nothing with their high-minded ideas. He'd just spent the summer raising money for charity.

The young men met at a cemetery — no joke — and ended up talking for hours and hours. They set up their first nonprofit soon after, based on a new idea they would dub *effective altruism*, or EA.

That first organization founded by Ord and MacAskill was Giving What We Can, which encouraged people to donate at least 10 percent of their incomes.[20] But that was just the beginning. Because once you decide you want to donate, the next question of course is: donate to what? There are millions of charities worldwide, and as we've seen, some are far more effective than others. If you want to do as much good as possible, the young philosophers realized, you have to prioritize relentlessly.

Say you want to help the blind. You could first save up $50,000, the cost of training one seeing-eye dog in the U.S. Or you could opt for Sightsavers, an organization that can take that money and treat 500 people with trachoma, a bacterial infection that's prevalent in poor countries and can lead to blindness.[21]

What to do, what to do? Of course it's good to donate to organizations like Guide Dogs for the Blind. Seeing-eye dogs are a fantastic support for the visually impaired, helping them fully take part in society. But if you can help 500 times as many people for the same amount of money, shouldn't you choose to do so?

Most people think that the best charities are at most one and a half times as effective as your average charity.[22] But when Toby Ord delved into a report from the World Bank — a study comparing around a hundred public health interventions — he found it's more like a factor of fifty.[23] That is, the best charities are fifty times (!) more effective than the median charity and a whopping 10,000 times more effective than the worst ones. Seems the economics of altruism is also subject to a *power law*, with at least 80 percent of results attained by just 20 percent of what we do.[24]

Every little bit helps, sure, but most little bits only help a little. And if you want to do some good, then why not do as much good as possible? Or if that sounds too calculating, try turning the question around: Would you prefer to focus on people who need your help less? And then help fewer of them and help them less?

The implications of all those power laws are enormous, Ord concluded in a piece with the thrilling title, "The moral imperative toward cost-effectiveness."[25] When you focus on the biggest problems and fund the best solutions, then you can achieve as much as fifty people who support "regular" interventions. In other words, you can save as many lives with an office job and a median salary as Arnold Douwes saved during World War II.

The best interventions are far more effective than the rest

Government and NGO interventions (grouped by topic), in order of cost-effectiveness

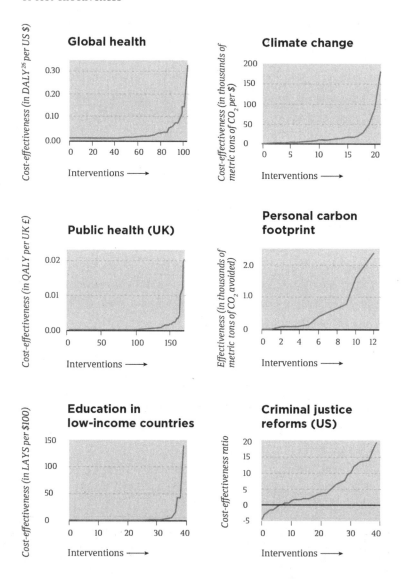

Source: Todd (2023)

Now think back to Rob Mather: by switching from helping Terri to fighting malaria, his own impact got an explosive boost. Researchers at GiveWell have since estimated the cost of saving one child's life by donating to the Against Malaria Foundation. The figure in cold hard cash? About $5,000.

People often get uncomfortable when the figures get this concrete, but then we live in an uncomfortable world. Yes, $5,000 is a lot of money. More than 90 percent of the world's people could never cough up that figure. With a standard starting salary at a major bank or law firm, on the other hand, you easily earn ten times that in your first year on the job. And college students spend that much on restaurants and takeout every year, without thinking twice.[27]

When it comes to saving people in our own countries, by the way, we already pay far more. When the U.S. builds levees, for instance, or reinforces buildings to protect people in hurricane-prone areas, the government is prepared to shell out up to $12.5 million in taxpayer money for each life spared.[28] For that figure, you could save the lives of 2,500 children elsewhere!

Doctors speak of *triage*, a French word meaning "sorting." When there's an emergency, you have to decide who you can help and who you can't. In a world where 14,000 children die every day from preventable causes, you could say we're in an ongoing emergency.[29]

Now, you can endlessly make these sorts of calculations and be plagued by guilt, thinking of all the children you let down because you decided your own comfort was more important. And it's true that one of the first effective altruists, when she was younger, even felt guilty going out for ice cream on occasion. When her father expressed worry that this lifestyle wasn't going to make her happy, she fired back in all seriousness: "My happiness is not the point."[30]

But Toby Ord and William MacAskill preferred to tell another tale to motivate others. They spoke of opportunities instead of obligations. Imagine for a moment that you save a kid from a burning building. Wouldn't that be one of the best days of your life? And if so, then isn't it fantastic that you — an ordinary person — can save as many lives as James Bond on one of his better days?

Some effective altruists indeed started to feel like superheroes. One of Singer's students first dreamed of becoming an engineer and building dams in Africa. Once the lessons sunk in, however, he set other priorities and ended up becoming a corporate banker in London. That way, he'd have more money and could donate more to effective charities. Or as he confided to a journalist, "I decided to be Superman."[31]

4

So much for my initial impressions of effective altruism.

To be honest, I'd already lost interest. Who wants to join a movement that insists on rubbing your nose in the fact that you can never do enough? That thought experiment of Peter Singer's — about all the drowning children — felt like a form of extortion. Sure, you've got to make sacrifices sometimes for a good cause. But if you've declared ice cream a sin, then I think you're missing something fundamental about the meaning of life.

Many effective altruists come across to me as somewhat robotic, with their obsessive pursuit of quantification and efficiency.[32] Of course the numbers are important, but you can overdo it. And what about all the things you can't measure?

Have you heard the one about the economist who dropped his wallet one night? He started looking for it once he reached the next streetlamp, because the light was better there. Effective altruists seemed to make a similar mistake. By fixating on what they could measure, they overlooked a world of possibilities.

Think back to Hans-Josef Fell, the German solar freak from the previous chapter. He wouldn't have been able to convince anyone in the nineties that solar panels were "cost-effective." But pumping billions into that technology turned out to be an excellent idea. The same was true for developing wind energy and electric cars. Or consider the fight against HIV/AIDS announced by President George W. Bush in 2003. More than a few economists warned the program would never be "cost-effective," and the money would be better spent elsewhere. We now know those efforts saved over 25 million lives, in part because they caused the price of HIV drugs to drop dramatically.[33]

What also bothered me about those effective altruists was that some went into finance so they could donate as much money as possible ("earning to give," they called it). This was right after the 2008 crash, when banks were being propped up using hundreds of billions in taxpayer dollars. At the height of the Occupy Wall Street protests in 2011, William MacAskill even managed to give a talk at Oxford titled "Want an ethical career? Become a banker."

Okay, I thought, so you guys want to steal from the poor to give to the poorest? And you think that after a few years on Wall Street you'll still want what's best for the world?

In 2012, MacAskill gave a presentation at the Massachusetts Institute of Technology (MIT). There he heard of Sam Bankman-Fried, a student who was said to be incredibly smart and a fellow Peter Singer fan. When they met for the first time over lunch,

Bankman-Fried expressed interest in working as an animal rights activist, but MacAskill had a better idea. Was the young man perhaps open to taking a high-paid job in the financial sector?[34] Then he could earn far more money and with it, do far more good.

It didn't take long before Bankman-Fried was the big hero of the EA movement. He set up a hedge fund and an online trading platform for cryptocurrency, became the youngest billionaire in the world, and promised to give away his fortune to the best charities. But the party didn't last. In 2022, Bankman-Fried was arrested at his penthouse in the Bahamas. His crypto exchange and hedge fund were bankrupt, billions had gone up in smoke, and the thirty-year-old entrepreneur was soon convicted of perpetrating one of the biggest financial frauds in U.S. history.

It was one big cliché: the guru turned out to be a con. He'd gambled away his followers' money in dubious investment schemes. Bankman-Fried was a symptom of a movement dripping with hubris, full of young idealists who thought themselves immune to moral corruption — people who took themselves for superheroes.

In the months following the bankruptcy, it became clear what kinds of harebrained schemes Bankman-Fried and his inner circle had cooked up for spending his billions. Paying Donald Trump not to run for president, for instance, or buying an entire country (the island nation of Nauru) to build a "bunker/shelter" and ensure "that most EAS survive" after a big disaster, so they could continue their good deeds.[35] Sounds like that relentless prioritizing had gone to their heads.

So yes, it's tempting to dismiss those effective altruists (a pretty pedantic term to start with) as charlatans. In their moral greed, they forgot that it's maybe not so nice to gamble away the savings of ordinary people on a crypto exchange. They worshipped their big hero, the billionaire Bankman-Fried, without asking too many questions about how he'd actually "earned" his money.

And there was another matter that bothered me. While busy doing all their endless prioritizing, many EAS seemed more than happy to accept our existing, extremely inequitable system.[36] To be sure, it's admirable to donate a considerable portion of your income to, say, the Against Malaria Foundation. At the same time, you have to keep asking yourself why you're so well-off, when other people are so poor they don't even have a few bucks for a mosquito net.

Let's see . . . Maybe it has something to do with our system of corrupt tax havens, unfair trade agreements, and neocolonial exploitation by western multinationals? The question then becomes: how do we get rid of that system?

Why don't EAS have a masterplan for that?

5

And yet the fierce moral ambition of the movement continued to fascinate me.

I went to a couple of EA conferences and, despite my reservations, I was amazed by it all. I'd never seen so many morally ambitious people in one place. Most donated a sizable portion of their income, and some had even donated a kidney to a complete stranger. Hard not to be impressed.

Next, I got introduced to GiveWell, Holden Karnofsky's nonprofit that made an appearance in Chapter 5. (I didn't let it slip in that chapter that GiveWell is an EA organization, but it was in fact one of the first.) GiveWell has encouraged over 125,000 donors to contribute more than $2 billion to effective charities, saving over 200,000 lives.[37] Hard not to be enthusiastic.

Meanwhile, I found that many effective altruists are quite open to criticism. On the GiveWell website there's a tab titled "Our mistakes," which seems to me good practice for any organization. Members of the movement now believe it was a mistake to send so many young people into the financial sector, and feel that in the early years, they were way too excited over a purely rational approach.[38]

And I have to concede that lots of EAS at the conferences did seem quite aware of how unequal and unfair a system they operated in. I met radical nerds who've lobbied to reform the criminal justice system. I spoke with EAS who were also Extinction Rebellion activists and were researching how the climate movement can be even more effective.[39] To top it all off, it was here I heard about Charity Entrepreneurship, the school from Chapter 6 that also came out of the EA movement.[40]

Finally, I found out that there's another billionaire active in effective altruism. Dustin Moskovitz was one of the cofounders of Facebook and became, at the urging of his EA friends, one of the biggest funders of vaccine research, animal activism, and anti-malaria measures in the world.[41] His Open Philanthropy foundation is continually on the lookout for sizable, solvable, and sorely overlooked problems, which they then put hundreds of millions toward each year.

When asked in 2013 how it felt to be one of the youngest billionaires, Moskovitz replied with a quote from the comedian Louis C.K.: "I never viewed money as being 'my money.' I always saw it as 'The money.' It's a resource. If it pools up around me then it needs to be flushed back out into the system."[42]

Admittedly, the role of this kind of generous billionaire remains an uneasy one. I'm sure it's a lot nicer to live on a planet where we can count on them paying lots more in taxes, and where governments do enough to fight poverty, child mortality, climate change, and whatever else we're facing. We must continue to fight for that world, but in the meantime, we also have to make do with what we've got.

Let me be clear: most rich-guy philanthropy doesn't amount to much. They generally donate a mere fraction of their net worth, and when they give, it's mostly for vanity projects, like paying huge sums to stick their name on the wall of an already well-funded university or museum. They'd love to be remembered, but with such cookie-cutter forms of giving, they're soon forgotten.

And yet there's always a small number of philanthropists who don't want to follow the herd and who choose to do something more meaningful with their fortunes. Take Katharine McCormick, who financed the pill when no one else dared cut a check. Or Bill Gates, who paid for developing a malaria vaccine when government and business weren't interested.

"In our past," Ralph Nader once said, "rich people donated essential money for the antislavery, women's right to vote, and civil rights movements."[43] American abolitionists were generously funded by Gerrit Smith, at the time the richest man in New York. Suffragists Susan B. Anthony and Elizabeth Cady Stanton found an ally in the entrepreneur George Francis Train, who bankrolled the production of their newspaper *The Revolution*. And at the start of the twentieth century, anti-lynching activists got a small fortune from Madam C. J. Walker, herself a child of enslaved people and, according to the *Guinness Book of Records*, the first female self-made millionaire in the U.S.

And then we have Charles Garland, son of a wealthy stockbroker. His story is too good to pass up. Picture a tall, handsome young man who, a century or so ago, attended prestigious Eton

College in England and then studied at Harvard. Everyone knew he stood to inherit big bucks. But then in November 1920, he made a shocking announcement: he refused to take the money. The 21-year-old felt he hadn't done a thing to earn the $1 million. And he didn't believe in a system that "starves thousands while hundreds are stuffed."[44]

Naturally, the press couldn't get enough of this eccentric fellow. Garland got bags full of mail about how he should spend his fortune, and big names of the time also weighed in. The influential Black activist A. Philip Randolph accused Garland of "criminal negligence," and writer Upton Sinclair called him crazy. "Do you realize," the latter wrote, "that never in the history of the radical movement has anybody had a million dollars or a tenth of that?"[45]

The young man held out for another year but was eventually persuaded to put his money into a trust. Garland had one condition: the funds had to be given away "as quickly as possible" to "unpopular" causes, such as the incarcerated and minority groups.[46]

Once he'd finally gotten rid of the money, the good man went to work as a farmer in Massachusetts. By his own account, he started an "experiment in social science"; by anyone else's, he started a commune for polygamists.[47] People came from far and wide to see this "love farm," until Garland was arrested for adultery.

Soon after Garland got out of jail, the sociologist W. E. B. Du Bois wrote in the NAACP's *The Crisis*, leading journal of the civil rights movement, that the Garland Fund could well prove "one of the main agencies for the emancipation of the American Negro."[48] And within a few years, the fund awarded the movement its largest grant yet. The NAACP could now hire its first full-time lawyer, kick-starting a legal struggle that in 1954 would turn into that historic case, *Brown v. Board of Education*.

That Supreme Court ruling was a watershed in the civil rights movement. There were many more fights to come, but racial segregation was now officially prohibited in public schools throughout the country. "Without the funding from the Garland Fund," writes one historian, "this landmark decision in constitutional law would never have occurred."[49] Charles Garland's inheritance made a historic difference.

The truth is that money and moral ambition need each other. Philanthropy doesn't have to get stuck in vanity and paternalism. It can lead to real systemic change, as long as you prioritize wisely and keep an eye out for damaging side effects. What's more, private individuals are in a unique position to support unpopular causes — when government and business steer clear.

And that brings us to the subject of the next chapter: what unpopular causes should we be fighting for today?

9

Expand your moral circle

Remember sitting in history, thinking: if I was alive then,
I would've . . . You're alive now. Whatever you're doing is what
you would've done.
David Slack, *television writer and producer (b. 1972)*

I

One of the most bizarre historical tales I ever read is from the memoirs of the English sea captain William Snelgrave. In 1734 he published an account of his life as a slave trader. He wrote about the time he was invited to a feast by the ruler of Ardra, a kingdom on the West African coast.[1]

Snelgrave didn't want to turn down the invitation because the king was a big supplier of slaves. But the captain thought the Africans "fierce, brutish cannibals," and as a precaution, took along ten sailors armed with muskets and pistols. The king was waiting for them, "sitting on a stool under some shady trees." As Snelgrave presented his gifts, he saw that he and his men were surrounded by at least fifty warriors with barbed lances and bows.

Fortunately, the mood under the trees soon turned friendly. The king was delighted with his gifts and the feast could begin, when suddenly, out of the corner of his eye, the captain spotted a little boy. He was very young — couldn't be more than eighteen months old. The child's leg was tied to a stake, with two African priests standing by.

Why, asked the captain, is that child tied up like that? The king answered that the little boy "was to be sacrificed that night to his god, Egbo." Snelgrave was furious. He ordered his sailors to free the boy at once, whereupon the king's warriors drew their weapons, and the Europeans and Africans stood pitted against one another.

The king shouted that Snelgrave couldn't "seize the child, it being his property." Snelgrave fired back that his faith "expressly forbids so horrid a thing, as putting a poor, innocent child to death." Had people in Ardra never heard of the Golden Rule, that "grand law of human nature?" Did his majesty not know that you were to do unto others as you would have others do unto you?

In the end, the conflict was resolved easily enough. Captain Snelgrave purchased the boy for a few blue beads and the festivities picked up again, with everyone in high spirits. The sailors and warriors drank together, finishing off liters of palm wine. On their way back to the ship, Snelgrave asked one of his men if he could find "a motherly woman" to care for the child. Certainly, said the sailor. Just yesterday, they'd bought a woman with "much milk in her breasts."

As soon as they again set foot on their slaving vessel, a Black woman made straight for the little boy "with great eagerness, and snatched him out of the white man's arms that held him." It was the woman the sailor already had in mind. Turns out she was the child's mother.

"I think," wrote Captain Snelgrave in his memoirs, "there never was a more moving sight than on this occasion, between the mother and her little son."

Not much later, the captain sailed to the Caribbean, where he sold mother and son, along with 300 other captives.

It's hard to wrap your head around today, but in the early eighteenth century, slavery was completely commonplace. Most people thought it made sense that some people bought and sold others, like you'd breed and trade chickens or pigs. Before 1800 in fact, some three-quarters of the world's people were serfs or enslaved.[2]

Forced labor and slavery were common practice in Africa, India, China, and the Arab world. It was widespread among the peoples of North America, from the Cherokee to the Chickasaw, and was the norm in czarist Russia. The ancient Greeks and

Romans also considered it perfectly acceptable to hold slaves, as did the Maya, Aztecs, and Incas.

And starting in 1492, the year Columbus set foot on land in the Bahamas, the Europeans began building one of the biggest slaving empires in history. Over a period of 350 years, they would end up enslaving some 12 million Africans. While genteel philosophers penned lengthy treatises on "the rights of man," merchants like William Snelgrave bought great numbers of people on the African coast and shipped them to the New World.

This was the world eighteenth-century abolitionists like Thomas Clarkson woke up to every day. A world where papers ran ads for enslaved people. A world where smiths marketed padlocks "for blacks or dogs" or instruments like the *speculum oris*, used to pry open the mouth of a lockjaw patient — or a slave who refused to eat. A world where it wasn't uncommon for an enslaved man to be renamed in ridicule after a Roman emperor, a French king, or the British prime minister.³

How would people have reacted 300 years ago if you stood on a street corner in London or Amsterdam, Philadelphia or Paris, and called for slavery to end? You would likely have been laughed at or called crazy. A popular author of the time, James Boswell, believed that abolishing slavery would be an "extreme cruelty to the African savages" because they were now "save[d] from massacre or intolerable bondage in their own country."⁴ A slaveholder wrote that "nine out of ten rejoice at falling into our hands," and another said the voyage from Africa to the West Indies was "one of the happiest periods of a Negro's life."⁵

History is teeming with celebrated philosophers, free thinkers, and intellectuals who thought it was fine that people were enslaved. Aristotle had written centuries before that some people are slaves by nature. Church father St. Augustine contended that slavery was tragic but unavoidable. And philosopher Immanuel Kant wrote that Black people were "created" for the brutal conditions on Caribbean sugar plantations.[6]

Or what about the American founding fathers, proponents of all kinds of revolutionary ideas but unwilling to change anything about slavery. George Washington had nine rotten teeth replaced with nine teeth pulled from the mouths of slaves.[7] Thomas Jefferson asserted that "all men are created equal" and owned 600 slaves, four of them his own children.[8]

It's true that some did express doubts about slavery. Kant later became an outspoken critic of the colonial project; Jefferson's conscience continued to trouble him. But what jumps out today is the hypocrisy of these so-called free thinkers. The British philosopher John Locke thought slavery "so vile and miserable" and so "directly opposite to the generous temper and courage of our nation" that he found it inconceivable that "an Englishman, much less a gentleman, would plead for it."[9] And yet Mr. Locke himself invested a small fortune in the Royal African Company's slave trade.[10]

Equally hypocritical was his French counterpart Voltaire. On paper, Voltaire was against slavery, but he couldn't mask his enthusiasm when in 1768 a slaving vessel was named after him. And he wasn't the only Frenchman who felt that way. In 1789 the French Revolution broke out under the motto "liberté, égalité, fraternité" (liberty, equality, fraternity). French merchants promptly renamed their slave ships *Liberté*, *Égalité*, and *Fraternité*.[11]

Throughout history, people seen as enlightened or progressive often upheld practices we now consider absolutely abhorrent. Makes you wonder: What practices of ours will future generations think barbaric?

When are you on the right side of history?

2

It's a key question if you want to go the moral ambition route. Anything we're doing now that we'll later see as horrific should top our list of priorities. What if Thomas Clarkson were alive today? What would he be fighting?

It's tempting to believe that we, modern people, have reached some plateau of good behavior. That we no longer need the likes of Clarkson. After all, we don't sacrifice small children or sell the enslaved. We don't burn witches at the stake, and it's been some time since we've taken a criminal and drawn and quartered him. Women have the right to vote, gay marriage has been legalized in over thirty countries, and in my own country of the Netherlands, I'm proud to say, there's even an animal ambulance on call day and night. Who could possibly be more civilized than us?

The remarkable thing here is that nearly every civilization, in nearly every period of world history, had the same high opinion of themselves. Take the ancient Romans. They thought themselves highly evolved because they — in contrast to barbarian tribes — didn't sacrifice children to the gods. But killing unwanted infants? That was fine. Feeding naked women to hungry lions in the Colosseum? Also not a problem. That was simply good fun during halftime.[12]

The past is full of practices we now think vile. The torture and strangulation of "sodomites," or homosexuals, was once a regular occurrence. Less than a century ago, white Southerners picnicked at the lynching of a Black man. "Whole families came together, mothers and fathers, bringing even their youngest children," wrote the Raleigh *News & Observer* in 1930 about a lynching in North Carolina.[13]

If so many people were blind to those misdeeds of the past, how will historians of the future look back on us? Could it be that we too — like Captain Snelgrave, like the King of Ardra — are blind to our own wrongdoing? I mean, it would be quite the coincidence if we're the first civilization ever that's got it all figured out. Isn't it far more likely that in some ways we're still doing things wrong?

Every year, law professor Robert P. George asks his students at Princeton University what they would have thought of slavery if they'd been white and living in the American South 200 years ago. "Guess what?" he posted online. "They all would have been abolitionists! They all would have bravely spoken out against slavery and worked tirelessly against it."[14]

Nonsense, of course. In reality, only a tiny fraction of the white population was abolitionist, and they paid a high price for their ideals. George always says to his students he's happy to believe them, as long as they can show that they stand up for the rights of unpopular victims of injustice today — even when it damages their own reputation, sets back their career, or costs them friendships.

The big question is how we figure out what we're still doing today that will seem clearly wrong down the road. No one has a time machine, and there's no way we can look into the hearts of generations to come. But I do think there are at least six alarm bells to be aware of. Six warning signs to look out for as a morally ambitious trailblazer.

First, if a practice later turns out to be wrong, then we've heard the arguments against it before. It's not that a group of activists in the late eighteenth century suddenly, for the first time in history, thought "wait a minute, perhaps there's something wrong with slavery." That view had been voiced for centuries but had never grown into anything like a movement.[15] So when we hear the rumblings of protest, it's good to seriously look into the matter — despite how odd it sounds at first.

The second alarm bell goes off when people don't defend their practices, but instead say things like, "That's how it's always been," "That's human nature for you," or "We don't have a choice." Social psychologist Melanie Joy speaks of the three N's: we normalize wrongful acts by calling them *normal*, *natural*, and *necessary*.[16] Slave traders like William Snelgrave did precisely that. Slavery has been around since time immemorial, they'd say: some people were slaves "by nature," and if you abolished slavery, the entire economy would collapse.

The third warning sign is when people avoid unpleasant facts. When you find a cool t-shirt, you don't want to think about sweatshops in Bangladesh. When buying flowers for your sweetheart, you don't want to think about exploited migrants laboring in the fields. When you're trying to catch a plane, you don't want to think about sea-level rise, forest fires, or millions of climate refugees.

Psychologists note that there are two forms of not-knowing. You can genuinely have no idea what's going on, but you can also show *willful ignorance*.[17] In the case of the latter, you know enough to know you don't want to know more. Then it's awfully irritating when someone reminds you of the uncomfortable truth.

That brings us to the fourth alarm bell: the angry response that moral pioneers face. Time and again, they're hated, harangued, harassed. Take someone like Mary Wollstonecraft, seen by many historians as the "mother of feminism."[18] In 1792, she published a revolutionary plea for equal rights for men and women: *A Vindication of the Rights of Woman*. A prominent London philosopher soon penned a response called *A Vindication of the Rights of Brutes*, in which he sarcastically pondered whether dogs, cats, or horses also deserved equal rights.

Wollstonecraft's reputation was smeared in verse and lampooned, and she was portrayed as a "maniac" and a "hyena in petticoats."[19] It would take a century before her name was cleared and two before a statue was erected in her honor.[20] As an American journalist once wrote, "Every society honors its live conformists and its dead troublemakers."[21]

A fifth alarm bell goes off when it's hard to explain a particular practice to children, who can be remarkably adept at spotting our hypocrisy. We teach them to share, and then have no good answer for why we have more than enough, while children in poor countries go hungry. Only as we get older do we learn to live with such contradictions.

A century ago, parents in the American South had to explain to their children why racial segregation existed and why white children and Black children couldn't always do things together. In the memoirs of union leader Harry Mitchell, we read about his Tennessee childhood and about the time he asked his mother if he and his friend Johnny could have a sleepover. "Neither of us could understand," Mitchell wrote about his Black friend not being allowed to spend the night. Harry's mom told her son they didn't have room for a guest, but Harry wasn't having it. "I got lots of room in my bed," he said.[22]

And finally, it's worth asking yourself the question: What will future generations see as our gravest offense? What practice of ours will most appall them?

When you study the past few centuries, you see a remarkable pattern of moral progress emerge. Some 250 years ago, in the time of the American Revolution (and the French), people fought for the rights of citizens (albeit male citizens), and the first abolitionists stood up. Next came the women's movement and the fight against child labor, while the unions also grew. Once the right to vote was secured, a second wave of feminism followed, followed by a fight for the emancipation of gay men and women. Each step seemed a logical extension of the previous one.

In 1981, philosopher Peter Singer (of Chapter 8 fame) published a book titled *The Expanding Circle*. Humankind, he wrote, long had a tight moral circle. But in time, we see the Golden Rule — to treat others the way you'd want to be treated — applied more and more broadly. And once you start expanding your moral circle, the question soon becomes: *Why not go further?* Is it a coincidence that many early feminists were also abolitionists? And that the first gay rights advocates were also active in the women's movement?

Take the big moral milestones of the last few hundred years, and connect the dots. Then you might be able to tell what future generations will judge us for. And if you think you already know the answer? That's the sixth alarm bell.

Six signs a common practice might be wrong

1. ✓ We've long heard what's wrong with it.

2. ✓ We say, 'That's just the way it is.'

3. ✓ We avoid uncomfortable facts about the practice.

4. ✓ We ridicule its opponents.

5. ✓ We find it hard to justify it to our children.

6. ✓ We suspect future generations will see it as barbaric.

3

So with these warning signs in mind, let's take a closer look at our own times. What contemporary practices might be wrong? What do we need to resist or fight or abolish if we want to follow in the footsteps of trailblazers like Mary Wollstonecraft and Thomas Clarkson?

It's not hard to come up with ideas:

- Is it justifiable to spend billions on luxury items, when 47 million children are suffering from acute malnutrition?[23]
- Is it defensible that we're doing so little to mitigate existential threats like pandemics and climate change, thus jeopardizing the future of humankind?
- Is it possible that someday we may look upon punishing criminals very differently, and consider retribution barbaric?[24]
- Is it okay to read storybooks to your children about farm animals frolicking free, when the average Westerner eats half their own weight each year in animals raised on factory farms?[25]

That last one — the way we treat animals — is perhaps the best example of a practice where all the alarm bells are going off. Let's go through the list.

The first warning sign is that the arguments against exploiting animals have been heard for centuries. Throughout history, we find many vegetarians, from Pythagoras to Tolstoy, from Mary Shelley to Leonardo da Vinci. And resistance to modern factory farming has also been around for years. The animal rights movement got its start in the 1970s, when factory farms and battery-cages for laying hens became prevalent.

And the sheer scale of animal exploitation has grown ever since. Today, over 200 million land animals worldwide are slaughtered every day. That's 80 billion animals a year. To give you an idea, the number of people who have ever lived is estimated at 117 billion.[26]

Of course, there are farmers who keep animals in a traditional manner, with pigs in the mud and calves in the pasture. But unfortunately, they're the exception. The modern farm is an animal factory, designed to produce enormous quantities of cheap meat. Billions of cows, pigs, and chickens are bred to grow as fast as possible. They're confined to small stalls and continually fed antibiotics to keep them alive just long enough.

And yet industrial-scale livestock production is invariably defended with — second alarm bell — the three N's. It's seen as "normal" because most people eat meat, "natural" because people are said to have always been omnivores, and "necessary" because we're thought to need the protein we get from meat.

The third alarm bell is already loud and clear, because there are some things about modern animal farms we'd rather not know. More than that, most consumers are not aware of even the most basic facts about how their meat and dairy is produced. In a recent study, test subjects were shown a photograph of a typical industrial-scale chicken coop and then asked, "Would you be happy to buy chicken from here?" Over 75 percent said no.[27] A UK study showed that the vast majority of the population was unaware that all male chicks (who therefore can't lay eggs) are gassed or macerated.[28] A Dutch study showed that only 18 percent of people asked knew that calves are taken away from their mothers shortly after birth. Nearly half of the respondents (44 percent) didn't know that a cow only gives milk after bearing a calf — and that cows have to continue to bear calves every year or so to keep producing milk.[29]

Our tendency to stick our heads in the sand in the face of such facts may also explain some unexpected results in other studies. A 2018 study, for instance, showed that nearly half the people in the U.S. want to ban slaughterhouses. Other scientists couldn't believe that result and replicated the study, adding a follow-up question: "Were you aware that slaughterhouses are where livestock are killed and processed into meat, such that, without them, you would not be able to consume meat?" Three-quarters of respondents stood by their answer.[30]

In my country of the Netherlands, you can see the same ambivalence. A recent survey showed that more than 60 percent of the people support a ban on factory farming, while 95 percent eat meat.[31] "I only buy meat from the butcher," we might then say, but most people don't seem to realize — or don't want to realize — that nearly all their meat, even meat sold by upscale butchers and grocers here, comes from factory farms.

Perhaps that's why animal activists are met with such aggression — the fourth alarm bell. Beloved celebrity chef Anthony Bourdain once wrote that "vegetarians are the enemy of everything good and decent in the human spirit" and called vegans a "Hezbollah-like splinter faction."[32] A Canadian study from 2015 indicated that only drug addicts call up more negative associations than vegans.[33]

Remarkably enough, many children believe their diet is vegetarian. They often don't realize the meat on their plate comes from a slaughtered animal. A recent study showed that many four- to seven-year-olds think hotdogs and bacon are made from plants. Four out of five "older children" (in this study, that's ages six and seven) indicated it's not okay to eat cows or pigs.[34] Children also grant animals a higher moral status than do adults.[35]

You could think, *Yes, well, those kids still have a lot to learn.* But why do parents find it tough — alarm bell five — to honestly tell children how we get meat? Studies indicate that many adults will give vague answers if pressed by children to explain where meat comes from.[36] And once it sinks in that that slice of ham on their plate is cut from a slaughtered pig — not unlike that cheery Peppa Pig on their tablet — then children are often shocked.[37]

And finally, it pays to zoom out, so you can spot that sixth warning sign. After the civil rights movement, the movements for women's rights, gay rights, and children's rights, standing up for animal rights seems a logical next step. It's with good reason that many of the first people to oppose slavery were also against the exploitation of animals.

The revolution in our thinking on rights

Books in English containing these terms,
as a percentage of the 2000 levels

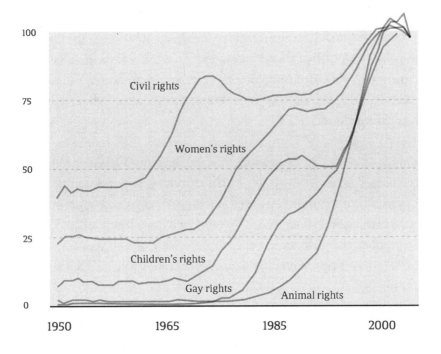

Source: Bookworm, *Steven Pinker (2011)*

Take the abolitionists from Chapter 3. The Quaker Benjamin Lay was essentially vegan, two centuries before we even had a word for it.[38] When fellow Quaker Anthony Benezet was asked whether he would like a piece of chicken, he said, "What? Would you have me eat my neighbors?"[39] Abolitionist William Wilberforce in his turn helped found the world's first animal rights organization, and abolitionist (and early feminist) Elizabeth Heyrick (1769–1831) once saved a bull from a bullfight by hiding the animal and waiting for the angry mob to pass them by.[40]

By the end of the eighteenth century, there was already a philosopher — the Brit Jeremy Bentham (1748–1832) — who dared to reason through the implications of the rights of people and animals. While the abolitionists were fighting against slavery, he was one of the first to speak out in favor of equal rights for men and women.[41] He also wrote that homosexuality should be removed from the penal code, though he didn't dare publish those passages.[42] And in a famous footnote dating to 1780, Bentham wrote "the day may come" when we include animals in our moral circle. Because what justifies excluding them?

> Is it the faculty of reason, or perhaps, the faculty of discourse? But a full-grown horse or dog is beyond comparison a more rational, as well as a more conversable animal, than an infant of a day, or a week, or even a month, old. But suppose the case were otherwise, what would it avail? The question is not, *Can they reason?* nor, *Can they talk?* but *Can they suffer?*[43]

This question posed by Bentham — where do we draw the line? — is key to the fight for animal rights. How big will we make our moral circle? I don't know anyone who takes this question more seriously than Andrés Jiménez Zorrilla. He's a former investment banker who worked for Morgan Stanley for years, managing a 2-billion-dollar real estate portfolio. Then he quit his job and enrolled at that charity-starting school in London (see Chapter 6). Jiménez had no idea what kind of charity he wanted to set up — until he heard about the suffering of . . . shrimp.

What's the next step in expanding your moral circle?

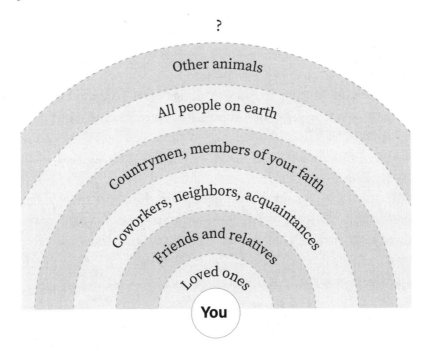

These days, Jiménez sports a shrimp tattoo and is CEO of the Shrimp Welfare Project. Does that come across as a little bizarre? You bet. But in the past few years, the scientific evidence has been piling up: even tiny shrimp can experience great suffering. Apparently shrimp react to harmful stimuli and respond to painkillers, indicating they suffer in ways we once thought only larger animals could.[44] If you then let the numbers sink in — 300 to 400 billion shrimp are farmed and killed each year — you could come to the conclusion that this may well be a wrong perpetrated on a massive scale.[45]

That is to say, maybe an odd guy like Andrés Jiménez Zorrilla will go down in history as a true zero, a modern-day Benjamin Lay (one of the first Quakers to take a stand against slavery; see Chapter 3). As we've seen, today's weirdos can be tomorrow's heroes.

4

But don't celebrate just yet.

Once you see that our moral circles have expanded through history, you could get the impression there's some natural law at work. And while idealists like to state that the arc of history "bends toward justice," I'm afraid that's a sixth illusion of the Noble Loser.[46]

History doesn't do things; people do things. If there's fairness in this world, it has to come from us. And if we fail to act, there's no justice. That's precisely why people risked their lives to help Jews during World War II. Because if they didn't step up, who would? And if not then, when?[47]

Yes, Captain Snelgrave's story is deeply troubling. It's hard to understand how he could appeal to the Golden Rule (even calling it "the grand law of human nature") while working as an actual slave trader. If someone can be that blind to their own vice, don't you think odds are we're also blind, however morally ambitious we may be?

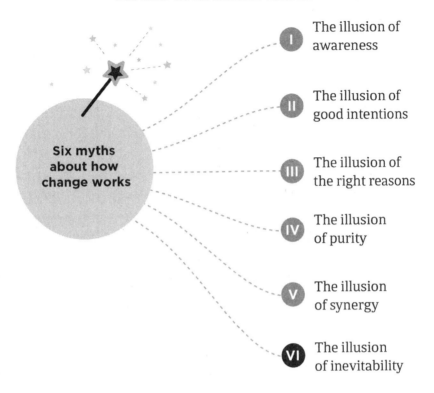

Six myths about how change works

I The illusion of awareness

II The illusion of good intentions

III The illusion of the right reasons

IV The illusion of purity

V The illusion of synergy

VI The illusion of inevitability

It's good to remember that courage is always relative. It's easy to speak out against slavery today, but in the eighteenth century, that could get you killed. And yes, moral pioneers do often take the lead in a number of ways, but they still have their own blind spots.

Take the abolitionist William Wilberforce, who fought against the slave trade with everything he had but thought the idea of women's rights nonsense. Or what about Elizabeth Cady Stanton, the feminist powerhouse who fought all her life for women's right to vote but felt less urgency about getting the vote for Black men and women? And MLK, one of the biggest civil rights leaders ever, once advised a young man with homosexual feelings to find a good therapist to rid himself of that "problem."[48]

Moral pioneers aren't saints. They're simply leading the way.

5

And then we finally get to the big challenge facing anyone who wants to strike out ahead. If you come to the conclusion that the people around you — friends, family, coworkers — are complicit in perpetuating a wrong, it's easy to get frustrated and lose yourself in bitterness and despair.

Think again about the fate of vegans. People who allow the truth to sink in about modern-day livestock practices will find it difficult to remain pragmatic. Those who expand their moral circle to include animals, stopping to consider the immense suffering they're subjected to, will find it tricky to work with the "perpetrators" of factory farming. But that's exactly what we need. "Sometimes we just want to scream loudly at injustice," wrote psychologist Herbert Simon, "but any serious revolutionist must often deprive himself of the pleasures of self-expression. He must judge his actions by their ultimate effects."[49]

That means it's not enough to keep shouting "Go vegan!" Animal activists have been doing that for over fifty years, while the number of vegetarians and vegans in the past few decades has only marginally gone up.[50] To spark a revolution, we must reframe the issue (see Chapter 4) to find fresh arguments against the meat industry and *for* a protein transition. For example: factory farms are not only horrendous for animals, they're also one of the top producers of greenhouse gasses.[51] Or: recent developments in cultivated meat present huge commercial opportunities. In addition to reframing, we'll need to build coalitions with avid meat eaters — and even meat producers — if we want to make serious strides.[52]

Someone who understands the importance of pragmatism and collaboration better than most anyone is activist Leah Garcés.

Her life is a picture of moral ambition, so let me wrap up this chapter with her story.

As a teenager in Florida, Leah Garcés was looking for a mission. She "craved struggle," she'd later write: "I felt flat without it."[53] One day she saw a documentary on animal abuse, and she knew: *This is my calling.*

Garcés got a degree in zoology and in the decades that followed, she traveled the world — advocating for bulls in Spain, dogs in Thailand, horses in Colombia, dolphins in Fiji, bears in South Korea, and whales in Norway. By thirty, she'd witnessed all kinds of animal abuses, but one stood out as the worst: industrial-scale livestock production, responsible for the untold suffering of billions of cows, pigs, and chickens.

In the spring of 2009, Garcés decided to return to the U.S. She was still bursting with ambition, but again, ambition is only raw energy. The question is what you do with it.

So what did Garcés do next?

She became friends with large-scale livestock holders.

Yep, you read that right. You see, Garcés had come to the critical realization that many U.S. farmers also can't stand the meat and dairy industry. She'd gotten to know a chicken farmer who had 25,000 birds in three giant, dark sheds in North Carolina. Craig Watts had gone in with Perdue, one of the biggest chicken companies in the country, back when he was just twenty-six. He'd taken out a huge loan to build chicken sheds on land his family had farmed for over a hundred years.

On paper, it seemed like a good idea. Watts was good with numbers, and he thought he knew what he was getting into. But the reality was grim. At regular intervals, he'd get a new shipment of day-old chicks to fatten up, and Perdue would pick them up again later and take them to slaughter. But Watts soon saw that something was wrong with the birds. The chickens grew so quickly their bones would break and organs burst. Turns out that's not unusual for industry broilers (chickens raised for meat). Scientists calculated in 2013 for the journal *Poultry Science* that if a newborn baby grew as quickly as a broiler, children would weigh over 650 pounds (300 kg) by the time they were two months old.[54]

Each morning, Watts removed dead chickens from the excrement-strewn floors of the big sheds amid penetrating ammonia fumes. Meanwhile, his finances took a hit — he was no match for the clever accountants at Perdue, who continually found new clauses in the fine print of Watts's contract. Watts realized he couldn't get out. Like many other farmers, he'd become a modern-day serf, compelled to keep working the land for someone else's profit. (Most U.S. chicken farmers today live under the poverty line and are deep in debt. They can't break free without selling their farmland, which has sometimes been in the family for generations.)[55]

Garcés had seen farmers like Watts as the enemy her entire life. But when she met Watts for the first time in the summer of 2014, she felt ashamed. Only now did she understand his side of the story. "I never had thought, 'He feels as trapped as the chickens.'"[56]

And so she decided to change tack. Just as Thomas Clarkson took on the plight of sailors on slaving vessels, Leah Garcés stood up for chicken farmers. Watts had never met an animal activist before — he half-jokingly called them ecoterrorists, but he got along well with Garcés.[57] At least she listened to his story. And like Garcés, Watts too was outraged when he saw a promotional video for Perdue showing happy, healthy chickens, clean barns, and a director proclaiming the birds were raised "humanely."

Watts let Garcés film inside his barns. Her camera rolled as he walked through the long, windowless buildings, past dead and crippled chickens and birds gasping for air. Then she sent the footage to the *New York Times*. For the next few weeks, both Watts and Garcés were super-nervous. He knew he could lose everything: his home, his land, his friends. She worked like a fiend to prepare for publication — and what was coming next.

The video went viral. Within twenty-four hours, they had a million views. "Torture one chicken and you risk arrest," wrote a journalist with the *New York Times*. "But scald hundreds of thousands of chickens alive each year? That's a business model."[58] Perdue was exposed, and everyone could now see for themselves what went on at their chicken farms. And no, this wasn't an isolated incident. This was the norm.

Garcés, meanwhile, had learned a crucial lesson. If she wanted to make a difference, she'd have to embrace her own discomfort. She'd soon get another chance to do so when she was contacted in February 2016 by none other than Jim Perdue — the villain of her video with Watts. It now seemed Mr. Perdue was prepared to remake his company and was asking Garcés for help.

"It was an unbelievable arc for me," she'd later write.[59] This was a company she'd exposed for being misleading, and that same company had now decided to improve conditions on their farms. Perdue even wanted to invest in developing plant-based alternatives to chicken.

These days, Garcés is helping dozens of chicken farmers find new ways to earn a living. Those dark barns are also suitable for growing mushrooms, for instance. No, Garcés doesn't think the animal rights movement should make peace with as many farmers as possible. She's also a fan of other activists with their hard-hitting campaigns — crucial for upping the pressure on companies.[60]

It's about the combination of tactics, she thinks. It's about building coalitions. It's about what works. She knows there's a long way to go before factory farming is outlawed. Garcés knows it could take a hundred years and she may not live to see it, like many abolitionists never saw the end of slavery. She realizes she's part of a much bigger story and that someday she'll pass the torch to a new generation of moral pioneers.

Make future historians proud

Your legacy is never one thing. Your legacy is every life you've touched, every person whose life was either moved or not. It's every person you've harmed or helped. That's your legacy.
Maya Angelou, *author (1928–2014)*

I

And then finally, there's something else we can put our moral ambition toward. It's perhaps the ultimate way to expand our moral circle.

Besides the struggle for the rights of everyone alive today, we can also take a stand for the world of tomorrow: for the future of humankind, and for all life on earth. To get a sense of how meaningful our actions might turn out to be one day years and years from now, it helps to pose a simple question. What's the most important thing that's happened in all of human history?

A few contenders come to mind. Was it maybe the invention of the wheel? Or gunpowder? Or the printing press? Or should we be thinking about the birth of religious figures, like Buddha, Jesus, Muhammad? Or perhaps instead, the rise and fall of one of the world's great civilizations, like the Egyptians, the Romans, the Vikings, or the Aztecs?

What was the most important thing to happen in human history?

A rather arbitrary selection of contenders

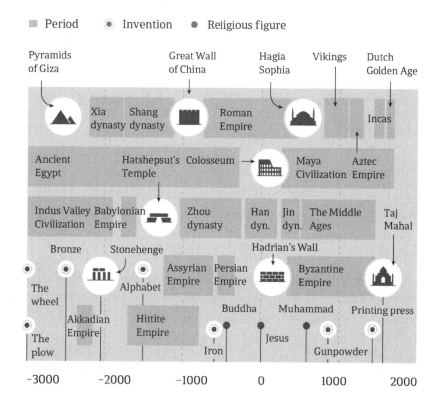

Naturally, there's something to be said for each of these milestones. Every one of them has great historical importance. But the most important one of all? Hard to say. You could even argue that the whole exercise is nonsense and that history, in the words of one British historian, is "just one damn thing after another."[1]

But suppose you go for a quantitative take on the past. What does history then look like? If you trace global population growth, for instance, can you find any pattern in the last 5,000 years?

Humankind takes off

━ Global population (in billions of people)

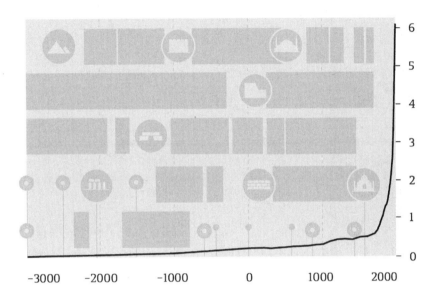

Source: Our World in Data

And voilà! Suddenly we have a clear contender for the most important thing ever. For thousands of years, the global population hardly changed at all. Then suddenly: an explosion. Around 1750, humankind took off. And to this day, we're in a rocket flying nearly straight up. So, what happened around 1750 that continues to have far-reaching consequences for us all? That's right, the start of the industrial revolution. Traditional tools and crafts made way for modern machines and factories.

Let's look at a few more graphs to see what's happened since.

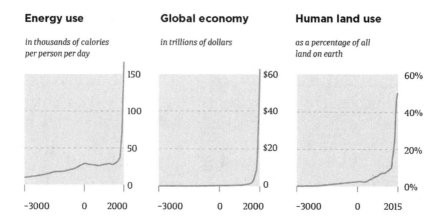

Energy use

*in thousands of calories
per person per day*

150

100

50

0

-3000   0   2000

Global economy

in trillions of dollars

$60

$40

$20

0

-3000   0   2000

Human land use

*as a percentage of all
land on earth*

60%

40%

20%

0%

-3000   0   2015

Sources: Muehlhauser (2018), Our World in Data

It's difficult to grasp how revolutionary the developments of the last few centuries have been. Historians speak of the "Great Acceleration" — in a short time, humankind has come to dominate the planet. We're suddenly wielding near-godlike powers. A single tractor today plows 450 times as fast as a yoke of oxen in 1800.[2] A single steel mill produces 170 times as much of the stuff as all of England did in 1720.[3] A single container ship transports three times the goods moved by the entire British fleet 400 years ago.[4]

And that could be just the beginning. Take another look at the graphs, at those lines that shoot up, and ask yourself: *Where will this explosion end? Where's this rocket taking us?* This century, maybe even within the next couple of decades, it should become clear whether we'll continue on this wild ride, stabilize our speed, or crash and burn. If you took the story of the human species and made it into a movie, we're at the point when the music builds, leading to the climax.

Until recently, most cultures and religions presumed we were living in the end times, that the journey of humankind was heading into the home stretch. But what if we're on the verge of something far bigger? What if the great acceleration is only the initial upturn on a graph shooting way up, way into the future? What if *we're* still the Ancients to all the people yet to come?

That would mean we bear tremendous responsibility for future generations. Because we find ourselves in the midst of massive change, we — the people who happen to live in the twenty-first century — have outsized power to shape the future. A small shift in direction today can mean a completely different destination years down the road. Our choices will be felt for ages.

I have to admit that, for a long time, I wasn't a big fan of this kind of analysis. I'm a historian by training, and historians speak disdainfully of *chronocentrism*, the naive idea that the times you happen to live in also happen to be especially important. But I'm now convinced that our times are indeed unique and critically important, perhaps determining everything to come. Of the 117 billion people who've ever lived, we're part of the 1 percent who can make a difference this century. We did nothing to deserve that role and we didn't choose to be here, but let's face it. We're at a historic crossroads. The future hinges on what we do next.

So what's it going to be?

Take a look at these three final graphs:

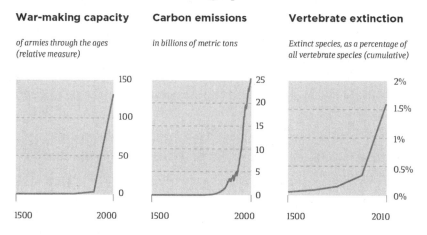

War-making capacity

of armies through the ages (relative measure)

Carbon emissions

in billions of metric tons

Vertebrate extinction

Extinct species, as a percentage of all vertebrate species (cumulative)

Sources: Ian Morris (2013), Our World in Data, Ceballos et al. (2015)

Over the last 300 years, we've not only made incredible progress, we've also left behind a trail of destruction. Every day, we pump over 100 million tons of carbon into the atmosphere.[5] We dump more than 2,500 tons of plastic into the oceans and clear more than 30,000 acres of forest, mostly in the tropics.[6] We're now using half of all habitable land for agriculture, and three-quarters of that goes to meat and dairy production.[7]

The sheer scale of our dominance over the animal kingdom is staggering. If you take all the wild mammals (from tigers to giraffes, from dolphins to whales) and somehow weigh them, and then do the same with all the mammals we keep as livestock (mostly cattle and pigs), what do you find? The livestock weighs over fifteen times as much as the wild bunch.[8] Or do the same thing with all wild birds versus all our poultry, and the poultry weighs more than twice as much. Some archeologists even predict that the bones of broiler chickens in the soil record will come to define our geological era, there are so many of them.[9]

What does all this mean for our quest for moral ambition? Well, we have to face up to the fact that our technological ingenuity has a dark side. In Chapter 7, we saw that technology can help us tackle some of the world's biggest problems, but now we have to address the flipside. Our power has become so great, so all-encompassing, that it's threatening our own existence — and that of all future generations.

Take the tempo alone with which the planet is warming up. Thanks to an army of activists, climate change is no longer an overlooked phenomenon, however hard the fossil fuel industry has tried to bury it. And yes, thanks to pioneers like Hans-Josef Fell (see Chapter 7), we have cheap and sustainable alternatives for generating energy.

But we're not there yet. The climate movement is one giant jobs fair, with work for millions of morally ambitious people. It's all hands on deck, because we have a mission to accomplish in the coming decades that knows no precedent. By 2050, greenhouse gas emissions worldwide must be brought down to zero. We have to get off the fossil fuels and kick the habit of eating animals — now, in a crazy short timespan — while at the same time devising and scaling up countless new green technologies.

Maybe you even want to take things a step further. Then it pays to ask yourself the question: *What was the best time to be a climate activist?* The best time was at least thirty years ago, when the movement was first taking off, and climate change an underreported issue. And then the follow-up question: What problems today are at the point global warming was back then?

What can you now tackle on time?

2

The uncomfortable truth is that we're facing a number of existential threats to humankind and life on earth. There are at least three looming dangers that get a lot less attention than climate change and urgently need people with moral ambition for that very reason.

The first threat's a familiar one. As I write this, over 3,000 nuclear weapons stand ready to be fired within minutes.[10] A hundred or so are all it takes to cause a nuclear winter, the apocalyptic scenario where there's so much dust in the atmosphere it blocks out the sun, the temperature on earth plummets, harvests fail, and billions of people starve to death.[11]

Experts estimate the odds of a nuclear weapon being used at 1 percent per year.[12] That may sound reassuring, but 1 percent a year is 63 percent in a century.[13]

More importantly, we've come close to nuclear conflict on a number of occasions. On October 27, 1962, for instance, "the most dangerous moment in human history,"[14] when the captain of a Russian submarine lost radio contact with Moscow, thought World War III had started, and wanted to fire a nuclear torpedo at the U.S. fleet above him. "We're gonna blast them now!"[15]

Russian protocol required a unanimous decision to fire, made with the two other officers on board. One agreed with the captain. The other voiced his veto. His name was Vasili Alexandrovich Arkhipov, and there should really be a statue of him in a public square in every capital city.

And there are other close calls in the history of the bomb. According to the U.S. Army, there have been thirty-two incidents since 1950 where nuclear weapons were accidentally dropped, damaged, or lost. Six U.S. atomic bombs are still unaccounted for, and the Russians have likely lost far more.[16]

Why did we ever start making these insane weapons? Why did America proceed with the Manhattan Project (the code name for developing the atom bomb) when it was already clear the Allies would win World War II?[17] In 1954, physicist J. Robert Oppenheimer, the "father of the atomic bomb," revealed one of the most important reasons: because we could. "When you see something that's technically sweet, you go ahead and do it and you argue about what to do about it only after you've had your technical success. That's the way it was with the atomic bomb."[18]

There's another technology being developed today whose power is feared by many experts: artificial intelligence, or AI. The computing pioneer, codebreaker, and war hero Alan Turing warned as early as 1950 about the dangers of a machine that surpasses our own capacity for thought.[19] Artificial intelligence can be used for propaganda, censorship, and surveillance, and can make it easier to build a weapon of mass destruction. Worst-case scenario? AI gets away from us and we lose control.

True, that's only speculation, and we may be far removed from such danger. Then again, maybe not. Development of the atomic bomb went much faster than expected, too. The groundbreaking atomic physicist Ernest Rutherford asserted on September 11, 1933, that it would be impossible to generate usable energy by splitting atoms. A former student of Albert Einstein's, the 35-year-old physicist Leó Szilárd, hit on the idea of a nuclear chain reaction the very next day.

What's the difference between the development of the atomic bomb and of artificial intelligence? Well, there's not one single Manhattan Project but a number of commercial labs racing to develop the most powerful AI possible. The Nobel-prizewinning computer scientist Geoffrey Hinton, considered one of the godfathers of AI, voiced his concerns as early as 2015 that the innovation would be used to terrorize people.

"Then why are you doing the research?" someone asked him.

"I could give you the usual arguments," he said. "But the truth is that the prospect of a discovery is too *sweet*."[20]

And then there's a third existential threat to humankind: pathogens that escape from a laboratory. The technological advances seen in biological labs can be weaponized, and that's deeply worrying. An atomic bomb is still pretty pricey, but the cost of a custom-made virus has been dropping for years now. The genetic sequence of smallpox can be downloaded for free, and while you still need the proper expertise and specialized equipment, it gets easier every year to manipulate the DNA of pathogens.[21]

In 2016, Canadian researchers synthesized horsepox, an extinct virus related to smallpox, with genetic material they'd ordered online. "Eradicating smallpox," wrote Kai Kupferschmidt in the journal *Science*, "took humanity decades and cost billions of dollars. Bringing the scourge back would probably take a small scientific team with little specialized knowledge half a year and cost about $100,000."[22]

And new pathogens can be far more dangerous. Picture a virus that's as virulent as Ebola and as contagious as the measles. "We cannot begin to imagine the devastation," two infectious disease specialists note, "possibly even a threat to civilization . . ."[23]

You'd expect research into dangerous pathogens to be strictly regulated. But you'd be wrong. More than 90 percent of all countries don't have policies in place addressing this kind of thing.[24] Not surprisingly, the history of biotechnology is filled with accidents. Between 1976 and 2016, there were seventy-one incidents where highly contagious and dangerous pathogens, like anthrax or Ebola, escaped.[25] And that's only the reported cases.

Meanwhile, bad actors can run off with ever-cheaper biotech. And no, that doesn't only happen in James Bond movies; it happens in the real world, too. In the 1990s, members of the Japanese doomsday cult Aum Shinrikyo were convinced the end was near. They thought non-believers were headed for hell but could be saved if they were killed by a true believer.

Aum Shinrikyo held tremendous appeal among students at Japan's top universities. The sect bought a patch of uranium-rich land in Australia and also tried to develop a biological weapon. One of its members had been a graduate student in virology at Kyoto University.[26] He led the sect to go in search of the Ebola virus in Africa.[27] Without success. But today they'd be able to order the necessary DNA sequence online.[28]

"No individual can make a nuke," notes a prominent biologist from MIT. "But a virus? That's very doable, unfortunately."[29]

Aum Shinrikyo built a $30 million facility in those days at the foot of Mt. Fuji. There, in a secret lab, they started producing sarin, a nerve gas first discovered in 1938 by the Nazis.[30] Their lab could handle huge volumes of the stuff — "not on a small terrorist scale, but in nearly battlefield quantities: thousands of kilograms a year."[31]

On a Monday morning in March 1995, during rush hour in Tokyo, five members of the sect toted plastic bags to the subway filled with liquid sarin. They boarded five trains and poked holes in the plastic with the tip of an umbrella, releasing the nerve agent. Hundreds of commuters were soon gasping for air at one station after another. Emergency personnel encountered horrific scenes, with passengers vomiting and convulsing on the ground, while others stumbled about, foaming at the mouth.

It's fortunate that sarin is a chemical agent and not a virus that can spread from one person to the next. That day "only" twelve people were killed.[32] It's terrible to think what a sect like this could do today using a biological weapon.

3

All in all, it's hard to overstate what a bizarre world we're living in.[33] Consider these four statements, all true:

The world's in awful shape. There's untold suffering among billions of people and animals.

The world's much better off than three centuries ago. We're healthier and wealthier than ever.

The world can be a wildly better place. Just look at how much money and talent we're still wasting.

The world's never been closer to its own demise.

Learn anything about the risks we're facing, and you'll be amazed at how little — how absurdly little — we're doing to protect ourselves and future generations. The rocket of human-kind has taken off, but we don't even have our seatbelts on.

Much like we spent next to nothing on coronaviruses before 2020, the entire world today is spending only a billion dollars a year on research into emerging infectious diseases like Ebola, Zika, and Marburg viruses.[34] For comparison, that's how much money Americans spend each year on whitening their teeth.[35]

Or take the sad state of the Biological Weapons Convention, the treaty banning biological weapons that was agreed in 1972 and signed by 185 nations. The organization behind this historic treaty has precisely four employees. Four! Its budget is smaller than that of your average McDonald's franchise, and the 2018 annual meeting had to be cut short due to lack of funding.[36]

Or consider the spotty attention paid to the risk of nuclear war. There were mass protests against nukes during the Cold War, but little remains of that movement today. For the first time in years, the number of nuclear weapons is going up again, while philanthropists give only a few tens of millions each year to the lobby against nuclear weapons — that's peanuts compared to what they donate to wealthy universities and museums.[37]

Or look at the limited number of researchers working on the safe deployment of artificial intelligence. Given the hype around AI, you'd expect they'd number in the tens of thousands, but 2023 counted at most a few hundred worldwide. And for every safety researcher, you have 300 programmers working to build more powerful systems.[38]

What we need is a new generation of Nader's Raiders for our times: morally ambitious people eager to be what Nader calls "good ancestors."[39] There are countless job openings with a towering VORP ("Value Over Replacement Player," see Chapter 6) — in government, with the private sector, or at nonprofits.

Trained as a biologist or engineer? You can make a difference in the fight against the next pandemic. Schooled in mathematics or computer science? You can help with the safe development of artificial intelligence. Working as an artist or in marketing? You can mobilize as many people as possible, by calling attention to things still under the radar. Have experience as a civil servant or politician? For instance, you can work for stronger regulations involving online sales of hazardous genetic material.

And there are many more roles to play, as entrepreneur, inventor, lawyer, diplomat, and so on and so on. Small nations — like my own little country of the Netherlands, but also Ireland, Austria, Costa Rica — can make a big difference, as they've done in the past. The Organization for the Prohibition of Chemical Weapons, for instance, has its headquarters in The Hague, while Ireland, Costa Rica, and Austria have for years had a major role in the campaign for nuclear disarmament.[40]

Does this all sound too abstract? I can give you a few concrete examples of morally ambitious pioneers who are trying to avert the biggest threats to humankind. In 2006, the Swedish lawyer Beatrice Fihn got an internship at a peace foundation in Geneva, Switzerland. At first, she was thrilled. But then she heard what the work mostly focused on: nukes. "I thought it would be super-boring, really old-school, irrelevant."[41]

Eleven years later, Fihn accepted the Nobel Peace Prize as Director of ICAN, the International Campaign to Abolish Nuclear Weapons. Under her leadership, the group has grown into a coalition of 652 partner organizations in 110 countries. One of their biggest successes to date was getting Nigeria to agree not to develop nuclear weapons. "Nigeria is the fastest-growing country in the world," Fihn said. "It's a massive thing that they are swearing off nuclear weapons forever."[42]

Or take a guy named Andy Weber, who saw many a friend head off to Wall Street in the 1980s. But to Weber, that seemed — and

I quote — "boring."[43] Weber decided he'd rather work as a diplomat. During a long flight, he read a piece in the *Wall Street Journal* with the headline: KAZAKHSTAN IS MADE FOR DIPLOMATS WHO FIND PARIS A BORE.[44]

The Soviet Union had just collapsed, and the new nation of Kazakhstan was in crisis. *Sounds like the perfect spot for me,* thought Weber. He asked the U.S. State Department to be assigned there, took a crash course in Russian, flew to what was then the capital, and had been at his post in Almaty for a few months when his car mechanic put him in touch with a local colonel, who passed along this note:

U-235
90%
600kg

Turns out that sitting in a warehouse in northeastern Kazakhstan with next to no security, was more than 600 kilograms of highly enriched uranium — enough for fifty atomic bombs.[45] Secret agents from Iran, Libya, and North Korea would gladly hand over bags of money for this material, Weber knew. And so he played a key role in Project Sapphire, a covert mission to pack fissile material into 55-gallon drums — 448 of them — and get them safely out of the country. (And yes, a Hollywood blockbuster is in the works.)[46]

Weber ended up devoting his entire career in diplomacy to the hunt for nuclear, chemical, and biological weapons. After Project Sapphire, he led a team of five — with the blessing of the Kazakh authorities — to an abandoned complex in Stepnogorsk, a secret city in the former Soviet Union. It wasn't on any map, but here's where the world's biggest factory for biological weapons was located during the Cold War. The Soviets had a huge — and hugely illegal — outfit called Biopreparat that produced all sorts of bioweapons (including a form of the plague even deadlier than the organic strain).

"It looked like a plant right out of the 1930s," Weber recalls. "There was nothing high-tech about it."[47] Yet the plant could produce more than enough anthrax to wipe out the entire world's population.[48]

Weber and his colleagues managed to bond with the Russians left on site. They drank vodka and ate salted fish together, as the U.S. diplomat played Russian folk songs on an old guitar. Soon after, he signed a contract with the plant's former personnel. He was hiring them to dismantle their own factory. Safely.

The result? Where one of the most dangerous factories in the world once stood, you'll now find only a grassy field.

Do people like Andy Weber get enough credit for their efforts? Public servants like him generally have one of two answers to that question:

1 Nobody gets credit for the disaster that didn't happen.
2 Government work is always teamwork.

That doesn't mean people like Weber are unambitious. Far from it. To this day, Weber emphasizes that his cult is still way too small. He's calling for a broad movement against climate change and the other existential threats we face.

When Weber was appointed by President Barack Obama in 2009 to serve as the principal adviser to the Secretary of Defense on these matters, he knew what to do: ask others to join in. That's why he started the Emerging Leaders in Biosecurity Initiative, a program for morally ambitious doctors, lawyers,

entrepreneurs, researchers, civil servants, engineers, and journalists from all over the world.

You could fill volumes with the stories of the now 200 alumni
from Weber's program. Let me introduce one of them, a young
doctor named Jassi Pannu. In her early twenties in Toronto, Pannu
seemed like a typical pre-med student. She was serious, worked
hard, and dreamed of one day becoming a specialist at a big hospital. She got good grades and in 2014 was accepted to medical
school at the prestigious Stanford University in California.

But once she got there, doubt set in. Was she climbing the
right ladder? "A common path in medicine," she tells me, "is that
you pick a rare disease and become an authority in your niche
field, instead of thinking about the biggest problems and how to
prevent them."

Pannu saw doctors all around her who were incredibly bright
and skillful — top in their fields. But what were they using their
talents for? Pannu wanted to help the needy, but the world's
poorest people don't have access to anything like the elite hospital in Silicon Valley where she practiced.

And so she decided to also work for Doctors without Borders.
Then she realized it could be more effective to focus on preven-
tive medicine. Next she found the field of biosafety, and now
she combines it all: her work as a physician in California, annual
service in Uganda to help HIV patients, and — as an alum of
Andy Weber's program — a key role in the fight against the
next pandemic.

As for what that last one entails? Dr. Pannu is part of a new
generation combating disease, a generation with a breathtaking
ambition. She believes in a world where we no longer have to
fear viruses escaping from a lab or spreading in the wild. With
a bold mix of policy and innovation, she believes we have a
shot at — ready? — making pandemics a thing of the past. In our
lifetimes.[49]

In the spring of 2020, when she was treating Covid-19 patients six days a week, Pannu used her evenings and Sundays to help draft the Apollo Program for Biodefense. That's a crazy ambitious plan with ideas from more than fifty experts for ending the pandemic age once and for all.[50] It's a package of proposals for the coming decades, put together at the request of politicians from across the U.S. political spectrum, and which will require the efforts of doctors and public servants, lobbyists and activists, scientists and entrepreneurs.

Like the historic moon mission the plan is named for, this mission needs vast amounts of money, talent, and knowhow. And just as in the sixties, when we didn't know for sure whether we could put a man on the moon, success today isn't guaranteed.

But the potential? Huge.

Full of enthusiasm, Pannu tells me about the program. First of all, we need to find quicker ways to detect new pathogens. The good news is that developments in this area are fast and furious. Researchers can already test a sample of water or mucus for all kinds of microorganisms, including viruses, bacteria, and fungi. That means we can build a worldwide network to keep an eye out for novel pathogens, at hospitals, say, or in wastewater.[51] It could even be possible to make a device you blow into every morning to find out on the spot if you're coming down with something.[52]

Second, all sorts of new medicines must be developed. Just imagine: a course of antivirals that works as well on viruses as antibiotics work on bacteria. Or picture the super-speedy production of new vaccines. It used to take years to develop a vaccine; now it's a matter of weeks. There are even universal vaccines in the works that guard against entire classes of viruses, like all flu viruses. And we could make it easier to administer a vaccine yourself, using a patch for instance or a nasal spray that comes in the mail.

Third, says Pannu, it's time for a giant clean-up program. There are already all kinds of things done to purify our food and water, making diseases like cholera nonexistent in many countries. Basic hygiene has made a bigger contribution to world health than all the expensive drugs and medical procedures combined.[53] But we can go much further. Because even though our drinking water is purified, we're still breathing polluted air, giving pathogens free rein. In addition to sewers for safely funneling away wastewater, we need something to whisk away dirty air. Or put another way: there's an urgent need for a new generation of radical nerds who'll fight for good, clean air.[54]

The fight for air quality starts with the air outdoors, Pannu emphasizes. It's with good reason that Nader's Raiders lobbied for the Clean Air Act fifty years ago, which *National Geographic* says grew into "one of modern America's most consequential laws."[55]

But we've still got a long way to go. Air pollution is linked to the premature death of some 10 million people every year, as well as to diseases like cancer, Parkinson's, Alzheimer's, and ALS. Polluted air claims more victims worldwide than fire, heat, traffic, homicide, war, drugs, alcohol, drownings, natural disasters, malaria, and tuberculosis combined. (Yet another good reason to stop with the fossil fuels!)[56]

Next, we have to realize that we breathe most of our air *indoors*, not out, with people in modern societies spending 90 percent of their time inside. That's more than some species of whales spend underwater.[57] And contagious diseases spread more easily indoors, so why don't we demand clear standards for indoor air quality? How come most countries don't have a Clean Indoor Air Act?

Legislation wouldn't be such a bad idea. For decades, buildings have had to comply with all kinds of fire safety regulations, which has saved tens of thousands of lives. Healthy drinking water contains no lead, or only tiny amounts, so in many countries we've got laws in place to regulate that. As a result, the brains of children develop better and crime rates have even dropped (because, research shows, less lead means less brain damage means less crime).[58]

According to Pannu and her colleagues, it's time to agree on some stricter rules for indoor air. We can start now by filtering and ventilating the air in public spaces, and in the near future, we could maybe install special lamps capable of disinfecting the air in seconds. This form of ultraviolet light, Far-UVC, appears in early studies to be safe for humans. Once the cost comes down, it could be installed in millions of LED bulbs.[59] Far-UVC appears to be at the stage where solar panels were in the 1950s: super-promising, but there's still lots of work to do.

Put all these plans together, Pannu decided, and the impossible can become reality. For thousands of years, people have been plagued by pathogens. Between 1347 and 1352, at least one-third of all Europeans succumbed to the Black Death. In 1918, Spanish flu took more lives than the entire Great War (WWI). And in its final century, smallpox sent 500 million victims to their graves, before Viktor Zhdanov led the way to eradicating it (see Chapter 7).[60]

If we play our cards right, we can protect ourselves from all twenty-six families of viruses that threaten us today. We'd no longer have to fear another pandemic and flu would be a thing of the past — we wouldn't even catch a cold. And no, this isn't some far-fetched scenario. According to experts like Jassi Pannu and Andy Weber, we can make it happen within decades.

But none of this is automatic. Just as with the malaria vaccine and the rise of solar energy, there's no law of nature ensuring everything turns out all right.

It's up to us.

Maybe reading about the existential threats facing us and future generations does your head in. Maybe you think it's brash to believe that you as an individual can do something about these gigantic risks. And maybe it feels a little cold to focus on potential nuclear conflicts or possible viral outbreaks instead of soothing some of the concrete suffering happening in the here and now.

But while Jassi Pannu fights for her dream of a world without pandemics, she doesn't lose sight of her patients. Her work in the hospital keeps her grounded, well aware of the fact that behind the huge numbers are people of flesh and blood. Covid-19 killed more than 20 million people worldwide, but you could perhaps better say that 20 million times, one person died.[61] We must continue to try to let these kinds of figures get through to us. That's 20 million times that a father or mother, brother or sister, friend or lover lost someone dear to them.

And as far as diseases go, Covid was relatively mild. A future pandemic could prove far, far worse.

There's no time to lose. Pannu feels the pressure acutely, which explains her ambition. She tells me that she and her colleagues at the Apollo Program for Biodefense draw inspiration from that famous speech given by John F. Kennedy. On a clear September morning in 1962, he addressed a crowd of 40,000 under the hot Texas sun at a university football stadium in Houston.

Kennedy opened his speech with a look to the past. Imagine the last 50,000 years, he said, unfolding in just half a century. Then it was only five years ago that we invented the wheel. The printing press came into being earlier this year, and just last month, we welcomed the electric lightbulb, the telephone, the automobile, and the airplane. Last week, we got antibiotics, television, and nuclear power.

"This is a breathtaking pace," said Kennedy, "and such a pace cannot help but create new ills as it dispels old . . ."

He spoke next of a bold plan to put a man on the moon by 1970: Project Apollo. A plan many thought impossible, requiring technologies that didn't even exist yet. "We choose to go to the moon in this decade and do the other things," Kennedy said in the most well-known passage of his speech, "not because they are easy, but because they are hard, because that goal will serve to organize and measure the best of our energies and skills . . ."

Kennedy himself wouldn't live to see it because he was assassinated a year after that speech. But before the decade was out, his prediction came true: in July 1969, a man walked on the moon.

Today, we're a few days further along on Kennedy's timeline of human history, and we need more moon shots. What about an Apollo program to end poverty and one to stop human trafficking, an Apollo program to eradicate malaria and one to end lead poisoning, an Apollo program to put a stop to global warming and one to wipe out the deadliest pathogens on the planet.

"We set sail on this new sea," Kennedy said, "because there is new knowledge to be gained and new rights to be won." But the president also warned that technology is only a tool; it has no conscience of its own. "Whether it will become a force for good or ill," Kennedy said, "depends on man."[62]

4

How much is at stake becomes even clearer when we zoom out more. On February 14, 1990 the unmanned space probe *Voyager 1* had been moving through space for over ten years. It had traveled 6 billion kilometers from the sun (3.7 billion miles) and was about to leave the solar system. Never before had something made by people ventured so far from our home planet.

That day, *Voyager* got instructions to turn its cameras back toward Earth one last time. It took a picture and saved it on its tape recorder, then radioed it back. The signal took more than five hours, moving at the speed of light, before it was picked up by one of the 70-meter radio antennas back on the planet *Voyager* came from.

That last *Voyager* photo became world famous. On the grainy image, Earth is but one-tenth of a pixel, a pale blue dot in a sea of darkness. "Look again at that dot," wrote astronomer Carl Sagan. "That's here. That's home. That's us. On it everyone you love, everyone you know, everyone you ever heard of, every human being who ever was, lived out their lives."[63]

On that minuscule dot a wondrous thing took place. A miracle that, as far as we know, hasn't happened anywhere else in the universe. Life. Our living planet is a flickering little light in a vast and lifeless cosmos. Look at us from this distance, and you see just how vulnerable we are. You sense how great our responsibility is to protect and keep this world — this spark of consciousness — this, our only earth.

Epilogue

I did not believe that a Cause which stood for a beautiful ideal
[. . .] should demand the denial of life and joy.
Emma Goldman, *activist (1869–1940)*

I

And now for a question that's been hanging over this book for ten chapters.

When have you done enough for a better world? When are you allowed to climb down off your horse and rest at the side of the road?

To answer that question, let's go back in time to June 12, 1840. That's the day the world's first international antislavery convention opened in London's grand Exeter Hall. After a nearly fifty-year struggle, success was finally here: slavery was now abolished throughout the British Empire.

People came from all over to attend — 5,000 of them, from Canada and France, Spain and the U.S., Haiti and Sierra Leone. And the keynote speaker? None other than Thomas Clarkson, now eighty. Of the twelve men who started the Society for the Abolition of the Slave Trade, he was the only one still living. The audience was urged to hold their applause, lest it prove too much for the aged man. Clarkson shuffled to the stage on the arm of a Quaker friend and stood for a moment in silence. He then spoke with "dignity, clearness, and feeling," his daughter-in-law later wrote. "Tears I believe ran down his cheeks, as they did from most eyes."[1]

The father of the movement laid out his vision for a world without slavery. "Take courage," he said. "Go on, persevere to the last." When he finished speaking, a resounding "Amen, amen!" rose up from the crowd. Unable to contain themselves, the audience got to their feet and applauded with abandon. "The women wept — the men shook off their tears," one attendee remembered. "It was many minutes before I recovered."[2]

But no sooner had the old fellow left the stage than the squabbling started.

Many women abolitionists attended the conference, for it was women who had taken the lead during the last years of the movement. In 1826, the women's society of Sheffield, England, was the first to call for fully abolishing slavery *now* — "without reserve, without limitation, without delay."[3] While men were still discussing "gradual" abolition, the women were far more radical. Because sometimes you have to aim higher if you want to hit your target.

"Men may propose only *gradually* to abolish the worst of crimes," a woman in Wiltshire wrote, "and only mitigate the most cruel bondage, but [. . .] we must not talk of gradually abolishing murder, licentiousness, cruelty, tyranny, keeping stolen men, parting husbands and wives, and so on. I trust no Ladies' Association will ever be found with such words attached to it."[4]

The straitlaced politician William Wilberforce had grumbled all along that women shouldn't take part in politics, as that would be "unsuited to the female character as delineated in scripture."[5] But other men in the movement were more clear-eyed about who was doing what. "Ladies Associations did everything," one later acknowledged. "In a word they formed the cement of the whole antislavery building — without their aid we never should have kept standing."[6]

So, what happened that June day in 1840? After Clarkson's speech, the question arose as to what role women could play at the conference. Upon giving the matter due consideration, the male delegates decided women were more than welcome.

To watch. From the balcony.

Two women who'd traveled from America to attend, Lucretia Mott (a Quaker) and Elizabeth Cady Stanton, went home furious. They would go on to organize an event in Seneca Falls, New York, eight years later that's now famous for launching the women's rights movement in the U.S.

The fact of the matter is that it's never enough. There's always a new hill to climb, a new mission to complete, a new mountain to move. There will always be toddlers in ponds who need saving. There's no end to what you can do to help. But that's also the danger. Moral ambition can take over your life.

Think again of those Dutch Resistance heroes from Chapter 2. A number of them later looked back on the war with some measure of satisfaction. Bert Bochove and his wife, Annie, provided thirty-six Jews with a place to hide, in the attic above their drugstore in Huizen. "In some ways," Bert recalled, "the war was the best time of my life."[7]

Others wrestled with the choices they'd made, still wondering years later whether they'd done enough. The war took a toll on their physical and mental health, and some suffered from post-traumatic stress disorder.[8] "It got to be too much for him, all the strain and horrors of those years," Max Léons wrote after the war about his buddy Arnold Douwes.[9] And Léons struggled with the past, too. "Around fifty, it all came back. Had a complete breakdown," he said. "I managed to recover, but you're never really the same after that."[10]

You can also go down fighting. In August 1793, after seven years of campaigning for change — seven years of protesting, mobilizing, debating, coordinating, organizing, challenging, and inspiring (plus lots and lots of horseback riding) — young Thomas Clarkson was worn out. Though only thirty-three, he looked like an old man. If he had to speak, he'd break out in a sweat. When he took the stairs, he'd stumble over the steps. There was still so much he wanted to do, but his frail frame balked.

Maybe Clarkson could have achieved more if he didn't get hit with burnout. Carry the weight of the world on your shoulders, and sooner or later, you'll buckle. And that doesn't help anyone.

Plus there's another, more essential reason to rein in your moral ambition. When all you see is gross injustice and drowning toddlers, try to justify "wasting" time or money on art or music, love or friendship. Then the good you do is never good enough.

But people are more than tools for getting things done. We're worthwhile in our own right. In one of his acclaimed essays, George Orwell wrote about the life of Mahatma Gandhi, a man remembered to this day as a saint. "I've never been able to feel much liking for Gandhi," wrote Orwell.[11] There was something exasperating, even unbearable, about India's celebrated fighter for freedom.

The fact that Gandhi didn't drink or smoke? Fair enough. But the mahatma also avoided herbs and spices, so as not to derive any pleasure from food. He saw sex as merely a means of making more people and took a vow of *brahmacharya*, swearing off erotic desire.[12] On top of that, Gandhi renounced every form of personal affection or friendship. He thought loyalty a dangerous thing and wished to love no one in particular. Gandhi simply loved everyone.

Most of us, wrote Orwell, have a word for such a life-style: inhuman. In a memorable passage in his essay, the British writer notes:

> The essence of being human is that one does not seek perfection, that one *is* sometimes willing to commit sins for the sake of loyalty, that one does not push asceticism to the point where it makes friendly intercourse impossible, and that one is prepared in the end to be defeated and broken up by life, which is the inevitable price of fastening one's love upon other human individuals.[13]

Gandhi, thought Orwell, hadn't understood what life was about. Most people don't want to be saints — and rightly so. We're on this earth to wonder and to wander, to seek and to sin. We're here to live life. And it seems saints, in their all-encompassing love for humankind, understand little of what it is to be human.

Speaking of, I'd like to go back to that Buddhist monk from the prologue of this book. In October 2015, Matthieu Ricard was invited to come to Princeton University and speak with Peter Singer. The philosopher asked the monk whether those 60,000 hours of meditation might have been put to better use.[14]

Ricard gave an honest answer. He said surely we don't blame a musician like Yo-Yo Ma for devoting so much time to the cello? There's more to life than morality and guilt. What about beauty, happiness, wisdom, truth?[15]

And yet Ricard had to admit struggling with that same issue. Someone had asked him back in the nineties if he had any regrets, and he replied, "Not to have put compassion into action."[16]

Fortunately, it's never too late for moral ambition. At fifty-four, Ricard set up a nonprofit that does humanitarian work in Tibet, Nepal, and India. He's donated the proceeds from his talks and books to the group ever since.

Thomas Clarkson, on the other hand, took an eleven-year sabbatical after his nervous breakdown. He bought some land in the north of England and built a house. He became a shepherd, grew wheat and barley, and wrote three thick tomes on the history of the Quakers. And for the first time in his life, he fell in love. He married the daughter of a yarn maker and, ten months later, became the proud father of a son.[17]

In short: there are limits. Morality plays a big role in a rich and full life, but it's not everything. And if your inner fire burns bright, no need to stoke it hotter. In any case, don't let yourself be fueled by a sense of guilt or shame, but rather by enthusiasm and a lust for life. Be ambitious, not perfect. There comes a point when you're fine just the way you are.

Why am I writing this now, and not at the start of the book? Simple: because most of us aren't there yet. Most people still have a long way to go and haven't come close to reaching the bounds of their moral ambition. And then the message is clear: stop wasting your talent and start making a difference.

2

There's one last thing I'd like to emphasize: this book is written for you and no one else. Don't wield it as a weapon, but to whip yourself into shape. See the good in others; demand more of yourself.

True, there's a lot you can criticize about self-help books and their focus on the individual. It's always irritating when gurus with exorbitant salaries drone on about "taking responsibility," while showing little awareness of poverty, inequality, or their own dumb luck. Call it the right-wing excuse: whenever structural injustice comes up, start hollering about bootstraps and how success is a choice.

Hogwash, of course. "If wealth was the inevitable result of hard work and enterprise," writes the journalist George Monbiot, "every woman in Africa would be a millionaire."[18]

But sometimes I wonder if the opposite also holds. Is there such a thing as the left-wing excuse? I'm talking about those privileged types who, whenever personal responsibility comes up, start hollering about changing "the system." That we first need an in-depth analysis which of course will show it's all the fault of corporations and government, advertising and algorithms, capitalism and crooks — anything to avoid looking in the mirror.

"One of the most difficult things," Nelson Mandela said after stepping down as South Africa's president, "is not to change society, but to change yourself."[19]

But if you manage to do it, and choose to go the moral ambition route, the ripple effect can be enormous. Your behavior is contagious, so a better world does indeed begin with you. In fact, the fallacy that one individual *can't* make a difference relies on a hyper-individualistic view of humanity. Humans are social creatures through and through, and that means your choices can in turn influence the choices of dozens, hundreds, or even millions of other people.

In this book, I've shared stories of towering figures past and present. It's easy to think they're fundamentally different from you and me, that we could never follow in their footsteps. But think again. They're people, too, with their own flaws and failings. Besides, moral ambition isn't a trait; it's a mindset. And it's catching. I hope reading this book has given you the bug.

At the start of his career, on a summer evening in 1787, Thomas Clarkson was alone on horseback as he approached the city of Bristol. It was hazy, and he could just make out the slaving port in the distance when the sound of church bells rang out through the fog. "I began now to tremble for the first time," Clarkson would later recount in his memoirs.[20] He looked toward the city where he knew not a soul and felt the immensity of the task ahead.

Then he spurred his steed onward. "In journeying on, I became more calm and composed. My spirits began to return."[21]

Nothing left to do but get started.

The School
FOR MORAL AMBITION

And now it's time to take action.

This book isn't meant to be the last word — more like the starting shot. If you want to move mountains, *you* have to get moving, and that's much easier to do together. That's why I went looking for idealistic entrepreneurs to build The School for Moral Ambition with me. (One of them — not a coincidence — is an alum of that magical school in Chapter 6.)

You'll find other inspiring stories on our website and learn how you can start your own *moral ambition circle*. That's a group of five to eight people who help each other out in the quest for positive impact. Maybe you can make a difference at your current job? Or maybe it's time for a change.

Discover how you, too, can go the moral ambition route, and support one another in taking the first steps. As a nonprofit, we make the tools you'll need freely available on our site.

moralambition.org

THE SEVEN FOUNDING PRINCIPLES OF THE SCHOOL FOR MORAL AMBITION

The School is founded on seven principles. They guide our decisions and express our commitment to making the world a wildly better place.

1 Action

We think awareness is overrated

We recognise that we're among the most privileged people in the history of humanity. That means we have an enormous opportunity to make a difference. We feel awareness is overrated and don't believe in pointing fingers. We're ambitious but uphold our own definition of success: we want to do as much good in the world as we possibly can.

2 Impact

We want to make a big difference

We don't aim for change alone, but for truly transformative impact. We know we must prioritise, and we choose to focus on the world's biggest, most neglected, yet fixable problems. At the same time, we're wary of the measurability bias because not everything that counts can be counted. In cases that aren't quantifiable, we do our best to construct a robust theory of change.

3 Radical compassion

We work to expand our moral circle

We consider all sentient beings to be members of our moral circle. All are uniquely valuable and have the inherent right to exist and flourish. We want to grow our compassion and help as many people and animals as possible. Like the abolitionists and suffragettes before us, we try to push the frontiers of humanity's moral circle. We care about future generations and seek to be good ancestors.

4 Open-mindedness

We cultivate a curious mindset

We strive to see the world as it truly is, not how we want to see it. We're epistemically humble: the world is complicated, and there are many things we don't know or aren't sure about. We cultivate a curious and inquisitive mindset, and we're not ashamed to change our minds. We encourage owning up to mistakes and admitting failures. We're not afraid to stand out from the crowd, even when our priorities and solutions seem outlandish to others. Our truth evolves with evidence, not ego.

5 Kindness

We believe in the good in people

For us, ambition is not about envy and resentment; it's about inspiration and encouragement. We try to bring out the best in one another, and we know it takes a team to make a difference. We don't treat people as a means to an end, but always as ends in themselves. We celebrate the heroes in the spotlight and those who work tirelessly in the wings. We believe everyone has talent, and we encourage all to live a morally ambitious life.

6 Zest for life

We want to live full, rich, well-rounded lives

We're not driven by feelings of guilt, but by sheer enthusiasm. We're excited about making the world a better place and about building a legacy that matters. At the same time, we know there's more to life than work and ambition. We have loved ones, hobbies and other interests. We want to live rich, full, well-rounded lives, both to sustain our ambition and as an end in itself.

7 Perseverance

We're determined not to give up

We understand this journey is a marathon, not a sprint. We know our mission could take years, decades, or even our entire lives. Of the sixty-eight women who convened in Seneca Falls for the first women's rights convention in 1848, only one lived to see women secure the right to vote. We know tough times lie ahead — times when all our efforts may seem in vain. In those moments of doubt, we'll remind ourselves that we are but a small part of a much bigger movement. And one day, we'll pass the torch to a new generation of moral pioneers.

THANKS

This book is dedicated to my mother, Peta Bregman-Veldhuis. Even when I was very young, she was already teaching me that it's more important to stand up for what's right than to make others feel at ease. My father says that's a Veldhuis thing, and my mother gets it from my grandfather.

When I leaf through the book, I see the ideas, advice, and suggestions of others everywhere I look. I'd like to thank Harminke Medendorp for being a phenomenal Dutch editor. Thanks to Bobby Vos for his invaluable help with the research. Thanks also to my early readers, who caught countless errors: Jurriën Hamer, Sigrid Bregman, Matthias van Klaveren, Jesse Frederik, Rob Wijnberg, Tamar Stelling, Simon van Teutem, Jelmer Mommers, Michiel de Hoog, Riffy Bol, Vera Schölmerich, Martijn Klop, Joshua Monrad, Vidur Kapur, Pepijn Vloemans, Bram Schaper, Marieke de Visscher, and James Herbert.

I'd also like to thank my Dutch copyeditors, Anna Vossers, Jelena Barišić, Roos van Tongerloo, and Hans Pieter van Stein Callenfels, for their keen eye and useful suggestions. I'm ever grateful to my Dutch publisher's stellar team, and in particular Milou Klein Lankhorst, Andreas Jonkers, Channa van Dijk, Anne Strunk, and Anna de Roest. Thank you to Leon de Korte for the infographics, and to Harald Dunnink and Martijn van Dam for the amazing cover.

For this English-language edition, I owe a special thanks to my translator, Erica Moore, whose expertise and mastery of her craft are unparalleled. She truly is the best. It was also a joy to work with my British editor, Alexis Kirschbaum, and my American editors, Alexander Littlefield and Ben George, who believed in this book from day one.

As I was writing, it began to dawn on me that this needed to be more than a book alone. Special thanks to Kellie Liket, a real zero (see Chapter 2), who encouraged me to crank up my own ambition to new levels. Thanks also to my cofounders at the School for Moral Ambition — Harald Dunnink, Jan-Willem van Putten, Julia van Boven, and Ruben Timmerman — for joining me on this adventure. Thank you to our board members Edmond Hilhorst, Heleen Dura-van Oord, Salmaan Sana, Saskia Bruysten, and Mustapha Abdellati for sharing their knowledge, dedication, and enthusiasm. Everything I earn on the book goes to the nonprofit.

And finally, thanks to Maartje, the love of my life and my rock of fifteen years. While writing this book, our little Kaat was born. You could fill libraries with everything that's been written about how to raise children to be good people. But working on this book made me see that we'd truly do better to start with ourselves. After all, doing good is infectious. So we'll do our best, sweet Kaat. And by the way, you've probably already seen the words on that little sign you got as a baby gift from one of your aunts: "Well-behaved women seldom make history."

NOTES

EPIGRAPHS

Prologue   Leo Rosten, *Passions & Prejudices*, McGraw-Hill Book Company (1978), p. 4.

Chapter 1   Allen Raine, quoted in: "As You Climb the Ladder of Success, Be Sure It's Leaning Against the Right Building," *Quote Investigator* (17 August 2017).

Chapter 2   Tyler Cowen, "The high-return activity of raising others' aspirations," *Marginal Revolution* (21 October 2018).

Chapter 3   Emmeline Pankhurst, "Speech from the Dock," at Bow Street Magistrates' Court in London on October 21, 1908.

Chapter 4   Joe Biden, quoted in: Justin Martin, *Nader: Crusader, Spoiler, Icon*, Perseus Publishing (2002), p. 268.

Chapter 5   Helen Keller, *The Open Door*, Doubleday (1957), p. 34.

Chapter 6   Coco Chanel, quoted in: Marcel Haedrich, *Coco Chanel: Her Life, Her Secrets*, translated by Charles Lam Markmann, Little, Brown and Company (1972), p. 255.

Chapter 7   Thomas Edison, quoted in George Sullivan, *Thomas Edison*, Scholastic (2001), p. 5.

Chapter 8   Margaret Thatcher, "TV Interview for London Weekend Television *Weekend World*," Margaret Thatcher Foundation (6 January 1980).

Chapter 9   David Slack, @slack2thefuture, Twitter (28 January 2017).

Chapter 10   Maya Angelou, quote from an interview with Oprah Winfrey, who talked about it in a 2013 interview with Chris Witherspoon.

Epilogue   Emma Goldman, *Living My Life: An Autobiography of Emma Goldman*, Gibbs M. Smith (1982), p. 56. Originally published in 1931.

NOTES

PHOTOS

- Photo, page 23: Scherl/Süddeutsche Zeitung Photo
- Photo, page 24: Eckler family photo
- Photo, page 43: © John G. Zimmerman Archive
- Photo, page 48: © Robyn Twomey
- Painting, page 50: Quaker Meeting by Egbert van Heemskerck II (with permission of Y Lanfa Powysland Museum)
- Painting, page 73: Portrait of Olaudah Equiano, artist unknown (1789). Wikimedia Commons, published by Project Gutenberg
- Photos, page 84: Scherl/Süddeutsche Zeitung Photo (left), Wegert family photo (right)
- Photo, page 204: Blue Marble, 7 December 1972, NASA
- Photo, page 216: Pale Blue Dot, NASA/JPL

PROLOGUE

1   Brian Mattmiller, "Dalai Lama Coming to UW to Probe Science of Emotions," University of Wisconsin-Madison (27 April 2001). The lead scientist, Richard Davidson, tells in Chapter 9 of his book about the excitement in the lab when they first saw Matthieu Ricard's brain scan. See: Richard J. Davidson and Sharon Begley, *The Emotional Life of the Brain*, Hudson Street Press (2012).

2   The high level of gamma waves was registered using electroencephalography, or EEG, a method for measuring the brain's electrical activity. See: Davidson and Begley, *The Emotional Life of the Brain*, Chapter 10. See also the resulting scientific study: Antoine Lutz et al., "Long-term Meditators Self-Induce High-Amplitude Gamma Synchrony During Mental Practice," *PNAS*, Vol. 101, Issue 46 (2004). Neurologists now question Davidson's left-right brain model. See: Guido Gainotti, "Emotions and the Right Hemisphere: Can New Data Clarify Old Models?" *Neuroscientist*, Vol. 25, Issue 3 (2019).

3   Anthony Barnes, "The Happiest Man in the World?" *Independent* (21 January 2007).

CHAPTER I

1   *Poverty and Shared Prosperity 2022: Correcting Course*, World Bank (2022), p. XIII.

2   Carolina Sánchez-Páramo et al., "COVID-19 Leaves a Legacy of Rising
    Poverty and Widening Inequality," *World Bank Blogs* (7 October
    2021); "UN Report: Global Hunger Numbers Rose to as Many as 828
    Million in 2021," World Health Organization (6 July 2022).

3   Bastian Herre, "The World Has Recently Become Less Democratic,"
    Our World in Data (6 September 2022). See also: "UNHCR: Ukraine,
    Other Conflicts Push Forcibly Displaced Total over 100 Million for
    First Time," UN Refugee Agency (23 May 2022).

4   So says noted economist Nicholas Stern, for example. See: "Net Zero
    Will Require the Biggest Economic Transformation Ever Seen in
    Peacetime, Says Nicholas Stern," Grantham Research Institute on
    Climate Change and the Environment, London School of Economics
    and Political Science (26 October 2021). The UN Panel on Climate
    Change speaks of "rapid, far-reaching, and unprecedented changes
    in all aspects of society": "Summary for Policymakers of IPCC Special
    Report on Global Warming of 1.5°C Approved by Governments,"
    Intergovernmental Panel on Climate Change (8 October 2018).

5   And if "pointless" makes you think of government employees, think
    again. The same study found that of the people who consider their
    jobs meaningless for society, three times as many work in the private
    sector as in the public sector: Robert Dur and Max van Lent, "Socially
    Useless Jobs," *Industrial Relations: A Journal of Economy and Society*,
    Vol. 58, Issue 1 (2019).

6   David Graeber, "On the Phenomenon of Bullshit Jobs. A Work
    Rant," *STRIKE! Magazine*, Issue 3 (August 2013).

7   Jeff Hammerbacher, quoted in: Ashlee Vance, "This Tech Bubble Is
    Different," *Bloomberg Businessweek* (14 April 2011).

8   Florian H. Schneider, Fanny Brun, and Roberto A. Weber, *Sorting
    and Wage Premiums in Immoral Work*, Working Paper No. 353,
    Department of Economics, University of Zurich (2020). See also: Jiri
    Novak and Pawel Bilinski, "The Wages of Sin — Social Stigma
    Premium in Executive Compensation," *SSRN* (11 January 2016).

9   Popular titles include *Rich Dad, Poor Dad* (1997) by Robert
    T. Kiyosaki and *The 4-Hour Workweek: Escape 9–5, Live Anywhere,
    and Join the New Rich* (2007) by Timothy Ferriss. And then there's
    the FIRE movement (Financially Independent, Retire Early) where
    people pass along money-saving tips and ways to earn returns as
    swiftly as possible in order to retire as soon as possible.

10 Kristine E. Guillaume and Jamie D. Halper, "After Harvard," Nenya A. Edjah et al. (eds), *The Graduating Class of 2020, By the Numbers, The Harvard Crimson* (24 May 2020).

11 *"Wat maakt management consultancy zo populair onder (top)studenten?,"* Consultancy.nl (24 July 2017).

12 Lockwood shared this in an interview with me. See also: Sachin Waikar, "Higher Taxes Can Make Altruistic Jobs More Attractive," *Kellogg Insight* (2 November 2016).

13 Benjamin B. Lockwood, Charles G. Nathanson, and E. Glen Weyl, "Taxation and the Allocation of Talent," *Journal of Political Economy*, Vol. 125, Issue 5 (2017).

14 Just think of the 2008 financial crisis, when hundreds of millions of taxpayer dollars were spent propping up the banks. Or what about widespread practices used to avoid paying taxes, facilitated by armies of accountants, attorneys, and financial consultants. See: Benjamin Todd, "Which Professions Are Paid Too Much Given Their Value to Society?," *80,000 Hours Blog* (27 June 2017). See also: Eilis Lawlor, Helen Kersley, and Susan Steed, "A Bit Rich: Calculating the real value to society of different professions," New Economics Foundation (December 2009). Bankers see their work as useless with above-average frequency. See the "Supporting Information" for the study by Dur and van Lent, "Socially Useless Jobs."

15 To name but a few examples: for every dollar a teacher earns, two dollars are created elsewhere in the economy. And many a researcher creates far more wealth than she gets paid. An average biomedical researcher, for instance, creates nearly $1 *million* in benefits to society each year. That is to say, education and research is cheaper than free. See Todd, "Which Professions Are Paid Too Much?"; Lawlor, Kersley, and Steed, "A Bit Rich?"

16 Anna Gross, "Millennial Management Consultants Yearn for Meaning at Work," *Financial Times* (29 January 2020).

17 Jeremy M. Grimshaw et al., "De-implementing Wisely. Developing the Evidence Base to Reduce Low-value Care," *BMJ Quality & Safety*, Vol. 29, Issue 5 (2020), p. 409.

18 Lightyear (solar-powered car, now unfortunately bankrupt), Meatable (cultured meat), and Leyden Labs (an antiviral nasal spray).

19 "25 onder de 25 van 2021," *MT/Sprout*.

20 Marit Willemsen, "De nieuwe start-up verkoopt matrassen," *NRC Handelsblad* (28 April 2017).

21 Max Roser, "Child Mortality: An Everyday Tragedy of Enormous Scale That We Can Make Progress Against," Our World in Data (21 July 2021).

22 Kim Parker, Nikki Graf, and Ruth Igielnik, "Generation Z Looks a Lot Like Millennials on Key Social and Political Issues," Pew Research Center (17 January 2019). See also: Niall Ferguson and Eyck Freymann, "The Coming Generation War," *The Atlantic* (6 May 2019); Joseph de Weck and Niall Ferguson, "European Millennials Are Not Like Their American Counterparts," *The Atlantic* (30 September 2019).

23 "Gen Z Wants to Work Less," *Newsweek* (25 May 2023). See also: Leila Latif, "The Soft Life: Why Millennials are Quitting the Rat Race," *Guardian* (2 April 2024).

24 Tanner Greer, "Honor, Dignity, and Victimhood: A Tour Through Three Centuries of American Political Culture," *The Scholar's Stage* (16 September 2015). See also: Gal Beckerman, *The Quiet Before: On the Unexpected Origins of Radical Ideas*, Crown (2022).

25 Quoted in: Akiba Solomon and Kenrya Rankin, *How We Fight White Supremacy: A Field Guide to Black Resistance*, Bold Type Books (2019), p. 3.

26 According to UN estimates, global livestock includes some 26 billion chickens: "Crops and Livestock Products," FAOSTAT, Food and Agriculture Organization of the United Nations (24 March 2023). Exactly how many of them are factory farmed is hard to say, but an estimate by the Sentience Institute puts the figure at 74 percent: Kelly Anthis and Jacy Reese Anthis, "Global Farmed & Factory Farmed Animals Estimates," Sentience Institute (21 February 2019).

27 Thomas Clarkson, *The History of the Rise, Progress and Accomplishment of the Abolition of the African Slave-Trade by the British Parliament: Volume I*, R. Taylor & Co. (1808), p. 214.

28 Clarkson, *The History of the Rise: Volume I*, p. 209.

29 Thomas Clarkson, *An Essay on the Slavery and Commerce of the Human Species, Particularly the African, Translated from a Latin Dissertation, which was Honoured with the First Prize in the University of Cambridge, for the Year 1785, with Additions*, J. Phillips (1786), p. 256.

30 Clarkson, *The History of the Rise: Volume I*, p. 210.

31 Adam Hochschild, *Bury the Chains: The British Struggle to Abolish Slavery*, Houghton Mifflin (2005), p. 89. See also: Robert Wiblin, "Christopher Brown on Why Slavery Abolition Wasn't Inevitable," *80,000 Hours Podcast* (11 February 2023). In this interview, the historian Christopher Leslie Brown — one of the foremost experts on British abolitionism — was asked who the most consequential individual was in the British antislavery movement. Brown answered that at the start of his career, he was determined not to give too much attention to individual heroes, but to focus more on the structural causes of abolitionism. But the more time he spent with the archives, the more he realized some individuals did indeed have outsized influence — Thomas Clarkson in particular. Brown: "As far as the movement goes, I just think that Thomas Clarkson is really essential to what ends up emerging."

32 One in ten Atlantic crossings saw an uprising on board. Christopher Leslie Brown, "Abolition of the Atlantic Slave Trade," Gad Heuman and Trevor Burnard (eds), *The Routledge History of Slavery*, Routledge (2011), p. 283.

33 Clarkson, *The History of the Rise: Volume I*, pp. 210–211.

34 They were primarily Quakers, but Clarkson also met lawyer Granville Sharp, who argued against slavery for more than twenty years, minister James Ramsey, who had recently penned a shocking account of conditions in the Caribbean, and the formerly enslaved writer Olaudah Equiano (see Chapter 4).

35 Clarkson, *The History of the Rise: Volume I*, p. 225.

36 Christopher Leslie Brown, *Moral Capital: Foundations of British Abolitionism*, University of North Carolina Press (2006), p. 442.

37 Brown, *Moral Capital*, p. 441.

38 That was Samuel Taylor Coleridge, quoted in: Ellen Gibson Wilson, *Thomas Clarkson*, Palgrave Macmillan (1990), p. x.

39 Quoted in: Hochschild, *Bury the Chains*, p. 237.

40 Thomas Clarkson, *The History of the Rise, Progress and Accomplishment of the Abolition of the African Slave-Trade by the British Parliament: Volume II*, R. Taylor & Co. (1808), p. 471.

41 Kwame Anthony Appiah, *The Honor Code: How Moral Revolutions Happen*, W. W. Norton (2010), p. 16.

CHAPTER 2

1   Irene Eckler, *A Family Torn Apart by "Rassenschande": Political Persecution in the Third Reich*, Horneburg Verlag (1998).

2   Isabel Wilkerson, *Caste: The Origins of Our Discontents*, Random House (2020), p. xv.

3   Nassim Nicholas Taleb, "The Most Intolerant Wins: The Dictatorship of the Small Minority," *Medium* (14 August 2016).

4   Johannes Houwink ten Cate and Bob Moore (eds), *Het geheime dagboek van Arnold Douwes, Jodenredder*, Boom (2018), p. 61.

5   The quote is the main thesis of my book *Humankind*, Bloomsbury (2020), p. 2.

6   "Our national resistance," said Dutch Prime Minister Willem Schermerhorn, for instance, in 1945, "will be regarded as the most notable stance of our people in this period of history." Original Dutch quote in *Het Parool* on September 1, 1945. See also Rob van Ginkel, *Rondom de stilte: Herdenkingscultuur in Nederland*, Bert Bakker (2011), p. 730.

7   Bart van der Boom, *"Wij weten niets van hun lot": Gewone Nederlanders en de Holocaust*, Boom (2012), pp. 139–140.

8   Van der Boom, *"Wij weten niets van hun lot,"* p. 179.

9   The standard work on this issue that comes to a nuanced conclusion is *"Wij weten niets van hun lot": Gewone Nederlanders en de Holocaust* by Dutch historian Bart van der Boom. He shows that ordinary Dutch people did know their Jewish countrymen were in great danger but were not aware that they were being gassed on arrival at Auschwitz and other concentration camps. Most Dutchmen weren't indifferent to the persecution of the Jews, but thought they couldn't do anything or were too afraid of the risks involved to resist.

10 Eva Fogelman, *Conscience and Courage: Rescuers of Jews During the Holocaust*, Anchor Books (1995), p. 60.

11 Fogelman, *Conscience and Courage*, p. 47.

12 Samuel P. Oliner and Pearl M. Oliner, *The Altruistic Personality: Rescuers of Jews in Nazi Europe*, Free Press (1988), p. 123.

13 Fogelman, *Conscience and Courage*, p. 68.

14 Max Léons and Arnold Douwes, *Mitswa en christenplicht: Bescheiden helden uit de illegaliteit*, BZZTÔH publishers (2000), p. 111.

15 Now California State Polytechnic University, Humboldt.

16 Fogelman, *Conscience and Courage*, p. 253.

17 Fogelman, *Conscience and Courage*, p. 254. See also: Stephanie Fagin-Jones, "Prosocialization: Lessons Learned from the Upbringing of Holocaust Heroes," *Heroism Science*, Vol. 4, Issue 2 (29 May 2019).

18 Quoted in: Pearl Oliner, *Saving the Forsaken: Religious Culture and the Rescue of the Jews in Nazi Europe*, Yale University Press (2004), p. 55.

19 Fogelman, *Conscience and Courage*, p. 59.

20 As early as the February Strike of 1941, Communists led the way in Dutch resistance to the German occupation. Conservative estimates are that over 20 percent of Dutch Communist Party members joined the resistance. By comparison, only 1 percent of the general population in the Netherlands took part. (Some 2,000 members of the CPN, or Communistische Partij Nederland, were active in the organized resistance. Before the war, the CPN had about 9,000 members. The Dutch resistance is estimated to have numbered around 45,000 people during World War II, while the country's adult population at the time was 5.5 million. Source: the author's correspondence with Rense Havinga, curator at the Dutch Freedom Museum.) Many of the Communists, by the way, had experience with resistance work from their time volunteering in the Spanish Civil War, where they'd fought against the fascists. Members of the Orthodox Reformed Church (*de gereformeerden*) also played a prominent role in the resistance. They made up only 8 percent of the country's population but helped an estimated 25 percent of the Jews saved. See: Oliner and Oliner, *The Altruistic Personality*, p. 38. In the east of the country, entire communities were mobilized by local Protestant ministers; Johannes Houwink ten Cate and Bob Moore, "De Jodenvervolging door de Nazi's in de jaren 1940–1945," Cate and Moore, *Het geheime dagboek van Arnold Douwes*, p. 42.

21 Cate and Moore, *Het geheime dagboek van Arnold Douwes*, p. 42.

22 Federico Varese and Meir Yaish, "The Importance of Being Asked," *Rationality and Society*, Vol. 12, Issue 3 (2000), p. 328.

23 Oliner and Oliner, *The Altruistic Personality*, p. 115.

24 Varese and Yaish, "The Importance of Being Asked," p. 320.

25 Varese and Yaish, "The Importance of Being Asked," p. 319.

26 Varese and Yaish, "The Importance of Being Asked," p. 327.

27 Cass R. Sunstein, *How Change Happens*, MIT Press (2019).

28 That's what the *Morning Chronicle* reported on February 14, 1788, quoted in: Christopher Leslie Brown, *Moral Capital: Foundations*

of British Abolitionism, University of North Carolina Press (2006), p. 449.

29 She says this in the short documentary *The Courage to Care* (1985), directed by Robert H. Gardner.

30 Anton Howes, "The Relevance of Skills to Innovation During the British Industrial Revolution, 1547–1851," Brown University, unpublished manuscript (2017), p. 16.

31 Anton Howes, "How Innovation Accelerated in Britain 1651–1851," *Capitalism's Cradle*, tumblr-blog (21 April 2016). See also: Alex Bell et al., "Who Becomes an Inventor in America? The Importance of Exposure to Innovation," *The Quarterly Journal of Economics*, Vol. 134, Issue 2 (2019).

32 Also look at the way zeros like Arnold Douwes recruited people for the resistance. They couldn't ask everyone to take in and hide Jews of course — that was far too dangerous. There must have been some sort of selection mechanism, where potential helpers (consciously or unconsciously) somehow signaled that they could be trusted. Maybe they'd refused to do the Nazi salute at some point. Or maybe they'd pointed a German soldier in the wrong direction, like Douwes, with his "Keep going straight." In that sense, small acts of resistance could turn into something bigger, because once you did something small, you might just be asked to do more. See also: Varese and Yaish, "The Importance of Being Asked," p. 324.

33 Fogelman, *Conscience and Courage*, p. 65.

34 Oliner and Oliner, *The Altruistic Personality*, p. 50.

35 Quoted in: Stanley D. Levison, interview with James Mosby, Ralph J. Bunche Oral History Collection, Moorland-Spingarn Research Center, Howard University (14 February 1970).

36 Anne Applebaum, "History Will Judge the Complicit," *The Atlantic* (July/August 2020).

CHAPTER 3

1 The legal nerds may know what I'm referring to here: the legendary Cellar Hatch Ruling, from a landmark Dutch court case that established criteria for determining negligence and liability under civil law. Critical to the historic 2015 climate lawsuit, *Urgenda v. State of the Netherlands*, this precedent helped frame the argument that the Dutch government was negligent in failing to take sufficient

precautions against the severe and foreseeable risks of climate change. The case made headlines around the world, as the first successful climate lawsuit against a national government. It inspired similar cases in other countries, including Germany, Ireland, and France.

2   Mark Green, *Bright, Infinite Future: A Generational Memoir on the Progressive Rise*, St. Martin's Press (2016), p. 45.

3   Paul Sabin, *Public Citizens: The Attack on Big Government and the Remaking of American Liberalism*, W. W. Norton (2021), p. 25.

4   Mark Green, "How Ralph Nader Changed America," *The Nation* (1 December 2015). See also: Ralph Nader, "On Harvard Law School and Systems of Justice in America," YouTube (14 September 2015), from 6:35.

5   See: "FORTUNE 500: 1965 Full list," *CNN Money*.

6   Ralph Nader, *Unsafe at Any Speed: The Designed-In Dangers of the American Automobile*, Grossman (1965).

7   Sabin, *Public Citizens*, p. 31.

8   "On 50th Anniversary of Ralph Nader's *Unsafe at Any Speed*, Safety Group Reports Declining Death Rates Have Saved 3.5 Million Lives," Center for Auto Safety (1 December 2015).

9   Peter Thiel and Blake Masters, *Zero to One: Notes on Startups, or How to Build the Future*, Currency (2014), p. 124.

10 Belinda Luscombe, "Who's Afraid of Peter Thiel? A New Biography Suggests We All Should Be," *TIME* (21 September 2021).

11 Pink Dandelion, *The Quakers: A Very Short Introduction*, Oxford University Press (2008), p. 89.

12 Catie Gill, *Women in the Seventeenth-Century Quaker Community: A Literary Study of Political Identities, 1650–1700*, Routledge (2005).

13 Patricia Crawford, "Women's Published Writings 1600–1700," in Mary Prior (ed.), *Women in English Society 1500–1800*, Routledge (1985).

14 Harry Mount, "Egbert van Heemskerck's Quaker Meetings Revisited," *Journal of the Warburg and Courtauld Institutes*, Vol. 56 (1993), pp. 209–28.

15 Marcus Rediker, *The Fearless Benjamin Lay: The Quaker Dwarf Who Became the First Revolutionary Abolitionist*, Beacon Press (2017), p. 149.

16 Quoted in: Christopher Leslie Brown, *Moral Capital: Foundations of British Abolitionism*, University of North Carolina Press (2006), p. 399.

17 Maurice Jackson, *Let This Voice Be Heard: Anthony Benezet, Father of Atlantic Abolitionism*, University of Pennsylvania Press (2009), p. 154.

18 In 1775, England's abolitionist network was tiny. But Clarkson and Co. soon recruited the charismatic politician William Wilberforce as their voice in Parliament. Wilberforce was somewhat of a cultish figure, who lived in a commune in the town of Clapham along with a handful of other abolitionists (including the brilliant lawyer James Stephen). They had a communal garden and were welcome in one another's homes. Many marriages ensued. They were referred to in jest as the "Saints" at the time and later dubbed the "Clapham Sect."

19 Adam Hochschild, *Bury the Chains: The British Struggle to Abolish Slavery*, Houghton Mifflin (2005), p. 97.

20 Chaim D. Kaufmann and Robert A. Pape, "Explaining Costly International Moral Action: Britain's Sixty-Year Campaign against the Atlantic Slave Trade," *International Organization* (Fall 1999), pp. 631 and 634. See also: Christopher Leslie Brown, "Abolition of the Atlantic Slave Trade," in Gad Heuman and Trevor Burnard (eds), *The Routledge History of Slavery*, Routledge (2011), p. 292.

21 Yes, a cult leader like Elon Musk sparked a revolution in the auto industry and aerospace (that is, before taking over Twitter/X, spreading conspiracy theories, and joining forces with Donald Trump). But Peter Thiel acquired his fortune through online advertising, digital surveillance, and tax avoidance.

22 See Belinda Luscombe, "Who's afraid of Peter Thiel? A New Biography Suggests We All Should Be," *TIME* (21 September 2021). And Thiel has bankrolled the political career of JD Vance. See: "What J.D. Vance really believes: The dark worldview of Trump's choice for vice president, explained," *Vox* (July 2024).

23 Thomas Clarkson, *The History of the Rise, Progress and Accomplishment of the Abolition of the African Slave-Trade by the British Parliament: Volume I*, R. Taylor & Co. (1808), p. 571.

24 That's how the *New York Times* put it, in Patrick Anderson's "Ralph Nader, Crusader: Or, the Rise of a Self-Appointed Lobbyist," *New York Times Magazine* (29 October 1967).

25 For these five lessons of Nader's and the cited quotes, see: Justin Martin, *Nader: Crusader, Spoiler, Icon*, Perseus Publishing (2002), pp. 67–68, 92, 124 and 133.

26 Martin, *Nader: Crusader*, p. 70.

27 Sabin, *Public Citizens*, p. 11.

28 Sabin, *Public Citizens*, p. 74.

29 Martin, *Nader: Crusader*, p. 75.

30 Sabin, *Public Citizens*, p. 11.

31 *Christian Science Monitor* wrote this that same month (Sabin, *Public Citizens*, p. 40).

32 Jack Doyle, "Nader's Raiders, 1968–1974," *The Pop History Dig* (31 March 2013).

33 William Greider, "Law Students, FTC Tangle over Apathy," *Washington Post* (13 November 1968).

34 Sabin, *Public Citizens*, p. 87.

35 "Agencies: Up Against the Wall, FDA!" *TIME* (20 April 1970).

36 Jack Newfield, "Nader's Raiders: The Lone Ranger Gets a Posse," *Life* (3 October 1969).

37 See: "Conscientious Objector to Fashion," *Telegraph* (20 August 1991), p. 25. His socks and shoes were legendary. Nader purchased twelve pairs of the exact same shoes and four dozen sturdy cotton army socks on sale in 1959. He was still wearing them in the eighties.

38 Philip Shenon, "Nader, After 8 Years, Is Back on the Inside," *New York Times* (10 May 1989).

39 Julius Duscha, "Nader's Raiders Is Their Name, and Whistle-blowing Is Their Game . . . ," *New York Times* (21 March 1971).

40 Sabin, *Public Citizens*, p. 88.

41 Thomas A. Stewart and Darienne L. Dennis, "The Resurrection of Ralph Nader," *CNN Money* (22 May 1989).

42 Quoted in: *TIME*, Vol. 108, Issue 19 (1976), p. 41.

43 Martin, *Nader: Crusader*, p. 203. See also: Nicholas Lemann, "The Last Battle Over Big Business," *New Yorker* (31 May 2021).

44 Michael Greenstone, "The Connection Between Cleaner Air and Longer Lives," *New York Times* (24 September 2015).

45 She said this in the documentary *An Unreasonable Man* (2006), directed by Henriette Mantel and Steve Skrovan (about forty-one minutes in).

46 Sabin, *Public Citizens*, p. 115.

47 Karen Aptakin, "Good Works: A Guide to Social Change Careers," Center for Study of Responsive Law (1980). See also: James T. Yenckel, "CAREERS: Guide to Good Works," *Washington Post* (20 May 1980).

48 Sabin, *Public Citizens*, p. 163.

49 Nader, "On Harvard Law School and Systems of Justice in America," YouTube (14 September 2015), from 17:20.

50 "An Open Letter To Ralph Nader," *https://web.archive.org/web /20010415013029/http://www.nadersraidersforgore.com/printversion .htm*. This letter is accessible on the Wayback Machine.

51 Lisa Chamberlain, "The Dark Side of Ralph Nader," *Salon* (1 July 2004).

CHAPTER 4

1 That was my suggestion as well — too simplistic, I'm afraid — in the final chapter of an earlier book of mine. See: Rutger Bregman, *Utopia for Realists*, Little, Brown and Company (2017).

2 Quoted in: Juan Williams, *Eyes on the Prize: America's Civil Rights Years, 1954–1965*, Penguin Books (2002), p. 66.

3 Jeanne Theoharis, *The Rebellious Life of Mrs. Rosa Parks*, Beacon Press (2013), p. 37.

4 Paul Hendrickson, "The Ladies Before Rosa: Let Us Now Praise Unfamous Women," *Rhetoric and Public Affairs*, Vol. 8, Issue 2 (2005).

5 Rufus Burrow Jr., *Extremist for Love: Martin Luther King Jr., Man of Ideas and Nonviolent Social Action*, Fortress Press (2014), p. 179.

6 Jo Ann Robinson, *The Montgomery Bus Boycott and the Women Who Started It: The Memoir of Jo Ann Gibson Robinson*, University of Tennessee Press (1987).

7 Theoharis, *The Rebellious Life*, pp. 83–84.

8 The Civil Rights Act of 1957, the Civil Rights Act of 1960, the Civil Rights Act of 1964, the Voting Rights Act of 1965 and the Civil Rights Act of 1968 (also called the Fair Housing Act).

9 Irene Eckler, *A Family Torn Apart by "Rassenschande": Political Persecution in the Third Reich*, Horneburg Verlag (1998), p. 41.

10 As far as flying goes, there's a clear link between climate awareness and the *resolve* to fly less. However: "We find no direct link between climate awareness and the actual number of flights taken," two Dutch researchers concluded in 2023. See: Toon Zijlstra and Gabrielle Uitbeijerse, "Klimaatbesef en minder vliegen?," Kennisinstituut voor Mobiliteitsbeleid (July 2023). As for giving to charity as prescribed by major religions, see the Book of Malachi in the Bible, Chapter 3, Verse 10; the Book of Deuteronomy in the Torah, Chapter 26, Verse 12; Volume 3, Book 8, Hadith 1790 of the Sunna. (The Sunna is the

collection of lessons from the Islamic prophet Muhammed. Holy for
Muslims, it is seen as a companion text to the Quran.)

11 Eitan Hersh, *Politics Is for Power: How to Move Beyond Political
Hobbyism, Take Action, and Make Real Change*, Scribner (2020).

12 Justin McCarthy: "Same-Sex Marriage Support Inches Up to New
High of 71%" Gallup (1 June 2022).

13 "Fact sheet: Public Opinion on Abortion," Pew Research Center
(13 May 2024).

14 David D. Kirkpatrick, "The Next Targets for the Group That
Overturned Roe," *New Yorker* (2 October 2023).

15 Larissa Hesketh-Rowe, "How Effective is Fair Trade?" *Giving What
We Can* (9 April 2015). See also: Nathan Nunn, "The Economics of
Fair Trade," *Reporter*, No. 2 (June 2019). This in-depth study into
fair-trade coffee in Costa Rica found that the largest and poorest
group in the sector — unskilled laborers — had literally zero benefits
from fair trade.

16 Sally McDonald et al., "Medical Donations Are Not Always Free: An
Assessment of Compliance of Medicine and Medical Device
Donations with World Health Organization Guidelines (2009–
2017)," *International Health*, Vol. 11, Issue 5 (2019).

17 Annika Stechemesser et al., "Climate Policies That Achieved Major
Emission Reductions: Global Evidence from Two Decades," *Science*
(22 August 2024).

18 David Anderson, "Proven Programs Are the Exception,
Not the Rule," *The GiveWell Blog* (18 December 2008). See
also: evidencebasedprograms.org.

19 Nurith Aizenman, "Why This Charity Isn't Afraid to Say It Failed,"
NPR (7 January 2019).

20 Matthew Feinberg and Robb Willer, "Moral Reframing: A Technique
for Effective and Persuasive Communication Across Political
Divides," *Social and Personality Psychology Compass*, Vol. 13, Issue 12
(2019).

21 Marcus Rediker, *The Slave Ship: A Human History*, Viking (2007),
p. 244.

22 Christopher Leslie Brown, "Little Ships of Horror," *Nation*
(17 January 2008).

23 John Bugg, "The Other Interesting Narrative: Olaudah Equiano's
Public Book Tour," *Publications of the Modern Language Association*
(October 2006), p. 1,424.

24 Bugg, "The Other Interesting Narrative," p. 1,436.

25 Olaudah Equiano, *The Interesting Narrative and Other Writings*, Penguin Classics (2003), p. 147. Originally published in 1789.

26 Equiano, *The Interesting Narrative*, p. 68.

27 Vincent Carretta, *Equiano, the African: Biography of a Self-Made Man*, University of Georgia Press (2005), p. xviii.

28 Ike Anya, "Fireworks fly at Equiano Conference," *Nigeriaworld.com* (28 March 2003).

29 It could be, for instance, that Equiano didn't dare give his true birthplace when asked as a child during the rite of baptism. For an excellent overview of the many arguments for and against, see: Brycchan Carey, "Where Was Olaudah Equiano Born? (And Why Does It Matter?)" *brycchancarey.com*.

30 Quoted in: Maartje Janse, " 'Holland as a Little England?' British Anti-Slavery Missionaries and Continental Abolitionist Movements in the Mid Nineteenth Century," *Past & Present*, Vol. 229, Issue 1 (2015), p. 140.

31 The painful truth is that there was never much of a Dutch anti-slavery movement to speak of. In 1842, abolitionists brought three separate petitions: from the Calvinists, from the liberals, and from a group of Rotterdam women. The last was the largest, but still had only 128 signatures. Compare that with the 1853 petition from the Dutch April movement against the Catholics, which 200,000 signed.

32 Quoted in: Maarten Kuitenbrouwer, "Nederlandse afschaffing van de slavernij in vergelijkend perspectief," *Bijdragen en Mededelingen betreffende de Geschiedenis der Nederlanden*, Vol. 93, No. 1 (1978), p. 86.

33 William Wilberforce, *A Practical View of Christianity*, Hendrickson (2011), Appendix I. Originally published in 1797.

34 Helen Lewis, *Difficult Women: A History of Feminism in 11 Fights*, Jonathan Cape (2020), p. 67.

35 And no, despite their success, the suffragettes didn't all become friends. On the contrary. Journalist Helen Lewis writes: "Even the suffragettes found the memory of their great triumph soured by personality clashes." See: Lewis, *Difficult Women*, p. 67.

36 Burrow, *Extremist for Love*, p. 182.

37 See: Ryan Grim, "Elephant in the Zoom," *Intercept* (14 June 2022).

38 Albert O. Hirschman, *The Rhetoric of Reaction: Perversity, Futility, Jeopardy*, Belknap Press (1991), p. 151.

39 Climate activist Naomi Klein argues for a "holistic vision for social and economic transformation." See: Naomi Klein, *On Fire: The (Burning) Case for a Green New Deal*, Simon & Schuster (2019).

40 Martin Luther King Jr., "Transformed Nonconformist," *A Gift of Love: Sermons From "Strength to Love" and Other Preachings*, Beacon Press (2012), p. 18.

41 Charles Stuart, *A Memoir of Granville Sharp*, The American Anti-slavery Society (1836), pp. 59–60.

42 Stuart, *A Memoir*, p. 56.

43 Clarkson, *The History of the Rise: Volume I* (1808), p. 236. The stone-cold reasoning was this: death rates in the Caribbean were soaring, so the colonies were dependent on the ongoing supply of newly enslaved people. If that stopped, then two things could happen. Either slavery would quite literally die out, or slaveholders would have to treat their slaves better. The latter choice, the abolitionists reasoned, would lay the basis for fully abolishing slavery.

44 Saul D. Alinsky, *Rules for Radicals: A Pragmatic Primer for Realistic Radicals*, Vintage Books (1989), p. xviii. Originally published in 1971.

45 Isabel Ortiz, Sara Burke, Mohamed Berrada, and Hernán Saenz Cortés, *World Protests: A Study of Key Protest Issues in the 21st Century*, Palgrave Macmillan (2022), pp. 13–15.

46 Vincent Bevins, *If We Burn: The Mass Protest Decade and the Missing Revolution*, PublicAffairs (2023).

47 Larry Buchanan, Quoctrung Bui, and Jugal K. Patel, "Black Lives Matter May Be the Largest Movement in U.S. History," *New York Times* (3 July 2020).

48 Zeynep Tufekci, "I Was Wrong About Why Protests Work," *New York Times* (21 July 2022).

49 Zeynep Tufekci, "Online Social Change: Easy to Organize, Hard to Win," TEDGlobal (2014).

50 John Blake, "What Did MLK Think about Gay People?" CNN (16 January 2012). This article can be accessed on the Wayback Machine.

51 Julian Bond, "Planning the March on Washington," interview with John Lewis in the series "Explorations in Black Leadership" at *blackleadership.virginia.edu*.

52 Zeynep Tufekci, "Do Protests Even Work?" *The Atlantic* (24 June 2020).

53 Carrie Blazina and Drew DeSilver, "A Record Number of Women Are Serving in the 117th Congress," Pew Research Center (15 January 2021).

54 Anna North, "The Women's Marches Are Shrinking. Their Influence Isn't," *vox.com* (17 January 2020).

55 Tufekci, "I Was Wrong."

56 See: *wegert-familie.de*.

57 King, "Transformed Nonconformist," p. 17.

1 Quoted in: Derek Thompson, "The Greatest Good," *The Atlantic* (15 June 2015).

2 *Being Terri* (2003), made by Ron Trickett.

3 "Terri's touched the world," *Ipswich Star* (26 February 2005).

4 Katy Weitz, " 'Every Day My Terri Inspires Me. I'm Lucky to Have Her': Amazing Bravery of the Baby Burned Alive," *People* (25 May 2003).

5 Dulcie Pearce, "I gave my baby 90 per cent burns . . . years on she has forgiven me," *Sun* (13 June 2012).

6 Armena Saleem, "Salute Our Bravest Kids: We Bring You the Amazing Stories of How Britain's Little Heroes Triumphed Over Tragedy," *People* (9 December 2001).

7 Thompson, "The Greatest Good."

8 "Little Girl Suffered 90% Burns. Charity Swim? Email Help?" *mumsnet.com* (4 July 2003).

9 "Swimming for Teri," *Richmond and Twickenham Times* (21 November 2003).

10 "Total Raised," *swimforterri.org*.

11 Denver Frederick, "The Against Malaria Foundation: Lessons from a Perennial Top-Rated Charity," *denver-frederick.com* (31 May 2021). See also: "History," *againstmalaria.com*.

12 See: Gwyneth Lewis, "Maternal Mortality in the Developing World: Why Do Mothers Really Die?" *Obstetric Medicine*, Vol. 1, Issue 1 (2008), p. 4; Jennifer Bryce et al., "WHO estimates of the causes of death in children," *Lancet*, Vol. 365, Issue 9465 (2005), pp. 1,150–1151; "Malaria: A Major Cause of Child Death and Poverty in Africa," UNICEF (October 2004), p. 1.

13 "World Malaria Report 2008," World Health Organization (2008), p. 18.

14 "World Malaria Report 2005," World Health Organization (18 November 2005).

15 Frederick, "The Against Malaria Foundation."

16 "AMA: Rob Mather, founder and CEO of the Against Malaria Foundation," *Effective Altruism Forum* (22 January 2020).

17 Quoted in: Alexandra Frean, "Bold Stroke in Malaria Battle," *The Times* (20 June 2005).

18 This was the Global Fund, which works to fight HIV/AIDS, tuberculosis, and malaria.

19 Rob Mather, "Against Malaria Foundation: What We Do | Rob Mather | EA Global: London 2018," YouTube (4 February 2019), from 6:30. See also: Rob Mather, "Against Malaria Foundation: What We Do, How We Do It, and the Challenges," *effectivealtruism.org*.

20 Frean, "Bold Stroke in Malaria Battle."

21 Mather, "Against Malaria Foundation: What We Do," YouTube from 39:35.

22 The organization is now an officially registered charity in seventeen countries, but there's no headquarters. To this day, Rob works out of his home in London. Less than 1 percent goes to overhead costs — the salaries of thirteen employees and some travel expenses — and all the rest can be used to buy mosquito nets, which are then distributed by local partners.

23 "Holden Karnofsky's 2013 Speech," Harvard Class of 2013 (2013).

24 Stephanie Strom, "2 Young Hedge-Fund Veterans Stir Up the World of Philanthropy," *New York Times* (20 December 2007).

25 And this estimate comes from 2020, when the AMF had raised some $250 million. As noted on p. 96, they've now raised well over twice that.

26 "Long-lasting Insecticidal Nets: Market and Supply Update," UNICEF Supply Division (October 2022), p. 1.

27 OK, as with just about every other famous historical quote, it looks like Bertrand Russell actually said something a little different — but the point stands! See: "It Is the Mark of a Truly Intelligent Person to Be Moved by Statistics," *Quote Investigator* (20 February 2013).

CHAPTER 6

1 Q: Why in Mongolia or Lebanon? A: Tobacco is subject to very low taxes in those countries, so you can save a huge number of lives if you manage to lobby a tobacco tax into existence there. See: Ariuntuya Tuvdendorj et al., "Reducing the Burden of Disease Through Tobacco Taxes in Mongolia: A Health Impact Analysis Using a Dynamic Public Health Model," *Nicotine & Tobacco Research*, Vol. 24, Issue 2 (2022); and "Tobacco Tax: Lebanon," World Health Organization (2020).

2 On the contrary, most charities aren't set up to help as many people and animals as possible. Most focus on issues that already get a lot of attention from other organizations, like sick people in the world's richest countries or the suffering of cute and fuzzy animals, like dogs and cats.

3 The standard program lasts two months, but many students stay on and work from the Kilburn Lane location once they set up their charity.

4 Hannah Ritchie, "Around One-in-three Children Globally Suffer from Lead Poisoning: What Can We Do to Reduce This?" Our World in Data (25 January 2022).

5 "Update on the Global Status of Legal Limits on Lead in Paint," United Nations Environment Programme (March 2023).

6 See: James Hu, "How Cost-Effective Is LEEP's Malawi Program?" *leadelimination.org* (13 January 2022). Independent researchers have calculated that LEEP can prevent one case of lead exposure for as little as $1.66, making it one of the most cost-effective charities in the world. See: Tom Barnes, "Lead Exposure Elimination Project (LEEP)," Founders Pledge (8 August 2022).

7 "Investing in Sexual and Reproductive Health in Low- and Middle-Income Countries," Guttmacher Institute (July 2020).

8 Elizabeth A. Sully et al., "Adding It Up: Investing in Sexual and Reproductive Health 2019," Guttmacher Institute (July 2020).

9 "Family Empowerment Media," Charity Entrepreneurship.

10 This was Ben Williamson of the Maternal Health Initiative, a program that ran through 2023.

11 "What it really takes to found a high impact charity | Joey Savoie | EA Global: London 2021," YouTube (15 December 2021), from 37:33.

12 "Good Enough Teeth — Why Gum is More Important Than Flossing," YouTube (21 June 2021).

13 One of the books Joey read at the time was *The Bully, the Bullied & the Bystander* (2003) by Barbara Coloroso.

14 See also this review of the literature: Sharon Padgett and Charles E. Notar, "Bystanders Are the Key to Stopping Bullying," *Universal Journal of Educational Research*, Vol. 1, Issue 2 (2013).

15 See: "Where are you on the global pay scale?" *BBC* (29 March 2012).

16 GiveWell was looking for new, highly effective charities. See: "Charities we'd like to see," *GiveWell Blog* (15 October 2015).

17 "A High-level Review of Our Thoughts on Interventions," Charity Entrepreneurship (7 March 2016).

18 "Immunization Coverage," World Health Organization (14 July 2022).

19 Lawrence D. Frenkel, "The Global Burden of Vaccine-preventable Infectious Diseases in Children Less than 5 years of Age: Implications for Covid-19 Vaccination. How Can We Do Better?" *Allergy and Asthma Proceedings*, Vol. 42, Issue 4 (September 2021).

20 "Fortify Health," Charity Entrepreneurship.

21 What's more, the cofounder of Fortify Health, Nikita Patel, in turn inspired her friend Lucia Coulter, who went on to start the Lead Exposure Elimination Project.

22 While getting a cup of coffee that afternoon, one of the researchers told me he'd recently finished a report on *kangaroo care*, a simple method of skin-to-skin contact that can be lifesaving for hundreds of thousands of premature babies. "In a matter of weeks, one of the students founded the kangaroo care organization," the researcher said. "That's a level of impact most academics can only dream of."

23 Abhijit Banerjee et al., "Selecting the Most Effective Nudge: Evidence from a Large-Scale Experiment on Immunization," NBER Working Paper 28726 (April 2021).

24 See: Robert Wiblin and Keiran Harris, "Varsha Venugopal on Using Gossip to Help Vaccinate Every Child in India," *The 80,000 Hours Podcast* (18 October 2021).

25 Source: the author's correspondence with Joey Savoie.

26 One example of such a network is scouting, which got its start in 1907 with a week-long camp for twenty boys on an island in the

south of England. That little summer camp grew into the worldwide
network of Boy and Girl Scouts we know today.

CHAPTER 7

1 Max Roser, "Mortality in the Past: Every Second Child Died," Our
World in Data (November 2024).

2 Kathryn Warner, "Edward II's Brothers and Sisters," *Blogspot*
(10 April 2014).

3 Olivia Blair, "So Who Really Was Queen Anne? The Truth
About *The Favourite*'s Forgotten Monarch," *Harper's Bazaar*
(8 February 2019).

4 Roser, "Mortality in the Past."

5 Max Roser, "Extreme Poverty: How Far Have We Come, How Far
Do We Still Have to Go?" Our World in Data (27 August 2023).

6 Max Roser and Hannah Ritchie, "Optimism and Pessimism," Our
World in Data (27 July 2018).

7 Roser and Ritchie, "Optimism and Pessimism."

8 Jason Crawford, "Why Haven't We Celebrated Any Major
Achievements Lately?" The Roots of Progress (17 August 2020).

9 "The Polio Crusade," *pbs.org* (7 December 2022). See also: Nancy
deWolf Smith, "In a Time of Plague," *Wall Street Journal*
(30 January 2009).

10 Gilbert King, "Salk, Sabin and the Race Against Polio," *Smithsonian
Magazine* (3 April 2012).

11 Richard Carter, *Breakthrough: The Saga of Jonas Salk*, Trident Press
(1965), p. 1.

12 David M. Oshinsky, *Polio: An American Story*, Oxford University
Press (2005), pp. 214–215.

13 Oshinsky, *Polio*, p. 211.

14 Donald Henderson, "Smallpox Eradication: A Cold War Victory,"
World Health Forum, Vol. 19, Issue 2 (1998). See also: Karen Kruse
Thomas, "40 Years in a Post-Smallpox World," John Hopkins
(8 May 2020).

15 Gordon Irlam, "In praise of Viktor Zhdanov," *80,000 Hours Blog*
(23 February 2012).

16 "William, Duke of Gloucester (1689–1700)," Royal Collection Trust.

17 D. A. Henderson and Petra Klepac, "Lessons from the Eradication
of Smallpox: An Interview With D. A. Henderson," *Philosophical*

Transactions of the Royal Society B: Biological Sciences, Vol. 368, Issue 1623 (2013).

18 Ann Marie Nelson, "The Cost of Disease Eradication: Smallpox and Bovine Tuberculosis," *Annals of the New York Academy of Sciences*, Vol. 894, Issue 1 (1999).

19 A. G. Bukrinskaya, *Viktor Zhdanov — My Husband: Elena Tatulova's Diary* (1996), p. 38.

20 Bukrinskaya, *Viktor Zhdanov*, p. 23.

21 Ross Pomeroy, "Has Malaria Really Killed Half of Everyone Who Ever Lived?," *RealClearScience* (3 October 2019).

22 Nobuko Yoshida et al., "Hybridoma Produces Protective Antibodies Directed Against the Sporozoite Stage of Malaria Parasite," *Science*, Vol. 207, Issue 4426 (1980).

23 Kalifa A. Bojang et al., "Efficacy of RTS,S/AS02 Malaria Vaccine Against Plasmodium Falciparum Infection in Semi-immune Adult Men in The Gambia: A Randomised Trial," *The Lancet*, Vol. 358, Issue 9297 (2001).

24 I'm talking here about research into the vaccine, not all research on malaria. See: Jeffrey Sachs, "Sachs on development: Helping the world's poorest," *Economist* (12 August 1999).

25 This is calculated per casualty for each disease. And then I'm talking about all malaria research, which in 1993 amounted to some $84 million. See: J. Anderson, M. MacLean, and C. Davies, *Malaria Research: An Audit of International Activity*, Unit for Policy Research in Science and Medicine (1996), p. 29.

26 Pratik Pawar, "Why Did It Take 35 Years to Get a Malaria Vaccine?" *Smithsonian Magazine* (2 June 2022). See also: Saloni Dattani, Rachel Glennerster, and Siddhartha Haria, "Why we didn't get a malaria vaccine sooner," *Works in Progress* (7 September 2023).

27 This estimate was made at my request by researcher Bobby Vos, on the basis of data from the WHO. See, for example: "World malaria report 2022," World Health Organization (8 December 2022).

28 "War-torn Somalia eradicates polio," *bbc.co.uk* (25 March 2008).

29 Quoted in: Louise Dawson, "How the bicycle became a symbol of women's emancipation," *Guardian* (4 November 2011).

30 Quoted in: Adrienne LaFrance, "How the Bicycle Paved the Way for Women's Rights," *The Atlantic* (26 June 2014).

31 I'll admit, the origin of her fascination is slightly decadent. After one of her dinner parties, the well-to-do Cochrane saw that her best

dishes were chipped. She suspected that her servants had been a little rough washing her heirloom china, and swore she'd do the dishes herself from then on. But that didn't go so well. Rinsing, sudsing, scrubbing, drying — as your fingers got wrinkly and your hands chapped — it turned out to be more work than she'd bargained for. And so Cochrane decided she'd get rid of the onerous task once and for all. A few years later, she went to the Chicago World's Fair. Here, you could admire the greatest inventions of the day, like the telegraph, the phonograph, and Josephine Cochrane's dishwashing machine. Visitors gawked at the bizarre contraption with its gears, belts, and pulleys, amazed you could put 200 dirty dishes in and then two minutes later, take 200 clean ones out. See: Julie M. Fenster, "The Woman Who Invented The Dishwasher," *Invention & Technology*, Vol. 15, Issue 2 (1999).

32 Okay, a few men did try. Both Joel Houghton (in 1850) and L. A. Alexander (in 1865) had developed a prototype for a dishwasher, but neither design proved particularly successful. What set Cochrane apart from her predecessors was that she developed a machine designed to clean dishes with water pressure instead of brushes. Today's dishwashers are still based on that idea. See: Jocelyn Ram and Eric Atkisson, " 'I'll do it myself,' " United States Patent and Trademark Office (16 October 2019); Mary Ellen Snodgrass, *Encyclopedia of Kitchen History*, Fitzroy Dearborn (2004), p. 320.

33 Ram and Atkisson, " 'I'll do it.' "

34 Ram and Atkisson, " 'I'll do it.' " Some authors argue that these new technologies haven't won women much time, in part because of higher standards for cleanliness and neatness today. (We wash our clothes more frequently than a hundred years ago.) But empirical studies (based on diaries women were asked to keep, recording their work hour by hour) show that women today still devote far less time to cleaning, washing, and cooking. If that doesn't seem to be the case, one contributing factor may be that since the 1970s, the time women (and men too) spend on two other "household" tasks has only gone up: doing the shopping and caring for children. See: Jonathan Gershuny and Teresa Attracta Harms, "Housework Now Takes Much Less Time: 85 Years of U.S. Rural Women's Time Use," *Social Forces*, Vol. 95, Issue 2 (2016).

35 The figures here are for the average homemaker, including any domestic help. See: Jeremy Greenwood, Ananth Seshadri, and

Mehmet Yorukoglu, "Engines of Liberation," *The Review of Economic Studies*, Vol. 72, Issue 1 (2005), p. 113.

36 Helen Lewis, "The next battleground for feminism is simple: women's time," *penguin.co.uk* (3 March 2020).

37 Alexandra M. Lord, "The Revolutionary 1965 Supreme Court Decision That Declared Sex a Private Affair," *Smithsonian Magazine* (19 May 2022).

38 J. A. H. Heine, *Consensuspolitiek in Nederland: Een studie naar de politieke besluitvormingscultuur in de tweede helft van de twintigste eeuw*, doctoral dissertation, Leiden University (2019), Chapter 11.

39 Genevieve Wanucha, "A Mind of Her Own," MIT *Technology Review* (22 February 2011).

40 Jonathan Eig, *The Birth of the Pill: How Four Crusaders Reinvented Sex and Launched a Revolution*, W. W. Norton (2014), p. 96.

41 David Halberstam, *The Fifties*, Villard Books (1993), p. 289.

42 Eig, *The Birth of the Pill*, p. 61.

43 Suzanne White Junod, "FDA's Approval of the First Oral Contraceptive, Enovid," U.S. Food and Drug Administration (1998).

44 Hannah Ritchie, Pablo Rosado, and Max Roser, "Meat and Dairy Production," Our World in Data (August 2017).

45 Quoted in: Kat Eschner, "Winston Churchill Imagined the Lab-Grown Hamburger," *Smithsonian Magazine* (1 December 2017).

46 "Singapore approves sale of lab-grown chicken nuggets in world first," ABC *News* (2 December 2020).

47 That's from the Dutch title of an excellent book by Roanne van Voorst: *Ooit aten we dieren* (2019). See also: Rutger Bregman and Jesse Frederik, "Kijken we straks terug op het eten van dieren zoals we nu terugkijken op het verbranden van heksen?" *De Correspondent* (27 March 2021).

48 "Josh Balk," *Viva!*

49 "Why Does Wikipedia Work?" NPR (12 July 2013).

50 Vaclav Smil, *How the World Really Works: A Scientist's Guide to Our Past, Present and Future*, Penguin Books (2022), p. 19.

51 Steven Pinker, *Enlightenment Now: The Case for Reason, Science, Humanism, and Progress*, Penguin Random House (2019), p. 149.

52 J. Storrs Hall, *Where Is My Flying Car?* Stripe Press (2021), Chapter 18.

53 "From Benjamin Franklin to Joseph Priestley, 8 February 1780," National Archives and Records Administration.

54 Tom Wilson, "Fusion energy breakthrough by U.S. scientists boosts clean power hopes," *Financial Times* (11 December 2022).

55 See: "I'd Put My Money on the Sun and Solar Energy," *Quote Investigator* (9 August 2015).

56 Max Roser, "Why did renewables become so cheap so fast?" Our World in Data (1 December 2020).

57 "Vast Power of the Sun Is Tapped By Battery Using Sand Ingredient: NEW BATTERY TAPS SUN'S VAST POWER," *New York Times* (26 April 1954).

58 Quoted in: Linda Botts, *Loose Talk: The Book of Quotes*, Rolling Stone Press (1980), p. 7.

59 Thomas L. Friedman, "Revolutionary Changes For Solar Field," *New York Times* (18 August 1981).

60 "Das Green Old Deal," NPR (17 January 2020).

61 Evident from BP's data, which they share at *www.energyinst.org*. See also: Jesse Frederik, "De klimaatactivist, de zakenbankier, de wetenschapper: voor de groene revolutie zijn ze állemaal nodig," *De Correspondent* (23 May 2023).

62 Shi Zhengrong, "Suntech's Founder Dr. Shi on Leaving His Post and the Future of PV," *Greentech Media* (23 August 2012).

63 For more on Martin Green, Shi Zhengrong, and Hans-Josef Fell, see also this fascinating book on the history of solar energy: Gregory F. Nemet, *How Solar Energy Became Cheap: A Model for Low-Carbon Innovation*, Routledge (2019).

64 See also: Ezra Klein, "The Dystopia We Fear Is Keeping Us From the Utopia We Deserve," *New York Times* (8 January 2023).

65 Daron Acemoglu and Simon Johnson, *Power and Progress: Our Thousand Year Struggle Over Technology and Prosperity*, Basic Books (2023), p. 5.

CHAPTER 8

1 Here's an interesting article on this phenomenon: Jay Bhattacharya and Mikko Packalen, "Stagnation and Scientific Incentives," NBER working paper 26752 (February 2020).

2 The last one comes from the essay "On Denoting" by philosopher Bertrand Russell. The philosophical question is: Is the sentence true? The assertion can't be true, because France doesn't have a king. But if the assertion is false, then that means its negation ("The present

king of France *isn't* bald") must be true, right? But that doesn't seem to be true either. So does that mean the assertion is neither true nor false? Analytic philosophers could discuss such matters incessantly.

3   Peter Singer, "From Moral Neutrality to Effective Altruism: The Changing Scope and Significance of Moral Philosophy," The Tanner Lectures on Human Values (2015).

4   "Malcolm X: Oxford University Union Debate in 1964," *blackhistorymonth.org.uk*.

5   Singer wrote the article in November 1971; it was published the next year. Peter Singer, "Famine, Affluence, and Morality," *Philosophy and Public Affairs*, Vol. 1, Issue 3 (1972), p. 230.

6   Chris Gardner, "Spielberg Trading Up to 300-Foot Yacht," *The Hollywood Reporter* (7 August 2015).

7   On the website *givingwhatwecan.org* you'll find a calculator that can indicate, based on economics research, how rich you are in comparison to all the other people in the world.

8   Fyodor Dostoevsky, *Crime and Punishment*, P. F. Collier & Son (1917), p. 27. The Russian original came out in 1866.

9   Joe Myers, "These charts show the growing income inequality between the world's richest and poorest," World Economic Forum (10 December 2021).

10 See for instance: "Population growth rate vs child mortality rate, 2021," Our World in Data; "Will saving poor children lead to overpopulation?" *gapminder.org*.

11 "Levels and Trends in Child Malnutrition," World Health Organization (31 March 2020).

12 Keith Payne, "Why Is the Death of One Million a Statistic?" *Psychology Today* (14 March 2010).

13 "A Single Death Is a Tragedy; A Million Deaths Is a Statistic," *Quote Investigator* (21 May 2010).

14 Eric Schwitzgebel and Joshua Rust, "The moral behavior of ethics professors: Relationships among self-reported behavior, expressed normative attitude, and directly observed behavior," *Philosophical Psychology*, Vol. 27, Issue 3 (2014).

15 Eric Schwitzgebel, "Cheeseburger ethics," *Aeon* (14 July 2015).

16 Singer, "Famine, Affluence, and Morality," p. 242.

17 Quoted in: Shankar Vedantam et al., "Justifying The Means: What It Means To Treat All Suffering Equally," *Hidden Brain* podcast (1 June 2020), from 20:09.

18 Quoted in: Susanna Rustin, "The Saturday interview. Toby Ord and Bernadette Young on the joy of giving," *Guardian* (24 December 2011).

19 His name at the time was officially William Crouch. He would later take the surname of his wife, Amanda MacAskill. The two are now divorced, but William decided to keep the name.

20 You can sign the following pledge on the Giving What We Can website: "I recognize that I can use part of my income to do a significant amount of good. Since I can live well enough on a smaller income, I pledge that I shall give at least 10% of what I earn to whichever organizations can most effectively use it to improve the lives of others, now and in the years to come. I make this pledge freely, openly, and sincerely." Your name is then added to the public list of all the people who have pledged to give. You might think, *Do you really have to parade your generosity about?* Of course it's good to be modest, but it's also important to inspire others — behavior is contagious, after all. Plus it's easier to stick to your plans and principles if you've shared them with other people.

21 Lucius Caviola, Stefan Schubert, and Joshua D. Greene, "The Psychology of (In)Effective Altruism," *Trends in Cognitive Sciences*, Vol. 25, Issue 7 (July 2021).

22 Lucius Caviola et al., "Donors vastly underestimate differences in charities' effectiveness," *Judgment and Decision Making*, Vol. 15, Issue 4 (2020).

23 Dean T. Jamison et al. (eds), *Disease Control Priorities in Developing Countries: Second Edition*, World Bank and Oxford University Press (2006).

24 Benjamin Todd, "How much do solutions to social problems differ in their effectiveness? A collection of all the studies we could find," *80,000 Hours Blog* (14 February 2023).

25 Toby Ord, "The Moral Imperative toward Cost-Effectiveness in Global Health," Center for Global Development (8 March 2013).

26 A QALY (*quality-adjusted life year*) means one additional healthy year. A DALY (*disability-adjusted life year*) means one healthy year lost. A LAYS (*learning-adjusted years of schooling*) means one year of good schooling. QALYs, DALYs, and LAYS are units used to compare the cost-effectiveness of public health interventions.

27 Melanie Hansen, "Average Cost of Food per Month for a College Student," *educationdata.org* (10 August 2024).

28 FEMA, "Benefit-Cost Analysis Sustainment and Enhancements: Standard Economic Value Methodology Report, Version 12.0" (May 2023), p. 17.

29 Emi Suzuki and Haruna Kashiwase, "New UN estimates show 14,000 children die and 5,000 babies are stillborn every day mostly of preventable causes," *World Bank Blogs* (9 January 2023).

30 This was Julia Wise, who grew to have a more joyous take on giving (and ice cream). See: Julia Wise, "Cheerfully," *givinggladly.com* (8 June 2013) and "Live it up," *jdwise.blogspot.com* (January 2011).

31 Quoted in: Josh Lowe, "Being Superman," *Prospect Magazine* (15 May 2013). See also: Dylan Matthews, "Join Wall Street. Save the world," *Washington Post* (31 May 2013).

32 A philosopher colleague quipped that if Peter Singer was logically consistent, he'd let the kid drown in the pond, then sell his mint-condition shoes, and donate the proceeds. (Although a true effective altruist would only do that if they could get more than $5,000 for the shoes, so you could save more than one life with the money. And for that matter, a real effective altruist would of course never have bought such expensive shoes in the first place.)

33 Justin Sandefur, "How Economists Got Africa's AIDS Epidemic Wrong," *cgdev.com* (31 May 2023).

34 Eric Levitz, "Is Effective Altruism to Blame for Sam Bankman-Fried?" *New York Intelligencer* (16 November 2022).

35 Quoted in: Kelsey Ables, "The enduring appeal of remote Pacific islands for rich apocalypse preppers," *Washington Post* (26 July 2023). See also: Michael Lewis, *Going Infinite: The Rise and Fall of a New Tycoon*, Allen Lane (2023), pp. 187–91.

36 As early as 2015, a few years before the movement went off the rails, a young Oxford philosopher, Amia Srinivasan, wrote that "effective altruism doesn't try to understand how power works, except to better align itself with it." EA doesn't provide any radical social criticism, she wrote, and "in this sense, it leaves everything just as it is." Amia Srinivasan, "Stop the Robot Apocalypse," *London Review of Books*, Vol. 37, Issue 18 (24 September 2015).

37 "GiveWell Responds on Global Health and Effective Altruism," *Wall Street Journal* (2 August 2022).

38 Most EAs now emphasize there are many ways to do good — as civil servant, scientist, lobbyist, activist, and so on. The question is always: what can you, with your particular skills and talents, best spend your time on? As I wrote in Chapter 1, a full-time career consists of some 80,000 hours, and each hour you've spent is gone forever. More than money, the time you have left on this earth is

your most precious possession. (One EA organization is called 80,000 Hours and gives free career advice to aspiring world-changers.)

39 James Ozden, "Effective Altruism: Not as bad as you think," *Understanding Social Change*, Substack newsletter (24 November 2022).

40 In fact the school's director, Joey Savoie, was one of Toby Ord and William MacAskill's first hires at their nonprofit Giving What We Can.

41 Jacy Reese, *The End of Animal Farming: How Scientists, Entrepreneurs, and Activists Are Building an Animal-Free Food System*, Beacon Press (2018), pp. 135–136.

42 Quoted in: Jenna Goudreau, "Dustin Moskovitz, The Second-Youngest Billionaire In America, Discusses What It Feels Like To Be Filthy Rich," *Business Insider* (1 October 2014).

43 Ralph Nader (2020), "What it takes to create social change against all odds," *ted.com*, from 18:21.

44 *Harper's Magazine*, Issue 142 (February 1921), p. 397. Quoted in: Gloria Garrett Samson, *The American Fund for Public Service: Charles Garland and Radical Philanthropy, 1922–1941*, Greenwood Press (1996), p. 1.

45 Garland emphasized that he wasn't a socialist and that he hadn't come to his remarkable way of thinking during his time at Harvard ("a university that," according to him, "turns out hypocrites"). He simply wanted to be a good Christian, he said, and Jesus hadn't accepted a million bucks either, had he? See: Dick Cowen, *The Garland Book*, unpublished manuscript, Yale Law School, Lillian Goldman Law Library (undated), p. 64, p. 80, p. 93 (for Randolph's quote), and p. 74 (for Sinclair's).

46 James Weldon Johnson, *Along This Way*, Viking Press (1968), p. 386. Originally published in 1933.

47 Cowen, *The Garland Book*, p. 10.

48 Cowen, *The Garland Book*, p. 17.

49 Megan Ming Francis, "The Price of Civil Rights: Black Lives, White Funding, and Movement Capture," *Law and Society Review*, Vol. 53, Issue 1 (29 January 2019), p. 300. This historian makes the case that support from the Garland Fund meant "movement capture" by white philanthropists, and that the NAACP, which initially focused on the fight to stop the lynching of Black Americans, was influenced by the fund to shift its attention to education. Another historian asserts

the opposite was true: the NAACP used the Garland Fund for its own purposes. For more on this fascinating debate, see: Megan Ming Francis and John Fabian Witt, "Movement Capture or Movement Strategy? A Critical Race History Exchange on the Beginnings of *Brown v. Board*," *Yale Journal of Law and the Humanities* (9 July 2020).

CHAPTER 9

1   William Snelgrave, *A new account of Guinea, and the slave-trade*, J. Wren (1754), Preface. Originally published in 1734 under the title, *A New Account Of Some Parts Of Guinea, and The Slave Trade*.

2   Adam Hochschild, *Bury the Chains: The British Struggle to Abolish Slavery*, Houghton Mifflin (2005), p. 2.

3   The main source for this paragraph is also Hochschild's *Bury the Chains*. See p. 51 (on the silver padlocks), p. 118 (on the *speculum oris*), and p. 34 (on the enslaved being named after emperors).

4   James Boswell, *The Life of Samuel Johnson*, Encyclopedia Britannica (1952), p. 364. Originally published in 1791.

5   Quoted in: Board of Trade, Report of the Lords of the Committee of Council, Volume I (London, 1789) and Thomas Clarkson, *The History of the Rise, Progress and Accomplishment of the Abolition of the African Slave-Trade by the British Parliament: Volume I*, R. Taylor & Co. (1808), p. 536.

6   Quoted in: Pauline Kleingeld, "Kant's Second Thoughts on Colonialism," *Kant and Colonialism: Historical and Critical Perspectives*, Oxford University Press (2014), p. 51.

7   Jill Lepore, *These Truths: A History of the United States*, W. W. Norton & Company (2019), p. 120.

8   "Thomas Jefferson and Sally Hemings. A Brief Account", *monticello.org*.

9   John Locke, *Two Treatises of Government*, Cambridge University Press (1988), p. 141.

10 Hochschild, *Bury the Chains*, p. 87.

11 Hochschild, *Bury the Chains*, p. 87.

12 Evan G. Williams, "The Possibility of an Ongoing Moral Catastrophe," *Ethical Theory and Moral Practice*, Vol. 18 (2015).

13 Quoted in: Albert James Williams-Myers, *Destructive Impulses: An Examination of an American Secret in Race Relations*, University Press of America (1995), p. 58.

14 Robert P. George (@McCormickProf), Twitter (2 July 2020).

15 Kwame Anthony Appiah, "What Will Future Generations Condemn Us For?" *Washington Post* (26 September 2010).

16 Melanie Joy, *Why We Love Dogs, Eat Pigs and Wear Cows*, Red Wheel (2020), pp. 96–100.

17 Kristine R. Ehrich and Julie R. Irwin, "Willful Ignorance in the Request for Product Attribute Information," *Journal of Marketing Research*, Vol. 42, Issue 3 (August 2005).

18 Bridget Cotter, "Mary Wollstonecraft: An Introduction to the Mother of First-wave Feminism," *Conversation* (7 March 2023).

19 Bee Rowlatt, "The Original Suffragette: The Extraordinary Mary Wollstonecraft," *Guardian* (5 October 2015).

20 Something similar happened to Martin Luther King. MLK Day is now a national holiday in the U.S., but in the 1960s, most Americans didn't like him. A few months before he was assassinated in 1968, his popularity hit a low point — nearly 75 percent of the American public disapproved of him (and especially his stance on the war in Vietnam). See: James C. Cobb, "Even Though He Is Revered Today, MLK Was Widely Disliked by the American Public When He Was Killed," *Smithsonian Magazine* (4 April 2018).

21 Mignon McLaughlin, *The Neurotic's Notebook*, The Bobbs-Merrill Company (1963), p. 72.

22 Kristina DuRocher, *Raising Racists: The Socialization of White Children in the Jim Crow South*, University Press of Kentucky (2011), pp. 23–24.

23 Francisco Barba, Lieven Huybregts, and Jef Leroy, "Estimating the Burden of Child Acute Malnutrition Accurately," International Food Policy Research Institute (3 December 2020).

24 Jurriën Hamer, *Waarom schurken pech hebben en helden geluk: Een nieuwe filosofie van de vrije wil*, De Bezige Bij (2021). See also: Robert Sapolsky, *Determined: A Science of Life without Free Will*, Penguin Press (2023).

25 "Per capita meat consumption by type, 1961 to 2020," Our World in Data.

26 Hannah Ritchie, Pablo Rosado, and Max Roser, "Meat and Dairy Production," Our World in Data (August 2017); Toshiko Kaneda and Carl Haub, "How Many People Have Ever Lived on Earth?" Population Reference Bureau (15 November 2022).

27 "Majority Say They Would Shop Differently If Facts Made Known," Vegan FTA (19 January 2022).

28 Joe Loria, "Shocking: New Study Finds Public Knows Nothing About Factory Farming," Mercy for Animals (18 November 2016).

29 Frederieke Schouten, "Onderzoek: meeste Nederlanders weten weinig over lot kalfjes uit de zuivelindustrie," *Dier&Recht* (30 May 2022).

30 Amalia Zimmerman, "Sentience Institute Survey Analysis," Animal Charity Evaluators (28 June 2018).

31 Laura van Heck et al., "Wat vindt Nederland van de Eiwittransitie? De toekomst van de veehouderij," *Kieskompas*, study commissioned by ProVeg (January 2022).

32 Anthony Bourdain, *Kitchen Confidential: Adventures in the Culinary Underbelly*, Bloomsbury (2000), p. 101.

33 Cara C. MacInnis and Gordon Hodson, "It Ain't Easy Eating Greens: Evidence of Bias Toward Vegetarians and Vegans from Both Source and Target," *Group Processes & Intergroup Relations*, Vol. 20, Issue 6 (2015), p. 6.

34 Erin R. Hahn, Meghan Gillogly, and Bailey E. Bradford, "Children Are Unsuspecting Meat Eaters: An Opportunity to Address Climate Change," *Journal of Environmental Psychology*, Vol. 78 (2021), pp. 4–5.

35 Matti Wilks et al., "Children Prioritize Humans Over Animals Less Than Adults Do," *Psychological Science*, Vol. 32, Issue 1 (2021).

36 Hahn, Gillogly, and Bradford, "Children Are Unsuspecting Meat Eaters," p. 2.

37 Watch " 'I Won't Eat Animals,' Girl Tells Her Mother" on YouTube, one of my favorite videos illustrating this point.

38 Marcus Rediker, *The Fearless Benjamin Lay: The Quaker Dwarf Who Became the First Revolutionary Abolitionist*, Beacon Press (2017), p. 115.

39 Maurice Jackson, *Let This Voice Be Heard: Anthony Benezet, Father of Atlantic Abolitionism*, University of Pennsylvania Press (2009), p. 19.

40 The Royal Society for the Prevention of Cruelty to Animals (RSPCA) was founded in London in 1824. See: "The Story of the RSPCA," RSPCA. And for Heyrick's story, see: Julia L. Holcomb, "I Am a Man, Your Brother: Elizabeth Heyrick, Abstention, and Immediatism," *Moral Commerce: Quakers and the Transatlantic Boycott of the Slave Labor Economy*, Cornell University Press (2016).

41 Nick J. Booth, "Bentham the feminist?" *UCL Culture Blog*
    (3 March 2016).

42 Jeremy Bentham, "Offences Against One's Self: Paederesty Part 1,"
    Journal of Homosexuality, Vol. 3, Issue 4 (1978). Bentham wrote this
    article sometime around 1785.

43 Jeremy Bentham, *An Introduction to the Principles of Morals and
    Legislation*, T. Payne and Son (1789), p. 351.

44 See for instance: Jonathan Birch et al., *Review of the Evidence of
    Sentience in Cephalopod Molluscs and Decapod Crustaceans*, London
    School of Economics and Political Science (November 2021).

45 See: Kaneda and Haub, "How Many People."

46 The saying that the arc of history bends toward justice was first
    coined by the minister Theodore Parker in 1852, and only became
    truly well known when MLK used it. See: "The Arc of the Moral
    Universe Is Long, But It Bends Toward Justice," *Quote Investigator*
    (15 November 2012).

47 I'm paraphrasing Hillel the Elder here, a Jewish scholar and sage who
    lived in the first century BCE. He wrote, "If I am not for myself, then
    who will be for me? But when I am for myself, then what am 'I'?
    And if not now, when?"

48 Martin Luther King Jr., "Advice for Living," *Ebony Magazine*
    (January 1958), p. 34. Published online by Martin Luther King Jr.
    Research and Education Institute, Stanford University.

49 Herbert A. Simon, *Models of My Life*, Basic Books (1991), p. 281.

50 Half a century after the publication of *Animal Liberation*, Peter Singer
    came to that conclusion, too. See: Simon Coghlan, "Peter Singer's
    Fresh Take on Animal Liberation — a Book That Changed the World,
    But Not Enough," *Conversation* (12 June 2023).

51 Catherine C. Ivanovich et al., "Future Warming from Global Food
    Consumption," *Nature Climate Change*, Vol. 13, pp. 297–302 (2023).

52 That was something the world's oldest vegan organization — the
    Vegan Society, founded in 1944 — already realized. "An Associate
    makes no promise as to behaviour," wrote the founders about
    becoming a member, "but declares himself in agreement with the
    object. The door is thusly widely opened, and the Society welcomes
    all those who feel able to support it." Source: Tobias Leenaert, *How to
    Create a Vegan World: A Pragmatic Approach*, Lantern Books (2017).

53 Leah Garcés, *Grilled: Turning Adversaries Into Allies to Change the
    Chicken Industry*, Bloomsbury (2019), p. 45.

54 R. F. Wideman et al., "Pulmonary Arterial Hypertension (Ascites Syndrome) in Broilers: A Review," *Poultry Science*, Vol. 92, Issue 1 (2013), p. 65.

55 Audrey Miller, "Why This Chicken Farmer Is Growing Mushrooms," Stone Pier Press (25 May 2021).

56 Leah Garcés, "A Lesson in Turning Adversaries into Allies," TEDxSeattle (2020), from 3:27.

57 Garcés, *Grilled*, p. 82.

58 Nicholas Kristof (@NickKristof), Twitter (14 March 2015); Nicholas Kristof, "To kill a chicken," *New York Times* (14 March 2015).

59 Garcés, *Grilled*, p. 169.

60 See: Garcés, *Grilled*, Chapter 9.

CHAPTER 10

1 Arnold Toynbee used this line to poke fun at the position taken by fellow historian H. A. L. Fisher. See: Arnold J. Toynbee, *A Study of History: Abridgement of Volumes VII—X by D. C. Somervell*, Oxford University Press (1957), p. 267.

2 Hiram M. Drache, "The Impact of John Deere's Plow," *Illinois Periodicals Online*.

3 Brian Potter, "The Blast Furnace: 800 Years of Technology Improvement," *Construction Physics*, Substack newsletter (23 February 2023).

4 Gale Pooley, "Thinking More About Shipping Innovation," *Gale Winds*, Substack newsletter (30 December 2022).

5 Hannah Ritchie and Max Roser, "CO_2 emissions," Our World in Data (2020).

6 Hannah Ritchie and Max Roser, "Plastic Pollution," Our World in Data (2022); Ritchie and Roser, "Drivers of Deforestation," Our World in Data (2021).

7 Hannah Ritchie, "Half of the World's Habitable Land Is Used for Agriculture," Our World in Data (11 November 2019).

8 Hannah Ritchie, "Wild Mammals Make Up Only a Few Percent of the World's Mammals," Our World in Data (15 December 2022). Or what about this one: people make up only 0.01 percent of all the biomass on Earth, while our buildings, roads, ships, trains, planes, satellites, submarines, tunnels, dams, high-voltage power line towers,

and electric toothbrushes weigh more than all the whales, chickens, forests, insects, molds, and bacteria put together. Or put another way: all our metal, bricks, asphalt, glass, plastic, wood, gravel, and concrete (lots and lots of concrete!) is heavier than all life on Earth. See: Emily Elhacham et al., "Global Human-made Mass Exceeds All Living Biomass," *Nature*, Vol. 588 (2020).

9   Carys E. Bennett et al., "The Broiler Chicken as a Signal of a Human Reconfigured Biosphere," *Royal Society of Open Science*, Vol. 5, Issue 12 (12 December 2018).

10   Here, I'm referring to ready-to-be-deployed nuclear warheads on ballistic missiles or ready to be mounted under bombers. See: Max Roser, Bastian Herre, and Joe Hasell, "Nuclear Weapons," Our World in Data (6 August 2013).

11   Jonas Jägermeyr et al., "A Regional Nuclear Conflict Would Compromise Global Food," *PNAS*, Vol. 117, Issue 13 (2020).

12   Luisa Rodriguez, "How Likely Is a Nuclear Exchange Between the U.S. and Russia?" Rethink Priorities (19 June 2019).

13   The calculation goes like this: picture a bag of marbles with ninety-nine blue marbles and one red one. Each year, you pull a marble out of the bag (and put it back). The first year, your odds of getting a red one is one in a 100, or 1/100, or 1 percent. The odds of getting a blue marble is ninety-nine out of 100, or 99 percent. The next year, you again have a chance of 99/100 of getting a blue marble. You can compute the chance of drawing a blue marble over a period of two years by multiplying the odds for each year: 99/100 x 99/100 = 0.99 x 0.99 = 0.9801. That's a 98.01 percent chance you won't draw a red marble in two years (and a 1.99 percent chance you'll get a red one). Over a hundred years, the odds of getting a red marble will have grown to 63.4 percent. After 500 years, odds are 99.3 percent.

14   Quoted in: Marion Lloyd, "Soviets Close to Using A-Bomb in 1962 Crisis, Forum Is Told," *Boston Globe* (13 October 2002).

15   Quoted in: Svetlana V. Savranskaya, "New Sources on the Role of Soviet Submarines in the Cuban Missile Crisis," *Journal of Strategic Studies*, Vol. 28, Issue 2 (2005), p. 246.

16   David Roza, "The U.S. military is still missing 6 nuclear weapons that were lost decades ago," *Task & Purpose* (25 August 2022).

17   By the end of 1944, it became clear that Germany was no longer working to develop an atomic bomb. The only person who left the Manhattan

Project at that point was the Polish-British physicist Joseph Rotblat. He resigned and later became one of the most influential activists in the fight against nuclear arms. He won the Nobel Peace Prize in 1995.

18   Quoted in: *In the Matter of J. Robert Oppenheimer: Transcript of Hearing Before Personnel Security Board*, United States Atomic Energy Commission (1954), p. 81.

19   Alan Turing, "Computing Machinery and Intelligence," *Mind*, Vol. LIX, Issue 236 (October 1950), pp. 433–460.

20   Quoted in: Raffi Khatchadourian, "The Doomsday Invention," *New Yorker* (23 November 2015). In May 2023, Hinton left Google and joined the ranks of AI critics. See: Cade Metz, " 'The Godfather of A.I.' Leaves Google and Warns of Danger Ahead," *New York Times* (1 May 2023).

21   Michael Specter, "In a World of Synthetic Biology, Publishing Virus DNA Sequences May Mean Perishing," *Stat* (6 April 2023).

22   Kai Kupferschmidt, "How Canadian Researchers Reconstituted an Extinct Poxvirus for $100,000 Using Mail-order DNA," *Science* (6 July 2017).

23   Abraar Karan and Stephen Luby, "A Natural Pandemic Has Been Terrible: A Synthetic One Would Be Even Worse," *Stat* (19 August 2021).

24   *Advancing Collective Action and Accountability Amid Global Crisis*, Global Health Security Index (December 2021), p. 57. On top of that, three-quarters of the more than 100 high-risk labs are located in urban areas, and three-quarters in countries that don't score well on biosafety and biosecurity. See: Filippa Lentzos and Gregory D. Koblentz, "Fifty-nine Labs Around World Handle the Deadliest Pathogens — Only a Quarter Score High on Safety," *Conversation* (14 June 2021); *Global BioLabs Report 2023*, King's College London and Schar School of Policy and Government (2023).

25   David Manheim and Gregory Lewis, "High-risk Human-caused Pathogen Exposure Events From 1975–2016," *F1000Research*, Vol. 10, Issue 752 (2022).

26   David E. Kaplan and Andrew Marshall, "Aum's Shoko Asahara and the Cult at the End of the World," *Wired* (1 July 1996).

27   William J. Broad, "SOWING DEATH: A Special Report; How Japan Germ Terror Alerted World," *New York Times* (26 May 1998).

28   And no, there's nothing requiring the hundreds of companies that provide made-to-order DNA to screen their customers. Some

companies have decided to do rigorous screening of all orders, while others have not. See: Michael Schulson, "Experts Debate the Risks of Made-to-Order DNA," *Undark* (21 December 2022).

29 Quoted in: Schulson, "Experts Debate the Risks."

30 David E. Kaplan and Andrew Marshall, *The Cult at the End of the World: The Terrifying Story of the Aum Doomsday Cult, from the Subways of Tokyo to the Nuclear Arsenals of Russia*, Crown Publishing (1996).

31 Kyle B. Olson, "Aum Shinrikyo: Once and Future Threat?" *Emerging Infectious Diseases*, Vol. 5, Issue 4 (1999), p. 514.

32 Two more victims died later. See: Aya Sugiyama et al., "The Tokyo Subway Sarin Attack Has Long-term Effects on Survivors: A 10-year Study Started 5 years After the Terrorist Incident," *PLoS One*, Vol. 15, Issue 6 (2020); Richi Tanaka and Kenji Tatsumi, "Woman Bedridden Since AUM Cult's 1995 Sarin Gas Attack on Tokyo Subway Dies at 56," *Mainichi* (20 March 2020).

33 Based on the three-part saying "The world is awful. The world is much better. The world can be much better" by statistician Max Roser. I added a fourth. See: Max Roser, "The world is awful. The world is much better. The world can be much better," Our World in Data (July 20, 2022).

34 See: "Emerging Infectious Diseases," *gfinderdata.policycuresresearch.org*.

35 Ron Wolfe, "Why So White?" *Arkansas Democrat-Gazette* (9 March 2010).

36 Toby Ord, *The Precipice: Existential Risk and the Future of Humanity*, Bloomsbury Publishing (2020), p. 135. See also: Jenifer Mackby, "BWC Meeting Stumbles Over Money, Politics," *Arms Control Association* (January/February 2019).

37 Dylan Matthews, "The Biggest Funder of Anti-nuclear War Programs is Taking Its Money Away," *Vox* (17 March 2022).

38 Leopold Aschenbrenner, "Nobody's on the Ball on AGI Alignment," *forourposterity.com* (29 March 2023).

39 Ralph Nader, "Selling Our Children," *The Good Fight: Declare Your Independence and Close the Democracy Gap*, Regan Books (2004).

40 Emmanuelle Maitre and Pauline Lévy, "Becoming a Disarmament Champion: The Austrian Crusade Against Nuclear Weapons," *The Nonproliferation Review*, Vol. 26, Issue 5–6 (2019).

41 Quoted in: Naina Bajekal, "She's Spent a Decade Fighting to Ban Nuclear Weapons: The Stakes Are Only Getting Higher," *TIME* (4 January 2023).

42 Bajekal, "She's Spent a Decade Fighting."

43 This quote comes from an unpublished interview Andy Weber had with journalist Tom Ough in November 2022, shared with me for use in this chapter.

44 Andrew Weber, "Countering Weapons of Mass Destruction Without a Map," TEDxIndianaUniversity (October 2017), from 1:18.

45 Judith Miller, William J. Broad, and Stephen Engelberg, *Germs: Biological Weapons and America's Secret War*, Touchstone (2002), p. 169.

46 David E. Hoffman, *The Dead Hand: Reagan, Gorbachev and the Untold Story of the Cold War Arms Race and Its Dangerous Legacy*, Icon Books (2011), pp. 443–455.

47 Hoffman, *The Dead Hand*, p. 464.

48 Miller, Broad, and Engelberg, *Germs*, pp. 166 and 178.

49 Jassi Pannu and Jacob Swett, "What If There Was Never a Pandemic Again?" *New York Times* (28 May 2023).

50 Bipartisan Commission on Biodefense, "The Apollo Program for Biodefense: Winning the Race Against Biological Threats," (January 2021).

51 "The Apollo Program for Biodefense," p. 17.

52 This promising area of research is called *volatolomics*, a field in its early days. It's a technique for analyzing tiny chemical compounds emitted in breath, sweat, and tears, which can serve as fingerprints for thousands of diseases. See: Wenwen Hu et al., "Volatolomics in Healthcare and its Advanced Detection Technology," *Nano Research*, Vol. 15, Issue 9 (29 June 2022).

53 One great account took place in mid-nineteenth-century London. During the infamous Great Stink of the summer of 1858, the smell of the River Thames was unbearable. A layer of effluent and human waste floated on the water, and when the odor reached Westminster, politicians fled the House of Commons with handkerchiefs pressed to their faces. Two weeks later, Parliament voted for an ambitious plan by engineer Joseph Bazalgette to construct a gigantic system of underground pipes, pools, and pumps to move the wastewater along, out of the city. For sixteen years, 20,000 workers built the 130-kilometer-long sewer system. "The great sewer that runs beneath Londoners," read Bazalgette's obituary, "has added some 20 years to their chance of life." One historian notes that the engineer likely "saved more lives, than any single Victorian public official." See: Fin

Moorhouse, "First Clean Water, Now Clean Air," *finmoorhouse.com* (April 2023); John Doxat, *The Living Thames: The Restoration of a Great Tidal River*, Hutchinson Benham (1977), p. 41.

54 See also: Juan Cambeiro and Brian Potter, "Indoor Air Quality Is the Next Great Public Health Challenge," Institute for Progress (29 June 2023).

55 Beth Gardiner, "This Landmark Law Saved Millions of Lives and Trillions of Dollars," *National Geographic* (29 December 2020).

56 David Wallace-Wells, "Air Pollution Kills 10 Million People a Year: Why Do We Accept That as Normal?" *New York Times* (8 June 2022). See also: Hannah Ritchie, Fiona Spooner, and Max Roser, "Causes of Death," Our World in Data (December 2019).

57 See: Cambeiro and Potter, "Indoor Air Quality Is the Next Great Public Health Challenge."

58 Current EU standards stipulate no more than ten micrograms of lead per liter of drinking water. See: "Directive (EU) 2020/2184 of the European Parliament and of the Council of 16 December 2020 on the quality of water intended for human consumption (recast) (Text with EEA relevance)," EUR-Lex (23 December 2020); Anthony Higney, Nick Hanley, and Mirko Moro, "The Lead-crime Hypothesis: A Meta-analysis," *Regional Science and Urban Economics*, Vol. 97, Issue 1 (November 2022).

59 Ewan Eadie et al., "Far-UVC (222 nm) Efficiently Inactivates an Airborne Pathogen in a Room-sized Chamber," *Scientific Reports*, Vol. 12, Issue 4373 (2022). Some scientists have pointed out there could also be too little exposure to germs, especially in early childhood, due to increased hygiene, which could mean a weaker immune system. The *hygiene hypothesis* was coined in 1989 by immunologist David Strachan to explain the rise in asthma, eczema, allergies, and autoimmune diseases. Recent research, however, points in another direction. Large studies in Denmark, Finland, and the UK showed no connection between the incidence of childhood infections and the incidence of allergies (on the contrary, a greater number of viral infections seemed to raise the risk of asthma). All the same, it's important children are exposed to bacteria, fungi, and other microbes. Children with pets and children who play outside more, for instance, are less likely to be troubled by allergies. Far-UVC (like good handwashing habits) doesn't detract from that, and could prove useful in public spaces to combat airborne viruses. See also: Emily

Johnston Files and Philip Weinstein, "Early Exposure to Infections Doesn't Protect Against Allergies, But Getting into Nature Might," *Conversation* (6 February 2020).

60 See: Jenny Howard, "Plague Was One of History's Deadliest Diseases — Then We Found a Cure," *National Geographic* (6 July 2020); "Viewpoint: The Deadly Disease That Killed More People Than wwi," BBC (13 October 2014); D. A. Henderson, *Smallpox: The Death of a Disease*, Prometheus Books (2009), p. 12.

61 "The Pandemic's True Death Toll," *Economist* (3 July 2023).

62 John F. Kennedy, "We Choose to Go to the Moon," Rice University speech (12 September 1962).

63 Carl Sagan, *Pale Blue Dot: A Vision of the Human Future in Space*, Ballantine Books (1997), p. 12.

EPILOGUE

1 Quoted in: Ellen Gibson Wilson, *Thomas Clarkson: A Biography*, St. Martin's Press (1990), p. 183.

2 Wilson, *Thomas Clarkson*, p. 183.

3 Quoted in: Adam Hochschild, *Bury the Chains: The British Struggle to Abolish Slavery*, Houghton Mifflin (2005), p. 326.

4 Quoted in: Clare Midgley, *Women Against Slavery: The British Campaigns, 1780–1870*, Taylor & Francis (2005), p. 106. Originally published in 1992.

5 Robert Isaac Wilberforce and Samuel Wilberforce, *The Life of William Wilberforce: Volume 3*, John Murray (1838), p. 494.

6 This was George Thompson. Quoted in: Midgley, *Women Against Slavery*, p. 44.

7 Quoted in: Eva Fogelman, *Conscience and Courage: Rescuers of Jews During the Holocaust*, Anchor Books (1995), p. 274.

8 Fogelman, *Conscience and Courage*, pp. 282–3.

9 Max Léons and Arnold Douwes, *Mitswa en christenplicht: Bescheiden helden uit de illegaliteit*, Uitgeverij BZZTÔH (2000), p. 118.

10 Quoted in: Matthijs Smits, "Het eigen ik speelt geen enkele rol," *Het Financieele Dagblad* (4 May 2001).

11 George Orwell, "Reflections on Gandhi," *Partisan Review* (January 1949). This essay is available online through The Orwell Foundation.

12   To prove to himself he'd conquered lust, Gandhi engaged in a series
      of experiments we'd now consider abuse. After his wife's death in
      1944, he'd regularly sleep naked next to women followers many
      years his junior.

13   George Orwell, "Reflections on Gandhi."

14   "A Conversation About Altruism: Matthieu Ricard, Julia Wise,
      and Peter Singer," University Center for Human Values, Princeton
      University (26 October 2015), from 30:36.

15   A 1982 piece by philosopher Susan Wolf on "moral saints" is worth
      a read. She emphasized that there's more to life than morality.
      Being preoccupied day in, day out with *the good*, makes for a barren
      existence. "If the moral saint is devoting all his time to feeding the
      hungry or healing the sick or raising money for Oxfam," wrote Wolf,
      "then necessarily he is not reading Victorian novels, playing the oboe,
      or improving his backhand." (Or binge-watching a series, I'd add.)
      See: Susan Wolf, "Moral Saints," *The Journal of Philosophy*, Vol. 79,
      Issue 8 (1982).

16   "A Conversation About Altruism: Matthieu Ricard, Julia Wise, and
      Peter Singer," from 37:27.

17   Granted, Clarkson couldn't stop himself in this decade from
      helping support ten struggling families and raising money to assist
      a poor man who'd lost his cattle. And when the British abolitionist
      movement gained new momentum in 1804, Clarkson again made the
      rounds through England and Scotland to activate the old network.
      See: Hochschild, *Bury the Chains*, p. 247.

18   George Monbiot, "The 1% Are the Very Best Destroyers of Wealth
      the World Has Ever Seen," *Guardian* (7 November 2011).

19   Quoted in: John Battersby, "Mandela," *Christian Science Monitor*
      (10 February 2000).

20   Thomas Clarkson, *The History of the Rise, Progress and
      Accomplishment of the Abolition of the African Slave-Trade by the
      British Parliament: Volume I*, R. Taylor & Co. (1808), p. 293.

21   Clarkson, *The History of the Rise*, p. 294.

INDEX

philosophy, 147–8, 153–4

pill, the, 132–3, 163

Pincus, Gregory Goodwin, 132

Pinker, Steven, 135

polio, 125–6, 129

'political hobbyism', 68

population growth, 194–5

poverty, 18, 26, 70–1, 111, 113, 119, 124, 129, 150, 152, 163, 188, 214, 225

power laws, 27, 151–2, 155

Princeton University, 45, 174, 223

Project Sapphire, 207

public interest lawyers, 58

Pythagoras, 178

Pythagoreans, 49

Quakers, 16–17, 49–52, 76, 82, 182, 184, 219, 224

racial segregation, 176

racism, 12–13, 18, 44, 73, 75

Raine, Allen, 1

Raleigh *News & Observer*, 173

Randolph, A. Philip, 164

Reagan, Ronald, 138

refrigerators, 131

Ricard, Matthieu, viii, 223–4

Robinson, Jo Ann, 66–7, 76, 82, 108

Romans, 171, 173, 194

Rosten, Leo, vii

Rothschild, Nathan Mayer, 123

Royal African Company, 172

Royal Navy, 52

Russell, Bertrand, 98

Rustin, Bayard, 82

Rutherford, Ernest, 201

Sagan, Carl, 215

St Augustine, 171

St Paul, 17

Salk, Jonas, 125–7

Sanger, Margaret, 132

Sarek, Karolina, 116–17

sarin, 203

Savoie, Joey, 106–19

School for Moral Ambition, 227, 229–31

Science, 202

Scientific World Changers, 111

sea-level rise, 175

Second World War, 28, 33, 111, 126, 129, 155, 184, 200

Seneca Falls, 221, 231

sexism, 13, 18

sexual harassment, 12

Sharp, Granville, 79–80

Shelley, Mary, 178

Shi, Zhengrong, 139–41

shrimp, 183–4

Sightsavers, 155

Silicon Valley, 47, 52, 209

Simon, Herbert, 186

A NOTE ON THE AUTHOR

Rutger Bregman, a historian and writer, is one of Europe's most prominent young thinkers. His books *Humankind* and *Utopia for Realists* were both *New York Times* bestsellers. His work has been translated into 46 languages and has sold over two million copies. He lives in New York City.

@rcbregman | rutgerbregman.com

A NOTE ON THE TYPE

The text of this book is set in Fournier. Fournier is derived from the romain du roi, which was created toward the end of the seventeenth century from designs made by a committee of the Académie of Sciences for the exclusive use of the Imprimerie Royale. The original Fournier types were cut by the famous Paris founder Pierre Simon Fournier in about 1742. These types were some of the most influential designs of the eight and are counted among the earliest examples of the "transitional" style of typeface. This Monotype version dates from 1924. Fournier is a light, clear face whose distinctive features are capital letters that are quite tall and bold in relation to the lower-case letters, and *decorative italics, which show the influence of the calligraphy of Fournier's time*.